WE WILL NOT FIGHT

Will Ellsworth-Jones has worked as a journalist for *The Sunday Times*, the *Independent* and *Saga Magazine*. He is also the author of *Banksy: The Man Behind the Wall*, published by Aurum in 2012. He lives in London.

'An intensely moving history that gives a fresh insight into the First World War'
York Evening Press

'Will Ellsworth-Jones powerfully relates the moving story of conscientious objectors in the First World War'
Editor's choice, *Saga Magazine*

'This engrossing book gives a full outline of the many effects of the Great War . . . The battle between a moral conscience and national duty is fascinating and movingly described by Ellsworth-Jones . . . This is a touching and deeply moving account of the Brocklesby family'
Family History Monthly

WE WILL NOT FIGHT

The Untold Story of the First World War's
Conscientious Objectors

Will Ellsworth-Jones

Quarto is the authority on a wide range of topics.

Quarto educates, entertains and enriches the lives of our readers—enthusiasts and lovers of hands-on living.

www.quartoknows.com

First published in 2008 by Aurum Press Limited
74-77 White Lion Street
London N1 9PF
www.aurumpress.co.uk

This paperback edition first published in 2008 by Aurum Press

A catalogue record for this book is available from the British Library.

ISBN: 978 1 78131 148 6

Designed in Minion by Richard Marston
Typeset by SX Composing DTP, Rayleigh, Essex
Printed and bound by CPI Group (UK) Ltd, Croydon, CRO 4YY

Contents

For Barbara

Introduction

In the middle of June 1916 Philip Brocklesby, a young second lieutenant freshly promoted from the ranks, landed in Boulogne along with a hundred other newly trained officers. What they lacked in experience they made up for in enthusiasm – and they needed it. For they were being rushed to the front as part of the massive preparations for the battle of the Somme which was only two weeks away.

Before he took the last leg of his journey Phil had an extraordinary mission to fulfil. Just before he had left England he had been given forty-eight hours' special leave to visit his family in the South Yorkshire mining village of Conisbrough. He arrived home to discover that his mother and father were intensely worried. They already had one son, Harold, fighting in France and now Phil was about to join him. But they were even more concerned by a third son, Bert. They had just received a secret message from him telling them that he was being held in Boulogne.

Bert Brocklesby was not in France to fight; he was there because he refused to fight, one of the first of a very small but growing band of conscientious objectors (COs). He had never been in any sort of trouble in his life and he was a religious man who took the sixth commandment, 'Thou shalt not kill', very much at its face value. While two of his brothers had volunteered to fight Bert would have nothing to do with the war. Now he was up against an army that was determined to break him.

Bert and thirty-four other conscientious objectors had been shipped to France and court-martialled for their disobedience. There was no doubt that under army law he and his fellow COs were guilty: they had disobeyed almost every order given to them. Now there was only one question that mattered: would they be sentenced to death?

This book is the story of Bert and his fellow objectors who were prepared to die for their principles rather than kill for their country in the First World War. It is the story too of the price these men and their families had to pay when they were forced to balance conscience against duty. Conscription had been introduced early in 1916 when never-ending losses, particularly along the Western Front, left the British army desperate for more men. These thirty-five conscientious objectors, who were amongst the first to refuse to join the army, had been singled out to show others who might be tempted to follow their example the fate that awaited them.

Before he left home Phil promised his parents: 'If I cross to Boulogne I will try to find Bert and let you know the position.' So when, by chance, he found himself in the right port he knew this would be the first and last opportunity he had to keep his promise. While his fellow officers were being loaded on a train to take them a short distance to their base camp at Etaples Phil gambled that he would not be noticed and slipped away.

Boulogne was one of the key ports for the British army; through the base came the young men, the shells, the artillery, the horses – the whole multiple list of supplies that kept the army alive and ready to fight. With the biggest British assault of the war about to be launched the port was now throbbing with activity and finding Bert was not an easy task. It was not until late afternoon, having trekked from one camp to another, that Phil eventually discovered the right camp, high up on the southern edge of town where he could look back across the Channel and just see England. And there he had to sit down on a grass mound and wait impatiently. For the lice that infested every army did not differentiate between conscientious objectors and the ordinary soldier and Bert, along with about forty other prisoners, had been taken to the baths to be deloused.

Eventually Phil saw a troop of men come marching up the hill towards him. Bert was a handsome man, solidly built and taller than most around him. So it was easy enough to spot him in any crowd, and there he was in the middle of the column: 'I shall never forget how Bert's face lighted up when he saw me,' wrote Phil later.

Using his newly acquired rank, Phil managed to negotiate to spend thirty minutes with Bert. The only place they were allowed to meet was in the guardroom and with men and guards swirling around it was hardly a very private affair. Yet despite the fact that one brother had volunteered to join the army while the other was a defiant opponent of everything military it was a joyous meeting between them.

Their reunion came at critical time in the war. There was growing realisation and resigned acceptance of the fact that this was not to be the quick, easy war that people had imagined. Just ahead lay the battle of the Somme – 19,000 British volunteers were killed on the first day, moving obediently in line to their death – a disaster that would test British resolve and underline the fact that this was a war like no other, a war that was to claim the lives of 9.5 million soldiers before its end. But here in this bustling Channel port a very human story was being acted out. And although the consequences of Bert's stand would ricochet down the generations, what mattered for the moment was that both brothers were still alive and well – whatever tomorrow might bring.

A newspaper article in the *Daily Telegraph* in May 1999 is what inspired this book. The headline needed considerable decoding: 'Castle cell graffiti of Somme pacifists brought to life', but the story told of sixteen conscientious objectors to the First World War who had been held 'half naked' in the cells of Richmond Castle, an eleventh-century castle in North Yorkshire, before being sent to France to face execution. While in their cells they had drawn on the walls – messages of hope, despair and sometimes defiance. It was certainly not modern-day graffiti; there was no swearing or nudes, instead there were complicated verses from the Bible as well as more everyday thoughts on the war: 'You might just as well try to dry a floor by throwing water on it as try to end this war by fighting' was a typical example. These graffiti had been found during restoration work at the castle but because they were in such fragile condition they needed to be photographed. These photographs, together with a reconstruction of one of the cells and a computer simulation of the cell block brought the troubles of the early twentieth century back to life.

The article raised several questions. In a war in which men answered Lord Kitchener's exhortation 'Your country needs you' in heroic numbers, who then were these pacifists and why were they being held in prison and threatened with execution? And why were they being threatened with execution in France?

The cutting stayed hidden in my files until a couple of years later when I visited Richmond and managed to persuade the helpful assistants who look after the Visitors' Centre to allow me into the cells, which have had to be closed off to the public in order to preserve the surviving graffiti (one cell was used between the two world wars as a paint store and the painters unfortunately saw the walls as a natural place to clean off their brushes). The cells are dismal and dank: with thick forbidding walls, little light and cold flagstone floors there is something of the medieval dungeon about them. To be incarcerated in such grim conditions, with the rule of silence strictly enforced, in the intimidating surroundings of the castle, would be enough to test anyone's beliefs. And these men knew they were on their own. There was very little public sympathy or understanding for the cause they were fighting for.

In Richmond – a town proud of its long military history – the commemoration of the men's stand still stirs up some of the same passions and hostility that were ignited over ninety years ago. As well as setting up the exhibition telling the objectors' story, English Heritage, keepers of the castle, established a garden to 'incorporate the history' of the castle. The garden includes sixteen abstract topiary shapes which, when I first visited the castle, were too newly planted to make any impression but whose significance was immediately spotted by the critics: 'Why should we have a living memorial to sixteen people who refused to fight for their country?' asked one town councillor, while a retired major who lived in the town said the commemoration of these 'cowards' showed a 'twisted sense of values'.

Malcolm Brocklesby, the nephew of Bert Brocklesby (who was one of the sixteen imprisoned in Richmond before being shipped to Boulogne), was invited to the garden's opening ceremony. Soon after he wrote a letter to the *Yorkshire Post* defending his uncle from these modern-day attacks: 'Such action requires a particular type of calculated courage. When a soldier enlists he knows there is a possibility he might die in battle; Bert and the others knew there was a probability that they would face the firing squad. Misguided and intransigent they might be but not cowards.'

When I contacted Malcolm Brocklesby it soon became clear that the family's involvement with the war went far beyond one man sitting in a cell in Richmond Castle. In addition to Bert and Phil there was Harold, wounded in July 1916 during the battle of the Somme, and a fourth brother, George, who was ruled out of the army because of illness. Instead he became the Conisbrough recruiting officer. As the country had had to come to terms with a war which was supposed to have been over in a few short months, so too had this family.

Britain in August 1914 was a country where it seemed inconceivable that anyone would not want to fight. There was no need for conscription because volunteers were in danger of overwhelming the limited organisational skills of the army. Yet as the war went on and the casualty lists grew relentlessly, conscription had to be introduced and the State had to decide how to deal with the fact that there were men who would rather die than fight. In total there were about 16,300 conscientious objectors in the First World War; 6,000 of them served varying sentences in prison and among these 6,000 there were 1,300 who refused to compromise with the state in any shape or form. It was from the ranks of these absolutists, as they were called, that the thirty-five French COs were drawn (in addition to the sixteen from Richmond, nineteen others came from other parts of the country).

The way in which the country and especially the army dealt with these principled men who proved so awkward was to have a continuing effect down the rest of the century. The battle over conscience fought between 1914 and 1918 laid the groundwork for treatment of the conscientious objector both in the Second World War and in the wars that have followed in Vietnam and Iraq. But on 15 June 1916 none of this was going through the minds of the two Brocklesby brothers in France. They just wanted to see each other: they both knew it might be for the last time.

1

The August Bank Holiday

In the last days of July 1914, with the Bank Holiday weekend approaching, it was impossible for anyone to imagine what was about to become of the world. In London, which was enjoying a particularly warm summer, events on the Continent seemed a very long way off and in the Brocklesbys' home town of Conisbrough they seemed even more remote. How could an assassination in far-off Sarajevo possibly threaten their secure, settled world in South Yorkshire?

Although not quite a traditional pit town, Conisbrough had been transformed from its roots as a rural settlement by the opening of nearby coal mines in the second half of the nineteenth century. On the eve of the war the town was thriving – despite a major mine disaster two years earlier that had cost seventy-five lives – and so were the Brocklesbys. Bert's father, John, had decided against following the family tradition of farming; instead he served a seven-year apprenticeship as a grocer before buying his own small grocery business in Conisbrough in 1887. From there he prospered, adding a boot and shoe department to the grocery and as his business grew so too did his status in the community: he became a Justice of the Peace, overseer of the poor and chairman of the parish council, eventually serving on a remarkable twenty-two committees or sub-committees of the county council. A cartoon during an election race for the Doncaster rural district council in 1904 gives the pedigree of each candidate as though they are entering a horse race. Brocklesby is 'By honest Injun out of Courtesy' while one of his rivals is 'By Ignorance out of Fatuity'.

WE WILL NOT FIGHT

(Amidst accusations of unfair play this was one of the few elections he lost – albeit by only a few votes.) He was certainly prepared to stand up for what he believed in: during one election meeting his opponents came equipped with a brass band to drown him out. The local paper reported that his supporters vanished but he stood his ground and was eventually given a hearing. He was a man of whom the local paper said rightly on his death, 'If every town had one or two such men devoted to its common weal, there would be a noticeable rise in the standard of public life everywhere.' Another local obituarist suggested: 'Unlike some magistrates one could mention, he never had an exaggerated sense of his own importance.'

From the family photographs 'Old Brock', as he was sometimes known, comes across as the contented patriarch with a neatly trimmed beard and moustache. He and his wife Hannah had four sons and when war came George was twenty-seven; Bert, or John Hubert to give him his full name, was twenty-five; Phil was twenty-one; and baby-faced Harold just seventeen. Together with their spinster aunt Rebecca ('Bec'), who was a little bit more easy-going than her rather formal sister Hannah, the Brocklesby boys lived in a comfortable three-storey terraced house in Brook Square at the foot of the town. Conveniently the family's shop was on the ground floor. They were close to the main road to Doncaster and, as children, every time they heard the sound of a horn they used to run outside to see a car – one of the 'marvels' as they called them – pass by. They lived the sort of secure life based on home and church which it is impossible to even imagine today.

Old Brock was also a lay preacher who had given his first sermon to the occupants of the workhouse in Hull before he had reached the age of seventeen. The longest day's preaching he could remember started at 7 a.m. and finished at midnight; he walked 14 miles, preached three sermons and ate 'two breakfasts, one dinner, three teas and two suppers' as he visited believers along the way. His wife gained great comfort from the Psalms, which she used to read in the same way that people read novels. One neighbour remembers her as thrifty and 'very kind', taking her under her wing as a newcomer to the chapel. Hannah was a fundamentalist outside the church as well as in; she used to tell Bert, for instance, that the use of drugs was unnatural – particularly pain-killing drugs. As for fighting – of any kind – she told him it was 'subhuman – a shameful practice'.

So Bert was raised amidst a family of strict believers during the time of the great Methodist Revival, when visiting missionaries were driving the church forward to the height of its power in Britain. In 1877 a magnificent new chapel had been constructed by the Methodists in Conisbrough, designed with rather more of an elaborate flourish than most nonconformist chapels. In a town of about 4,000 the Methodists had between 300 and 400 members. The Anglican church on the opposite side of the town remained the choice of the establishment, but the Methodists, appealing both to the rising working class and to the town's tradesmen, had become powerful rivals.

At the heart of their mission was a simple question: Are you saved? Bert's mother – quite a fearsome woman – taught him that the Bible was the word of God and every word of it 'from cover to cover' was true. So even at the age of seven the question of whether he was 'saved' or not worried Bert, but it was not as though he was some sort of religious obsessive. He was an ebullient, popular boy who was both a bright spark and a bit of a joker. His faith was probably the strongest of the four brothers and he had emerged from the Methodist missions with a simple but clear belief in Divine Will, whereby everything was decided by God. It was here that his problems were to lie in the future. But for now he had no problems; while some boys dream of one day driving a fire engine, or becoming a millionaire, Bert's ambition from early childhood was to become a missionary in distant lands.

He taught Sunday school and his younger brother Phil remembers how an appeal for sinners to come forth and be saved was made. There was a Penitent Bench for the sinners to sit on while they waited to be 'saved'. It was simple: if they did not come forward they would be condemned to Hell. In their day George and a slightly hesitant Bert had come forward and now it was Phil's turn. But the appeal for sinners was a nightmare for Phil: 'Some went out, but I remained glued to my seat. I was not going to make an exhibition of myself. After a bit Mr Appleyard, the senior superintendent, a dear old man with a white spade beard which came down to his chest, came to me; he stroked my head and said "I know George is saved, and I know Bert is saved and, I think . . . you are saved." I refused the cue and remained stuck to my seat. That is why I know that I am not saved.' It was a brave decision for Phil to take at eleven. He would never be quite as overawed by religion as his older brother.

At fifteen, Bert, on the other hand, was proud to be put in charge of organising a torchlight procession as part of the grand climax of one of the ten-day Methodist missions. He invented his own torches out of old coffee tins held on four-foot rods with paraffin for fuel and 'wicks' made out of old rope. Running down the line re-lighting the wicks when they went out – which they did frequently – was all part of the fun. As he went home to wash off the dirt from the torches, his brother George came tearing after him to say he was needed on the organ. 'Oh Joy! My almost lifelong ambition to play the organ for a service! But who shall ascend the hill of the Lord? He that hath clean hands. Down I ran to our Brook Square home and panted back up the hill. The chapel was crowded to capacity . . .' This sense of innocence, of enthusiasm, was central to the brothers' lives and Bert was at the heart of it.

He joined the Mission Band which was under the leadership of a reformed drunkard, gambler and wife-beater who was determined to let the town know that it was God who had turned him around. Once or twice a week they were to be found around town playing lustily, encouraging sinners to come forward and be saved like their leader, who was as famous after his conversion as he was notorious before it. Bert was appointed organist at the Baptist chapel when he was only sixteen and five years later he became organist at the Methodist chapel – the ceremony welcoming a new organ had been presided over, inevitably, by his mother and the opening performance of Handel's *Messiah* took place under the direction of Bert.

If the church needed to raise money it was again the Brocklesbys who led the way. One Christmas the chapel held a two-day bazaar to raise funds for a new house for the minister. In a large room in the town's new school there were 'dainty stalls all neatly trimmed with holly and Christmas decorations'. Father Brocklesby was the treasurer, brother George was one of the three secretaries and Bert was in the parcels office as well as the cloakroom. In the evening there were competitions: potato peeling and spelling, and a reversal of the sexual stereotypes with the women racing to drive in nails with a hammer and the gentlemen competing as the quickest sock darners. The considerable sum of £100 was raised on the first day alone. The chapel was a warm, friendly place with a strong sense of community, and it exhibited the pride of a class bent on self-improvement.

Bert had started teaching younger boys at the local school when he was only twelve. But in 1907 he left the closed safety of Conisbrough to venture into the wider world: he trained to be a teacher at the Methodists' College, then located in Horseferry Road, Westminster, London. Here again he enjoyed himself; he even found another Mission Band to play in, visiting 'the slummiest streets I have ever seen'. Whether it was music or rugby, Bert was at the heart of things. Yet for the first time in his life he encountered a period of 'spiritual darkness, a timeless dreadful experience' as he came to doubt the literal truth of the Bible. He only resolved it when he was back home in Conisbrough where he went up to the room where he was born, threw himself on his knees by the bedside and waited until he heard 'a still small voice as clearly as I may ever hope to hear it in this life, and I had the distinct feeling of being spoken to'. The voice he heard brought spiritual rebirth: 'I realised the love of God as never before,' Bert wrote, and claimed that this was 'the greatest liberation of my life' – he had escaped 'Doubting Castle'.

Today, reading Bert's account of how he grappled with the consequences of sin as laid down in Hebrews, it sounds as if he is some sort of penitent monk eager to scourge himself until he finds the width of forgiveness expressed in Matthew. But follow his progress through Westminster College and a much more rounded picture emerges. In the 1908 formal photograph of the College Principal with his key officials around him, Bert – the College Precentor in charge of the college music programme – dominates the picture, standing, smiling slightly cockily in the back row. He was a regular in the college rugby side and when he finished at Westminster the team's captain wrote: 'We are sorry we shall not have you with us next season, as we are sure to miss you especially as you were the life of the team after matches if we won or lost, but fortunately we did not lose on many occasions.'

Bert could have gone on to take a music degree but his father – on the Conisbrough education committee – tipped him off about a possible schoolteacher's vacancy. His fatherly advice was straightforward: 'Don't be diverted from your true course which I think should be straight for your degree. You have marked out your own course and done well . . . we are all proud of what you have accomplished.' But the lure of his home town and a good job drew Bert back. Here he could be a figure of some considerable importance and in addition there was Annie Wainwright, the pretty daughter of a winder at the local coal mine. Not only was Bert the chapel's organist but he was also the chapel's choirmaster and Annie sang soprano in the choir. They were soon to be engaged and during the Christmas of 1910 he noted coyly in his diary 'oh, you naughty, naughty mistletoe'.

It was undoubtedly Bert who was the dominating force among the four brothers. Loud and jovial, he was a formidable force but a man who despite his warm sense of humour had a dogmatic and stubborn side to him too. He was the biggest of the four and probably the brightest. When a secondary school opened in nearby Mexborough Bert had been one of the first students to enrol and Phil, who followed him there, remembers always having to compete with Bert's 'virtue' and the disappointment of never quite managing to live up to his older brother's standards. Harold recalled later in life that Bert was 'my youthful hero' and Phil too describes him as 'my hero'.

By 1914 George was studying accountancy and helping his father run their shop. Bert was teaching and, although not a Socialist, he managed to slide out of any duty at the family shop by claiming – conveniently – that he disagreed with the 'profit motive'. Consequently, from the age of eleven Phil had to take Bert's place helping in the shop until he was apprenticed to a pharmacy. Harold had won a place at Sheffield University. This was a family moving up the social ladder and Bert was already a young star in the town. But the life they had known up to now was about to come to an abrupt end.

On Sunday, 2 August 1914, a Bank Holiday weekend, Bert, took the short walk up the hill from the family home to the chapel to play the new organ at the morning service. As usual, the chapel was full; however, his family were high up the pecking order and always had good seats reserved for them. The preacher, speaking from the imposing mahogany pulpit, warned the congregation that the 'dogs of war had been loosed'. All across the Continent armies were being hastily mobilised to confront each other – the preacher was not being melodramatic.

But Bert had made plans for a cycling holiday with Harold and a college friend – it had been a hot summer – and he was not about to change anything now. For it was still impossible for him or almost anyone else in Britain to imagine that this was Europe's last weekend of peace. Only a week earlier the Chancellor of the Exchequer, Lloyd George, had told the House of Commons that relations with Germany were 'very much better than they were a few years ago. There is none of that snarling which we used to see.' Ireland, and the threat of a civil war over Home Rule was what dominated politics. True, the Prime Minister, Herbert Asquith, did warn Parliament that the situation in Europe was one of 'extreme gravity'. But if there was to be a war, it should be a war that others fought: the Prime Minister still saw no reason why the British 'should be anything more than spectators'. The sea stood between Britain and the Continent and the all-powerful navy seemed to offer all the protection that was needed.

No one quite realised just how quickly the world was unravelling in Eastern Europe. On 28 June Franz Ferdinand, heir to the empire of Austria-Hungary, had been assassinated along with his wife, the Duchess of Hohenberg. The killer was a Bosnian Serb. Some three and a half weeks later the Serbs were presented first with an ultimatum from Vienna and then, on 28 July, with a declaration of war. In London a sophisticated woman could still ask 'Where is Serbia anyway?' and the Manchester *Guardian* could wish that it was physically possible for Serbia to be 'towed out to sea and sunk', but the reality was that across the Continent Europe's huge armies were on the move.

Whole books have been written about the outbreak of the war. In short, this is how events unfolded: Serbia, expecting a punishing attack from Austria-Hungary, mobilised what army it had; Austria-Hungary partially mobilised to attack Serbia; Russia partially mobilised to protect Serbia and then, desperate to have the advantage in any wider war, switched to full mobilisation on Thursday, 30 July. Austria, spurred on by Germany, decided on full mobilisation the next day; Germany, whose war plans were based on a swift and successful attack into France before turning in force on the Russians, mobilised too. France – bound by treaty with Russia, but more importantly fearing the Germans – subsequently mobilised. As reservists reported to their barracks, war became horrifyingly unstoppable. No nation dared pause for fear of being overrun on the battlefield before they had had time to gather their millions and put them on the precisely timed trains to the front.

In Britain *The Times* published a detailed and helpful graphic: not a guide to the movement of Europe's armies but instead a map helpfully supplied by the Automobile Association for the country's small but growing number of car drivers, showing them all the possible police speed traps 'in advance of the holiday weekend'. As for those still thinking of venturing abroad, *The Times* reported 'So far the outbreak of war has not greatly disturbed holidaymakers who are contemplating a continental journey next week.' On the night of Friday, 31 July, in London it was business very much as usual. According to *The Times*: 'the restaurants and music halls were filled with the usual throngs of pleasure seekers and although the possibility of a European Armageddon was here and there discussed the casual observer would not have gathered that we were in midst of a crisis the issue of which no man can foresee.'

On Sunday, 2 August, when Bert was playing the organ in Conisbrough, the Cabinet met twice in London – meeting once let alone twice on a Sunday was almost unprecedented. Asquith's assessment at this stage was that three-quarters of the Liberal Party's members were opposed to war. But Germany's ultimatum to Belgium, demanding the use of Belgian territory for its troops on their way to invade France, strengthened the war party. Despite an impressive peace rally in Trafalgar Square in the afternoon, walking back to Downing Street after dinner Asquith noted the first sniff of war hysteria: 'There were large crowds perambulating the streets and cheering the King at Buckingham Palace ... War or anything that seems likely to lead to war is always popular with the London mob.'

The Belgians rejected the German ultimatum the next day and on the Tuesday the Cabinet was told that the German army had violated Belgium's neutrality as it started on its meticulously planned journey of destruction, sweeping into France. For the doubters in Asquith's Liberal government, who still had to be convinced about the logic of going to war, this was what was needed. Under the Treaty of London signed in 1839 Britain was one of the guarantors of Belgian neutrality; here was a point of honour which, as Asquith had said, 'simplifies matters'. Germany was given an ultimatum demanding that its troops be withdrawn from Belgium. The deadline for a positive response from Germany was midnight Berlin time, but it was a deadline that meant little, for across Europe it was assumed it would be ignored.

Asquith himself went to the House of Commons to announce what the Cabinet had decided and then went for an hour's drive by himself.

As Roy Jenkins writes in his biography of Asquith, 'it was not perhaps the way that many men of power would have chosen to spend their time at this watershed of history. But it gave him a good opportunity to survey his feelings and collect his thoughts.'

By 7 p.m. London was heaving. The King and Queen appeared on the balcony of Buckingham Palace and were greeted with 'tumultuous cheering'. This sense of excitement, of adventure, was reflected across Europe. In Vienna the writer Stefan Zweig noted: 'Strangers spoke to one another in the streets, people who had avoided each other shook hands, everywhere one saw excited faces. Each individual experienced exaltation of his ego, he was no longer the isolated person of former times, he had been incorporated into the mass.' The *London Daily News* correspondent reported that in Germany too 'men were cheering and singing as people always cheer and sing when war is coming.'

The crowds kept on growing and as time moved on Trafalgar Square, Whitehall and Parliament Square were filled with a solid mass of people. Vic Cole, aged seventeen, saw it all: 'I don't remember getting home that night I was so excited.' He had been studying wireless telegraphy at a school in Clapham but now his mind was elsewhere. 'My work suffered greatly during the next few weeks. I wanted to be in the army with a gun in my hand, like the boys I had so often read about in books and magazines.' Within a month he was at the recruiting office with his sixteen-year-old friend. They both had to lie about their age – nineteen was the minimum age for going overseas – and then they were in the army. It was that simple. His friend was killed two years later.

Towards 11 p.m., when Britain's ultimatum to Germany expired, this cheerful crowd grew silent. Then *The Times* reported: 'As the first strokes rang out from the clock tower a vast cheer burst out and echoed and re-echoed for nearly twenty minutes.' Next came the National Anthem. The scene had the feel of New Year's Eve about it, but instead of New Year it was war that the crowd was welcoming in.

*

On the Bank Holiday Monday, Bert Brocklesby, together with his youngest brother Harold and Maurice Oliver, a good friend from his days at the teacher training college in Westminster, set off on their bicycling holiday. Their aim was to reach Land's End, an ambitious 350 or so miles away. But their first stop was about 30 miles away at Castleton, a lovely limestone village in the Peak District where the chapel choir was having its annual Bank Holiday outing. It was natural enough that the choirmaster would want to join the choir outing but it also gave him a chance to see Annie again before he departed. From Castleton the choir made their way up Winnats Pass, a stark, gloomy ravine that plunges into the darkness of the Derbyshire crags before emerging triumphant into the light again. Here in this primitive, earthy setting the three cyclists and the choir all sang hymns together. Bert noted: 'There seemed something very solemn and impressive about this, and we could not at the time realise that we were singing goodbye to Peace and indeed the funeral song of a whole era.' That same weekend in Germany the Chief of Staff, Helmuth von Moltke, predicted 'a war which will annihilate the civilisation of almost the whole of Europe for decades to come'.

Having reached the spa town of Buxton that night, the threesome were up early the next day and on their way to Wolverhampton. 'The whole countryside was seething with excitement as the Germans had invaded Belgium and Britain might be at war at any time,' writes Bert. 'People, seeing us with our camping equipment, asked if we were going to join up.' The Spartan trio eventually found a boggy lane close to the town which they had to make do with for the night even though the ground was soft and wet. Their next stop was Kidderminster but on the way they saw a newspaper placard announcing 'Britain declares war on Germany'.

'So that is how we received the most fateful news, and from that time the world became quite a different place. We were stunned. War with Germany! How could that be?' The papers the trio bought reported thousands of men 'volunteering for service at every recruiting station in the country'. But on this, the first day of the war, Bert had no doubts: 'However many might volunteer yet I would not. God had called me to work for his kingdom. God had not put me on earth to go destroying his own children.'

War fever had spread swiftly from London, but in Britain, as across most of Europe, the first emotion was not so much hatred of the enemy – that was to come soon enough – but concern about spies. On the outbreak of war the government announced the arrest of twenty-one German 'spies' but this did little to satisfy the press or the public, and within a month the Metropolitan Police had received more than 8,000 reports of suspected spying. The *Daily Mail* suggested that readers should 'refuse to be served by a German waiter. If he says he is Swiss demand to see his passport.' D.H. Lawrence's wife Frieda was among those who suffered for their German origins – in the first days of the war an incautious 'Auf Wiedersehen' as she left a London dinner party brought a succession of five detectives to investigate a report by a neighbour that there were spies about. In Essex an unfortunate surveyor, whose job it was to update the Ordnance Survey map of the area, was arrested no less than six times after the worried occupants in the different villages he had to work his way through called the police. Eventually he had to be given army protection. It was much the same with Bert and his cycling companions. 'Very soon the spy scares began to sprout. People wondered who we were, wandering with a tent around the country, just as though a spy would carry around some distinctive mark. At one village in Worcestershire the local policeman came to identify us. The only mark of identity we could show was Harold's Post Office Savings Bank book. Things were getting so uncomfortable we decided to abandon our tour and make a beeline for home.' Home offered the safety and comfort of the familiar – but it would not be long before all that changed too.

2

Toss of the Coin

The day after war was declared, Burberry's outfitters was advertising 'complete uniforms' in four days. A few days later the local Conisbrough paper announced it was time to 'enter a special word of appreciation of the gallant responses of South Yorkshiremen to their country's call . . . If the very worst comes to the worst England may rely on her male population to the last man.' The newspaper trumpeted a War of Nations and reported 'a great rush to the colours. Remarkable Situations – Tremendous Enthusiasms.' And the same scenes were being repeated across the country.

Britain might have declared war but in these early days the British army was not a significant force. Its most recent outing had been the Boer War and it had not covered itself in glory there – it had taken two years and 400,000 troops to subdue a force of no more than 90,000 men. The army's training had certainly improved since then, but its full-time strength was still only 200,000. It needed 35,000 recruits every year to keep up this number and most years it got no more than 30,000. The reserves were poorly trained and poorly led. Their nominal strength was 300,000 but the figure was usually at least 60,000 men short of this. Some reservists would desert regularly and with no proper system in place to keep track of them they would then join a different volunteer battalion and claim a fresh joining-up bounty every time they did so. The most enterprising were said to have joined eight different battalions in a year – while the story might be exaggerated, it illustrates how the reserves were regarded. So when, by 17 August, the British

Expeditionary Force had all arrived in France in impressive secrecy they numbered just 90,000 men, whereas the French field army assembled on the Western Front equalled about two million and Germany's army about 1.7 million.

With just a land frontier dividing France and Germany, huge armies fuelled by conscription had become an accepted part of life ever since the defeat of France in the Franco-Prussian war of 1870. Full-time service usually lasted two years and there were further yearly duties which kept a man involved with the army well into his thirties and beyond. In Germany in particular, conscription was a rite of passage: 'the moment when for the first time, the young man left his family and village to step into a wider world'. Army service was part of life's cycle and there were very few objections. It was much the same in Austria and Russia – all across the Continent there were millions who lived an everyday civilian life but who had endured tough army discipline and training and were ready to fight at short notice. France, with a smaller population than Germany and nervous about the size of its army, extended conscription to three years in 1913.

In contrast anyone who worried about the army's state of health in Britain in the pre-war years was usually condemned as a crank. In 1902 at a meeting presided over by the third Duke of Wellington at his home, Apsley House in Hyde Park, it was agreed to form the National Service League to press for two years' military service for all young men and compulsory drill in schools. By any measure the League, in these early years at least, was a complete failure. The word 'conscription' soon vanished from its literature, so negative was the reaction to it. The League's original demand was scaled down first to two months under canvas and eventually to two weeks of drill parade for three years – just about enough to train a good Boy Scout. The Royal Commission on the Militia and Volunteers, headed by the Duke of Norfolk, put much the same case – albeit with rather more authority. In a war against any one of the great European powers, the Commission argued, Britain would be at a 'grave disadvantage'.

However the reaction was exactly the same: almost universal denunciation.

Occasional conscription bills would come and go in Parliament and they were all defeated. In 1913 a routine conscription Bill failed again as did a rather more quixotic attempt by Lord Willoughby de Broke to conscript the sons of the upper classes as an example to the lower classes (it was defeated in the Lords by fifty-three votes to thirty-four).

Conscription had not been part of Britain's way of life for centuries although the Royal Navy sometimes used press gangs to round up 'recruits'. One such early 'recruit' was a fisherman, Richard Seller. In 1665, when Britain was at war with the Dutch, he was sorting his nets on Scarborough pier when a press gang arrived. After a good beating he was hauled through a gun port and on to the *Royal Prince*, the flagship of Admiral Sir Edward Spragge. On board he refused to do any work and, when asked why, was brave enough to declare that he was a Quaker whose warfare was spiritual, 'therefore I durst not fight with carnal weapons'. Intermittent beatings followed for two weeks. Anyone with any rank was encouraged to have a go: the boatswain's mate used a piece of the capstan, the captain used his cane. Apart from what Seller termed 'ordinary' beatings, he was hauled a considerable way up the mast and allowed to drop; forced to work the capstan; put into irons without food or water and beaten yet further 'so the blood and rotten stuff ran down my leg round about'.

After a council of war conducted by the captains of every ship in the fleet he was sentenced to be hanged at the yardarm. But as Seller stepped out along the gunwale towards the rope that was waiting for him, Sir Edward had a dramatic change of heart and told Seller 'Come down again. I will not hurt an hair of thy head, for I cannot make one hair grow.'

Seller was set free from his irons and in the battle that was soon to follow he acted as a non-combatant, caring for the wounded and keeping a look out for attackers sneaking up on them in the smoke – at one point he saved the *Royal Prince* from a fire ship. When the ship eventually reached Chatham he was rewarded by being set free.

Press gangs continued to play a considerable part in providing men for the navy's ships until the end of the Napoleonic Wars, although after the Restoration of Charles II in 1660 universal compulsory service in the army was unknown. While laws allowed the conscription of people of 'blemished character' or an 'unsettled mode of life', most recruits were tempted into the army by bounties. It was a tradition that Britain was proud of. The prevailing view was that 'if sacrifice was compulsory where was the moral glory?' Shortly after the end of the Boer War, Lord Salisbury, the Conservative Prime Minister, praised soldiers who had been attracted to the army 'not by coercion but by the emoluments and the honours of a great and splendid vocation'. Even as late as May 1915 Harold Tennant, Asquith's brother-in-law and Parliamentary Under Secretary for War, argued that conscription was 'foreign to the British nation, to the British character and to the genius of our people'.

But there was, of course, something rather more telling than the 'genius' of the British people, and that was the navy – the most powerful in the world. At the turn of the century Britain owned half of the world's twenty-four million tons of steam shipping. Imperial Britain was not only a dominant force in merchant shipping but also in naval power. In response to the Germans' attempt to match Britain on the high seas, the navy had simply out-built and out-designed them. In 1914 Britain had twenty-two of the revolutionary new Dreadnoughts whose combination of big guns, heavy armour and high speed made any other ship of comparable size virtually obsolete, and she was building thirteen more. By comparison Germany had fifteen with another five under construction. And the British advantage was repeated down throughout each class of ship.

Britain's shores were certainly safe but by Continental standards its army was hardly an army. The British Expeditionary Force (BEF) which almost immediately went into action on the Western end of the French line proved itself at the Battle of Mons, holding up the advance of a far larger German force for twenty-four vital hours before joining the fighting retreat towards Paris. It played a part in the crucial French victory at the Marne which finally brought the German advance to a halt and, at the first battle of Ypres, stopped the Germans reaching the channel ports. But by November 1914 the original BEF was no more; a third of the men who had arrived in France three months earlier were dead and total casualties, including the missing and wounded, were now almost 90,000. For Britain to play a continuing part in the war the army would need men in numbers that had never been contemplated.

What is remarkable about August 1914 is how happily men volunteered to go to war. For they were not being asked to defend their own homes in the way that the French and indeed the Germans were. They were being asked instead to defend France and Belgium – a far less emotive proposition. There are many reasons that help to explain this, which must all be put into one essential context: these men did not know what we know today, they had no concept of the horror they proudly lined up to share. In fact their worry was often that if they did not hurry the war would be over before they had the chance to join in.

The Hon. Aubrey Herbert, a Conservative MP, might have taken matters to the extreme, but he is an example of the overwhelming enthusiasm that existed. He ordered the Irish Guards' uniform from his tailor, found out the route one of the Irish Guards' battalions was going to take to the station on its way to France and simply fell in beside them as they marched. He was listed as an interpreter, but despite having appalling eyesight he was very much involved in the fighting at Mons until he was wounded then captured by the Germans before finally being freed by the French. (His life continued in much the same fashion in later years; the Albanians, grateful to him for helping save their country from being partitioned, twice offered him their kingship.)

A lieutenant with the Royal Engineers based in Scotland remembers how some of his men actually tried to desert in order to join fighting units like the Royal Scots or the Black Watch and get to the front before it was all over. In the first week of the war 8,193 volunteers came forward; in the second week this jumped to 43,354. News of the battle of Mons and the retreat to the Marne only increased the determination to fight, with 63,000 volunteering in the last week of August and 174,901 in the first week of September.

This unity of purpose was surprising, for Britain in 1914 was a country no longer at ease with itself. Although Britain remained the richest country in Europe, 20 per cent of the population lived below the subsistence level and a grumbling swell of discontent had resulted in a series of strikes in the docks, the railways and the mines. In 1912, the year when these strikes peaked, 40 million working days were lost. The suffragettes, women seeking the right to vote, were increasingly militant – in 1913 a suffragette died when she threw herself in front of the runners at the Derby. Despite or perhaps because of the rise of the trade unions and the newly formed Labour Party, the House of Lords appeared to believe that the Tories had a divine right to rule. In 1909 they blocked Lloyd George's people's budget, a package of social reforms aimed, so the Chancellor said, at waging 'implacable warfare against poverty and squalidness' and including a super tax on incomes over £5,000. It took another election before the budget was passed and a further election – and the threat of the government creating enough peers to secure a majority – before the Lords' powers were finally limited. Yet the Conservative opposition remained venomous and there followed an even more divisive fight over Home Rule for Ireland, with the Conservatives and – at a crucial point – some elements of the army siding with the Protestants of the North and their paramilitary 'volunteers' before war postponed the whole problem.

However much the Conservatives under Andrew Bonar Law hated Asquith they did support his entry into the war. But within his own government Asquith had to deal with a potential 'peace party' of no less than ten ministers including Lloyd George. As the war came ever closer he received resignation letters from four of them, although by the time war was declared he managed to reduce this number down to two. As for the Labour Party, which along with the Irish Nationalists gave the Liberals their solid majority in Parliament, the hope of its members on the left that Europe's workers and the parties representing them would 'stand together for peace' proved entirely misplaced. Ramsay MacDonald resigned as leader, having failed to convince the party that Britain should remain out of the war, and was replaced by Arthur Henderson who by the end of August 1914 had become one of the Joint Presidents of the Parliamentary Recruiting Committee. The party was not going to have its growing strength jeopardised by any accusation that it was unpatriotic. Keir Hardie, leader of the Independent Labour Party, despaired as his hopes of organising an international strike against the war disintegrated. 'I have never seen a man so broken,' said one of his supporters. 'He died a year later and just as much as any soldier who was shot he was a casualty of war.'

Although Asquith managed to unite the country in favour of a war that only a few weeks earlier had seemed unthinkable, he was too much the intellectual to be a leader who could inspire men into battle. He hated the idea of being perceived as some sort of cheerleader. During the final days leading up to war he found himself surrounded by cheering crowds as he made his way to the Commons: 'I have never before been a popular character with "the man in the street" and in all this dark and dangerous business it gives me scant pleasure,' he admitted. But he was clever enough not only to know his own limitations but also to realise that the country needed some sort of figurehead leading its battalions. He found that man in Lord Kitchener, whom he appointed Secretary of State for War. Kitchener was the soldier hero of the hour both in Sudan and South Africa. Slow he might be: 'he generally finds things out sooner or later – as a rule rather later' was Asquith's own verdict having sat in Cabinet with Kitchener on his right-hand side for a couple of months. But he was just what Asquith needed.

What Kitchener ignited – both the man and the famous poster his face appears on, emblazoned 'Your Country Needs You' – was patriotism so strong it surprised even the Field Marshal himself. At one early stage, without consulting anyone, he raised the height restriction and the chest measurement volunteers had to reach to be accepted into the army because he was concerned that the number of recruits was surpassing the army's ability to process them. He might have been, as Asquith's second wife Margot so bitingly put it, 'more of a great poster than a great man' but in these early days it did not matter.

The German army was soon inadvertently helping Kitchener's recruiting efforts as it entered Belgium. When the British Expeditionary Force moved through France every soldier carried in his Pay Book Kitchener's order of the day: 'Be invariably courteous, considerate and kind. Never do anything likely to injure or destroy property, and always look upon looting as a disgraceful act.' It is hard to imagine soldiers taking too much notice of Kitchener's thoughts in the heat of battle, but they were words that German soldiers could have heeded in Belgium. The German chief of staff Helmuth von Moltke wrote on 5 August: 'Our advance in Belgium is certainly brutal, but we are fighting for our lives and all who get in the way must take the consequences.' Innocent civilians – priests even – were shot and survivors bayoneted. At Dinant, more than 600 civilians were murdered including a three-week-old baby. In the small university town of Louvain the occupying German troops panicked, believing – wrongly – that they were being fired on by civilian snipers hidden amidst the buildings. After three days the losses amounted to 209 civilians killed, a library of 230,000 rare books burnt out and the population of 42,000 evacuated.

Certainly the British and French played up the Belgian atrocities in these first days of the war for all they were worth – Lloyd George's claim that the Germans had killed three civilians for every one soldier being just one example of the exaggerated claims made – but atrocities there were and the 'rape of Belgium' had an instant and dramatic effect on the country. The Dean of Durham reported on a meeting at the city's town hall where he was one of the speakers: at its close, 200 miners came forward to volunteer. The argument that swayed them was a 'genuinely altruistic' one: the treatment of Belgium 'stirred a flame of moral indignation' among them and they were determined to be the 'chivalrous rescuers'.

As war threatened, Gilbert Murray, Regius Professor of Greek at Oxford – a man much more influential in political circles than that title might imply – had joined a neutrality committee which included two bishops. But after the invasion of Belgium he wrote, 'The power whose good faith I had always championed . . . in part meant murder from the beginning.' John Percival, Bishop of Hereford, and one of the neutrality committee's supporters, was another who changed his mind, writing to *The Times* on 12 August that 'in obedience to our treaty obligations and in support of Belgium's just claim, our country had no choice to take up the sword.' Two months later his son was killed in the early fighting. The fate of Belgium finished off the neutrality committee, which disappeared just as rapidly as it had appeared.

Although the great majority of both the country and the government thought that war would be over by Christmas, Kitchener had doubts; doubts so strong that he planned for the army to come to its maximum strength in the third summer of the war. His view was not shared by others. Two weeks after the war began Raymond Asquith, the brilliant eldest son of the Prime Minister who had easy-going access to Downing Street, wrote a letter to a friend from Balliol College dismissing Kitchener's caution: 'King of chaos they call him. He seems to be a sad mixture of gloom, ignorance and loquacity; says the war will last three years.' Nevertheless men kept pouring in to the recruiting stations; within five weeks almost 480,000 men had volunteered.

Before the month of August was out, John Brocklesby was elected chairman of Conisbrough's local War Fund Committee and his wife took her place on the Ladies' Committee for Soldiers' Relief. The hall next to the Brocklesbys' house and shop in Brook Square was opened as the town's recruiting office. There, Sergeant J.M. Atkinson presided, helped by the eldest Brocklesby son, George, who looked after all the paperwork. He had barely survived a life-threatening bout of influenza and was medically unfit to join up even if he had wanted to. Sergeant Atkinson did not have to go far to find the right man to swear in his recruits for, conveniently, Brocklesby senior had been a Justice of the Peace for the last seven years. So by January 1915 when Sergeant Atkinson departed for active service, leaving George as the sole recruiting officer, this family conveyor belt had already delivered 500 volunteers into the army.

Bert, such an outgoing character, was on the road to becoming – like his father – something of a fixture in the town as a schoolteacher who had learned his craft in London, as an organist whom the local paper hailed as a 'brilliant executant', and as a young man who was already welcomed as lay preacher in the church. Now, at twenty-five and of prime military age, he only had to turn left out of the front door of the family house, take no more than four or five steps into the recruiting station and the picture of him as one of the town's upstanding citizens would have been complete. But he would not do it.

Yet for the second and perhaps last time in his life he did have doubts. His family was ready to fight, his friends were ready to fight and although he was firm in his belief in the commandment 'Thou shalt not kill', the message was being drowned out by clergymen on all sides, armed with many other passages from the Bible, urging their flock to war. Should Bert listen to these united voices or the text that he clung to so tenaciously? Amidst what he called the 'harvest of hatred' that surrounded him he needed some reassurance that he was right. They were doubts which in the end he decided to resolve in a slightly absurd way.

When the founder of the Methodist Church, John Wesley, fell inconveniently in love with a young American member of his congregation in Georgia in 1737 he ended up 'casting lots' in an attempt to decide whether he should propose marriage to her (he didn't propose and she very soon found someone else). Now Bert Brocklesby decided he too should cast lots.

He returned to the room where he had been born, the room where he had first heard the still, small voice that had rid him of his 'spiritual darkness'. There he demanded that 'God should give me a plain Yes or No to the question: Should I enlist? And like Gideon of old I determined the method. As I believed that God controlled everything, He could control the spin of a coin tossed in the air. So it was heads for one course, tails for the other.'

It was, he admits, a peculiar thing to do, 'not a method a maturer judgement would recommend', but it got results. 'There was a remarkable run of tosses saying I must not enlist; memory says about twelve, and possibly one in favour of joining up.' Given the sort of character that Bert was, there is absolutely no doubt that he would have gone on tossing coins through the night until he got the result he wanted.

Although this episode reads strangely now it did bring some sort of confirmation and thus comfort to a man who despite the closeness of his family and his friends was very much alone in his belief. Since there was no conscription in Britain at this stage there were no conscientious objectors and no organisation to turn to; every man was alone. Bert himself argued, 'It shows my lonely extremity, and also the love of God who is ready to help us in whatever way we may be helped.'

3

A Lone Voice

There were others who, in these early days, felt the same way as Bert, yet nevertheless felt equally strongly they should be doing something to help their country. Corder Catchpool, a thirty-one-year-old, rather intense Quaker, was one of them. What he and others like him wanted was a way of showing that they were patriots but not warriors.

Corder had been hiking in the Alps with his younger brother Guy when they dropped below the snowline and discovered that war had broken out. In their hotel 'the little French *femme de chambre* was in tears. Her father and brothers will have to fight. "Ils sont fort, ils sont fort les Allemands."' It was time for him to try to make his way back to England. This was easier said than done at a time when Europe's armies were girding themselves for war: in Dijon, while they were drinking the water from a fountain, they were arrested by the police on suspicion of poisoning the public water supply. Perhaps it was the fact that in Amiens he had crossed paths with the first divisions of the British Expeditionary Force 'on their way to meet the enemy at Mons' that made him feel that to do nothing was not enough.

He found his answer in *The Friend*, the Quaker weekly newspaper, which in its issue of 21 August carried a letter from Philip Noel-Baker (who went on in later years to win the Nobel Peace Prize and captain Britain's Olympic team) appealing both for volunteers and for funds for a Quaker ambulance corps. 'It is possible that it would in various ways involve some personal risk to the members of the corps. But it would probably result in the saving of a great many lives and in the alleviation of a great deal of suffering among the primary victims of war.'

Even though the letter was carefully crafted it still roused the opposition if not anger of other Quakers. A couple of weeks later Charles Gregory from Evesham wrote to *The Friend*: 'An ambulance corps at the rear, healing the fighters to fight again, is as much a part of the military equipment of today as the man with the bayonet doing his deadly work on the field of battle. It will be deplorable if any of our young Friends should so fall away from their peace principles as to take part in this work.'

Nonetheless Noel-Baker's letter raised £100 and led to the setting up of a training camp in Buckinghamshire for about forty men. The first recruits were to include Catchpool and others who were mostly students from Oxford or Cambridge. In class terms these Quakers were a step or two ahead of the Brocklesbys and the corps grew into a 'rather motley band of lawyers, doctors, students, engineers, surveyors, accountants, businessmen and workers in many arts and crafts'.

They were trained in first aid and stretcher bearing, toughened up by route marches and organised along semi-military lines complete with khaki uniforms. However they did not take orders from the army and they were not paid – although there was a maintenance allowance for the poorest members. Despite being pacifists there was a certain military air – however relaxed – about them. Here is Catchpool writing to his family about the day they left for France: 'Finally to the outfitter's in Regent Street, to pack my person into khaki. Then paraded and marched thirty-strong, to Charing Cross, chanting the inevitable "Tipperary".'

At Dover all forty-three volunteers, equipped with eight brand-new ambulance cars, managed to hitch a ride on a navy ship, the *Invicta*, which was on a mission in complete contradiction to their own peaceful intentions: transporting twelve-inch shells to France. Their introduction to warfare was much speedier than most soldiers ever experienced. In mid-Channel they came across the *Hermes*, a light cruiser transformed into a sort of aircraft carrier carrying seaplanes. It had been torpedoed by one of Germany's new breed of submarines and was sinking all too fast. Some of the ship's company had managed to escape into the sea where the *Invicta* and others circled, trying to pick up the survivors. But there were many others clinging to the ship – either wounded or frightened or both. Noel-Baker watched while the ship began to settle: 'Its bows suddenly shot up in the air and it went down stern first to the bottom with all those gallant British sailors on board. I had never seen anybody die before. It was to me a very harrowing experience.'

Worse was to follow. After dropping off the men they had rescued back in Dover they turned around and headed for Dunkirk once more. There they docked and were trying to get to sleep when a French doctor appeared on board begging for help. Casualties were arriving in such numbers from the battle now unfolding around Ypres, a little to the north, that the medical resources were completely overwhelmed. The Friends went straight to the railway sheds where they were given a vivid introduction to the horror of war. Noel-Baker remembers: 'We found between 2,000 and 3,000 British, French, Germans, Belgians who had first aid bandages put on them on the battlefield and most of them had no further attention for a fortnight. Their wounds had all turned septic. The stench of the place was absolutely appalling.'

'Consider this man,' wrote Corder Catchpool, 'with his arm hanging by a shred of biceps – or this, bits of bone floating in a pool of pus that fills up a great hole in his flesh, laughing bitterly when I turn away to vomit . . . We work on through the night, hurrying from one to another and only able to touch a fringe. The priests touch more than we, hurrying through the solemn rite – men are dying on all sides.'

Thus the Friends Ambulance Unit (FAU) was born and after the first long week of giving what help he could to the wounded who rotated through these sheds, Catchpool wrote 'the need of help is so urgent that I have never tasted purer happiness than during the past week'.

The unit was the exception; pacifists at this stage had to do nothing more than stick to their jobs and keep their mouths shut. But that simply was not Bert's way. Early in the New Year of 1915, with the war far from 'over by Christmas', he was asked to preach at the evening service in the Chapel. He chose as his text Romans 12:19–21: 'Dearly beloved, avenge not yourselves, but rather give place unto wrath: for it is written, Vengeance is mine; I will repay, saith the Lord.' If anyone didn't take the hint then two further texts made his feelings about the war very clear. The first was from Cardinal Bourne, the Catholic Archbishop of Westminster commenting that as the church had sons on both sides of the conflict all they could do was pray for the war's speedy end. The second was from Dr Alfred Salter, an East End doctor and later MP who drew a vivid picture of a warrior God only to dismiss it: 'Look! Christ in khaki, out in France, thrusting his bayonet into the body of a German workman. See! The Son of God with a machine gun, ambushing a column of German infantry, catching them unawares in a lane and mowing them down in their helplessness . . . No! No! That picture is an impossible one, *and we all know it.*'

The result was, as Bert noted, 'a bombshell'. There were the sectarian critics: 'You had no business to quote a Catholic in a Methodist Church,' one told him; there was another who said with considerable foresight, 'Bert has ruined his career.' But it was only Mrs Harry Appleyard, a member of another of the town's important families, who was confident enough to say what others were almost certainly thinking: 'He has only preached it because he is frightened to go himself.'

To be fair to Bert, a week later he was asked to preach at the nearby village of Swinton and he again delivered 'the Gospel of Peace'. But this time, when he paused in the middle of his sermon to apologise for the controversial nature of his subject, a member of the congregation encouragingly called out 'Go on brother, we hear plenty on the other side.' Nevertheless, no one else asked him to preach again. At a recruiting meeting in town a few days later the principal speaker read out what a local newspaper called an 'extraordinary' letter from someone who had heard Bert's sermon. Bert, the anonymous letter writer complained, 'had asserted that this country had no right to join Russia and France in opposing Germany. I am thankful to say that this person occupies a position of splendid isolation. I may further tell you that he is of military age. If I hesitate to charge him with want of courage, I have no scruples whatever in declaring that he is without a spark of patriotism in his soul.' At this stage, while people in the town might complain about Bert they did not yet know quite how far he would go to defend his beliefs – that was to come later.

By the end of November 1914, the Western Front had stabilised. Armies permitting, you could have walked a line of trenches that ran for 475 miles from the North Sea to neutral Switzerland. The development of the machine gun and the modernisation of both artillery and the rifle, as well as the efficiency of the railway system which could keep an army supplied with food, ammunition and new men, had turned the war into a creature far different from that imagined in those first exciting days of August. A war of movement had swiftly become a war of the trenches where any sort of advance came at horrifying cost to the attackers. Already along the Western Front the British had suffered 30,000 dead; the Belgians a similar number, the Germans 241,000 and the French 306,000 – excluding missing or wounded men. Until March 1917, when the Germans made a planned withdrawal to the fortified 'Hindenburg line', this front was hardly to move at all, but the army's appetite for men grew inexorably.

Almost 1.4 million men had volunteered in the first six months. Certainly they were untrained, recruits who could not just be thrown into battle, but they constituted, nevertheless, a remarkable response to Kitchener's call to arms. Many men decided to join together and fight together, giving Kitchener's Army a vital sense of comradeship that it would need in the years to come. General Henry Wilson suggested that these 'Pals' battalions, as they were known, would become 'the laughing stock of every soldier in Europe' but he was to be proved wrong.

The first Pals Battalion was the London Stockbrokers who became part of the Royal Fusiliers; 210 men joined within hours, 1,600 within a week. In contrast, in Glasgow the Fifteenth Battalion of the Highland Light Infantry – the 'Tramways Battalion' – was made up entirely of the drivers, conductors and mechanics of the city's tramways department. As big cities like Liverpool, Manchester and Sheffield showed how easy it was to raise a battalion, so it became a matter of civic pride for other towns to follow in their footsteps. In South Yorkshire the *Barnsley Chronicle* encouraged men to join the town's own Pals Battalion: 'It is an opportunity which will never present itself again for men to prove themselves men.' Two thousand men attended an outdoor meeting in mid-September – many of them miners who had just come up from their day shift – at which their Union representative assured them 'just as you have worked together in the pits, you will be able to work together as soldiers'. They heard too from a local council member who appealed to their sense of pride: 'You know very well that no one makes better soldiers than the brave lads from our coalfields. You men face death every day of your lives and on the field of battle you will be braver than any there'. They might lack officers, uniforms and even rifles – at first they all had to share just forty weapons – but, no matter, all of these could come later. It took just three weeks to raise 1,100 men – the first battalion of Barnsley Pals. The recruiting efforts had been so successful it was soon decided to raise a second battalion.

The officers were volunteers just like the men and among them there appeared an unlikely soldier, Reverend George De Ville Smith, curate of St Thomas's in Worsbrough Dale. In France 32,699 clergymen were conscripted and 4,618 were killed. But in Britain, from the very start of the war, the Archbishop of Canterbury Randall Davidson made it clear that for a clergyman to volunteer as a combatant was 'incompatible' with his ordination. When De Ville Smith first involved himself in helping to raise the battalion, he did promise his vicar that he would not take a commission with the Pals. But he was a military man in waiting. In 1912 he had formed a company of the Church Lads' Brigade and his tall, commanding figure was to be seen 'almost daily leading the boys whom he dearly loved'. Shortly afterwards he broke his vow, accepting the rank of temporary second lieutenant in the Thirteenth Battalion York and Lancaster Regiment – to give the Pals their full name. Naturally enough, his vicar asked him why he had broken his word. 'My country first, sir,' came the reply, and the vicar could only accept the inevitable.

However, by 1915 this early heady rush of volunteers had become a much more cautious flow, influenced perhaps by the stories seeping through from France of what life was actually like on the battlefield. Whereas the First Battalion of the Barnsley Pals had reached the required number in about a month, the Second Battalion was still not quite there after three months. The *Barnsley Chronicle* lamented the fact that the latter was 'not making the progress it deserves. This is all the more strange when one looks about the streets and picture palaces in an evening, where hundreds of young men, quite eligible to serve in the Army are whiling away their time.' The newspaper might complain, yet by the end of 1915 across the country almost 2.5 million men had volunteered.

In February Phil Brocklesby came home from the pharmacy where he was working in Headingley, worrying about whether he should enlist. His older brother had just enraged the town by preaching against the war. His younger brother Harold, who was more prepared to go along with things, was already an officer in the University Training Corps and gung-ho for battle – just to emphasise the point he was home too from University, resplendent in his uniform. Which way was Phil going to turn?

Phil was smaller than Bert and he shared with his brother a strong sense of fun (although sometimes he was laughed at rather than laughed with). Undoubtedly he looked up to big brother Bert, but Phil was a more gentle character. Not perhaps as clever or loud as Bert, he did not share Bert's one-track mind and was not always so sure that he was right.

At this stage in the war their father believed wholeheartedly that volunteering was the right thing to do. Harold, who of all the brothers was the one most inclined to follow the lead of others, was trying hard to persuade him to join – gingering him on – but Phil had an independent streak in him which made him hesitate. He had absolutely no hatred of the Germans, but he did have a sense of responsibility – of doing what was right – the feeling that if other people were fighting it was his duty to do his share too. One black sheep in the family was enough. Having thought about it over the weekend, on the Monday morning Phil asked his brother George for the enlisting form, and took the necessary oath before his father, the Justice of the Peace. It was just a month since Bert had preached his sermon against war. Years later Phil remembers this form rather proudly: 'it was probably unique, for George signed as recruiting official; it had my signature as a volunteer, and father's signature as magistrate, so it was signed by three Brocklesbys.' The next day he reported for service with the York and Lancaster Regiment at Pontefract barracks where a year later his brother would end up in very different circumstances. He was greeted by Corporal 'Sunshine', so nicknamed because he was anything but. He had his first army meal, tripe and onions in milk, followed by a bad night's sleep. There were some old sweats in his hut who had returned from France 'more or less badly wounded' who spent half the night chilling the brand new recruits with their experiences. But France still seemed a long way away; for now he was in the army and quite enjoying it. In April Harold left University – never to return – and was off to Jersey for more officer training.

As the number of volunteers began to decline, so, naturally enough, the call for the introduction of conscription intensified, but the idea of forcing men to fight remained alien to Prime Minister Asquith, Lloyd George, the Liberal Party, the Labour Party and the trade unions. Quite apart from the belief that going to war should be a matter of choice, there was also the feeling that a man forced to fight would not be the same calibre of fighter as the man who had volunteered. It was Under

Secretary for War Harold Tennant who asked if it would be desirable for men who had been 'spurred by patriotism to join the ranks' to have to serve side by side with the man 'who has been driven into service, not because he likes it, but because he is told he must'.

In April 1915 Raymond Asquith, whose efforts to join the fighting were still being frustrated, wrote to his wife Katharine about lunch with Lady Sybil Grant: 'She seems to want conscription. It is very odd how many people do nowadays. The idea that they have at the back of their minds seems to be that if their lovers are being killed, it is only fair that their footmen should be killed too. I don't feel that myself.'

But as the army's appetite for men grew ever more voracious the conscriptionists were becoming ever more powerful. The way that the battles of 1915 were fought and the consequent losses they brought only increased their case. At Neuve Chapelle in March, the British hoped to break the German line near Lille, but the initial gains were soon checked and very little ground was won – at a cost of 11,652 killed or wounded. Next followed the defence of Ypres, with the German attackers using gas for the first time. The line was held but at a cost to the British of about 60,000. Then, in May, there was a disastrous attack on Aubers Ridge where the British lack of high-explosive shells meant the German defenders were able to stop the attack in its tracks – this time costing 11,600 men. And finally, in September, came Loos where 16,000 men lost their lives and 25,000 were wounded. The Germans were so horrified at the massacre of line after line of men that they held their fire as the British retreated. In addition the attempt to open up a new front against the Turks at Gallipoli was proving to be a disaster.

The battle at Aubers Ridge might not have overthrown the Germans but it almost overthrew Asquith. The British Commander in Chief, Sir John French, used a *Times* journalist as well as military friends in London to suggest that the shell shortage had cost him the battle. This campaign when linked with the resignation of the First Sea Lord, Admiral Sir John Fisher, who had fallen out with his political superior, Winston Churchill, over the naval venture against the Turks meant that to survive Asquith had to invite the Conservatives, along with the Labour Party, into a coalition. Now the Conservatives could argue the case for conscription from within the government.

Asquith was genuinely worried by the strength of feeling against conscription both within his own party and among the increasingly powerful ranks of trade unions. In August he recorded a conversation he had had with the Liberal chief whip: 'Gulland, whom I saw this morning for the first time for weeks, tells me that he gets letters from Liberal chairmen, etc., all over the country . . . some of them predicting that conscription would bring us to the verge or over the verge of revolution. I have had several interviews with colleagues, all strong in the same sense.'

In September he wrote to the former Tory Prime Minister Arthur Balfour, who had replaced Churchill at the Admiralty in the new coalition government, pleading for his help in constructing a bridge over a 'growing and perilous chasm'. In this letter – nine pages and handwritten – he told Balfour that a 'government servant' had attended the Labour congress in Bristol and reported back regarding conscription: 'Believe me it would mean revolt if not revolution.'

It was not just the trade unions that Asquith had to deal with outside Parliament. He faced a very different type of pressure from two other sources. King George V studied the recruiting figures week by week and was not backward in privately pressing the conscription case. More important was the newspaper proprietor Lord Northcliffe, owner of the *Daily Mail* and *The Times*, who was leading a very public campaign in favour of conscription.

Registration had become the first goal of the conscriptionists. Its aim was ostensibly benign: 'to take stock of what we have got in the way of men'. The King pointed out in a letter to Asquith that 'no one could object to that'. But it didn't take a genius to see what would happen next, as the Labour MP Philip Snowden put it: 'the appetite grows by what it feeds on . . . if this register be compiled, then at once a violent press agitation will be begun for the use of the material of this register for the purpose of enforcing compulsory military service.' Nevertheless the National Registration Act took little over a week to get passed on 15 July 1915, and a month later 150,000 volunteers fanned out to distribute a simple form that everyone, both male and female between the ages of fifteen and sixty-five, had to fill in. The penalty for failing to do so was a large fine or imprisonment. When the numbers had been added up they showed almost 1.8 million men to be of the right age, not involved in a vital occupation like manufacturing ammunition, who were medically fit yet not in the army. They were commonly labelled 'slackers'. Some women worried that registration was part of a plan to 'take away their men folk' and they could not have been more right. Northcliffe, having won the fight over the Registration Bill, now went on to demand that these slackers be forced to serve.

But Northcliffe had not won yet. In the same month that registration took place, Sir John French, the Commander in Chief, was worrying about the effect that conscription would have on the army. He wanted men who were not only ready, but also eager to fight. He wrote to Kitchener: 'As you know I have for many years been a strong advocate for the application of Continental conscription in all parts of the British Empire. I am however somewhat doubtful as to the wisdom of bringing in so drastic a change while the war lasts.'

It was in August too that the hard-pressed Kitchener received an eight-page letter marked 'secret' from Margot Asquith. She had married Asquith after the death of his first wife and she played a tempestuous part in politics which would amaze the wives of today's politicians. Northcliffe and others, she told Kitchener, 'are running this campaign for conscription to put you in a hole'.

You must show pluck and beat them . . . If you are clever you will come and see Henry [as she called her husband] on Friday morning and say this to him: 'You must bring up conscription in the Cabinet next week. Say you are against it till the necessity arises. If your Cabinet is in favour of conscription I will threaten to resign.' The British public will take

conscription and anything else you like if you and Henry quite quietly
say you want it . . . Don't let Curzon [Lord Curzon, former Viceroy of
India and now in the coalition cabinet] score, he is an untrustworthy
fool. You have been weak over Northcliffe as I told you before. Very
[underlined] weak.

But Kitchener, the man who received this impassioned plea, had just
agreed with the French that Britain should put seventy divisions into
the field by the end of the year. He had no hope of doing it without
conscription. On 3 September 1914, 33,204 recruits had volunteered in
a single day. A year later it took two weeks to reach that figure, yet the
army was now looking for 35,000 men a week.

Asquith admitted in the Commons that there were 'differences' in
the Cabinet over the issue. In one final attempt to get the volunteers
required, in October 1915 the government introduced an unhappy
scheme named after the newly appointed Director-General of
Recruiting, Lord Derby. Under this scheme the men who had not yet
volunteered were encouraged to 'attest' that they were willing to serve
at some time in the future if they were asked to do so. The 'encouragement' was fairly heavy-handed; one canvasser said it was the most
unpleasant job he ever took on, 'to recruit your neighbours' sons, your
neighbours' men, your own men'.

It was a scheme that offered pleasure now – those who signed up
could tell friends and neighbours that they too had agreed to serve and
show them the armband they had been given to prove it – with the
prospect of pain and possible death some distant way down the road.
But it still did not conjure up the numbers the army wanted.

4

'Did She Call You a Coward?'

Month by month it was becoming harder to resist the call to fight. Even a religious man would find little comfort in his church if he had doubts. Bert Brocklesby decided almost instantly that he would not fight, but there were very few clergymen of any denomination who seriously questioned the war. Amongst the country's main Christian churches the only body that remained committed to peace was the Quakers, and individually a surprising number of Quakers – 33 per cent of men of military age – eventually enlisted. A month after war was declared the Bishop of Sheffield, preaching in a neighbouring town to Conisbrough, told the congregation: 'Let us stand or fall together. We know we are right and God will befriend the righteous, so that in the end we are certain to triumph.' This was mild in comparison to many of his fellow clergymen.

Archdeacon Basil Wilberforce, chaplain to the Speaker of the House of Commons, preaching at St Margaret's in Parliament Square at the beginning of the war, claimed that 'to kill Germans is a divine service in the fullest acceptance of the word'. The Bishop of Carlisle said the war was being fought on behalf of 'truth, justice and righteousness'. He saw it as a 'crusade' and British soldiers 'in a sense divinely ordained for this service'. The Bishop of Durham spoke of the 'holiness of patriotism'. It is hardly surprising that after sixteen months of war one MP observed: 'the clergy are preaching up and down the length of the land not "Thou shalt not kill" but "Thou shalt kill."'

Two days before war broke out the Archbishop of Canterbury,

Randall Davidson, had preached a prescient sermon in Westminster Abbey: 'What is happening is fearful beyond all words . . . the thing which is now astir in Europe is not the work of God but the work of the Devil.' But by the time of his Christmas pastoral letter the Devil was loose and now the question was not stopping the war but winning it: 'I think I can say deliberately that no household or home will be acting worthily if, in timidity or self-love, it keeps back any of those who can loyally bear a man's part in the great enterprise on the part of the land we love.'

In contrast to the Archbishop's careful wording, the Bishop of London, A.F. Winnington-Ingram, had no doubts at all. While the Archbishop was airing his worries about the Devil the Bishop was standing on a hay cart in a military camp, dressed in his army chaplain's uniform, quoting Shakespeare's Henry V to 5,000 reserves. He used Agincourt, Crécy, Inkerman, the Alma and Waterloo among his recruiting tools; rather more emotive, however far-fetched, was his rhetorical question: 'We would all rather die, wouldn't we, than have England a German province?'

Winnington-Ingram cut something of a glamorous figure with his cockney accent and hint of the East End. He was the Church of England at its most patriotic. His publishers liked to call him the 'Bishop of the Battlefields'. He was far less patrician than some of his fellow bishops (once Cosmo Lang became Archbishop of York he was said never to have entered a shop again) and he regularly visited troops both at home and abroad. In September he preached to soldiers at Bisley in a sermon which left no room for doubters: 'This is an Holy War. We are on the side of Christianity against anti-Christ. We are on the side of the New Testament which respects the weak, and honours treaties, and dies for its friends and looks upon war as a regrettable necessity . . . it is a Holy War, and to fight in a Holy War is an honour.'

There were some among the clergy, however, who saw the war not in terms of patriotism but as a divine punishment for the country's many sins over the years. It was a view put eloquently by J.E. Watts-Ditchfield, the Bishop of Chelmsford, in a sermon in St Paul's in Holy Week 1916 which reads more twenty-first century than early twentieth century. He said the war was a judgement on all nations, including the Allies:

Had not the Allies much to answer for in the past – Russia for her treatment of the Jews, Belgium for the Congo atrocities, France for her overthrow of God and religion . . . We should look on our own sins – the opium traffic forced on China, our refusal to interfere when Armenians were massacred, the neglect of Sunday, the prevalence of intemperance and impurity, the hastening to be rich, the division among the classes and the masses, the unhealthy public spirit as shown in the press, the neglect of the housing question, the begrudging of money for old-age pensions, and the removal of slums.

The Bishop of Oxford, Charles Gore, put it rather more succinctly. He saw the war as a judgement of God that had to be endured to the bitter end. 'I feel as if we must be greatly chastised before we can be strengthened.' Even politicians sometimes joined in this breast-beating. A month after the war began Lloyd George told an audience in London, 'A great flood of luxury and of sloth which had submerged the land is receding and a new Britain is appearing. We can see for the first time the fundamental things that matter in life and that have been obscured from our vision by the tropical growth of prosperity.' This breast-beating was certainly not confined to Britain. In Germany, for instance, a poem by A.W. Heymel looked forward to a war that would bring to an end 'the opulence of peace', while Thomas Mann saw war as a moral necessity, both 'a purging and a liberation'.

While today it is almost impossible to be considered an intellectual and to argue in favour of the war against Iraq, in August 1914 there were very few intellectuals who were in open opposition to the war. Perhaps the man most famous for his eventual opposition to the war is Siegfried Sassoon, but in July 1914 he felt rather differently. He realised that war was almost upon him at the end of the month when some of the cricketers with whom he was playing a two-day match at Tunbridge Wells received telegrams recalling them to their regiments. The next day he went on a 60-mile bike ride to Rye to think over how he should respond to this test of manhood and came back knowing that he had to volunteer – 'like most of the human race I had always wanted to be a hero'. By the time war was declared Sassoon had already enlisted as a private in the Sussex Yeomanry.

The poet and critic Edmund Gosse wrote of the possible cleansing quality of war while Rupert Brooke (in his sonnet 'Peace', written in 1914) welcomed the war in almost grateful tones:

> Now, God be thanked Who has matched us with His hour
> And caught our youth and wakened us from sleeping.

But others had little time for questions of morality, of duty, or the Day of Judgement. They saw war as fun and they wanted to be there before it was all over. It is a dirty little secret that war can on occasion actually be fun. Discussing conscientious objectors, a British naval officer who was involved in the Falklands war said that what surprised him was that they had chosen to miss out on something which he was delighted not to have missed: 'We had such an enjoyable time.' Similarly a sergeant from Texas, trying to persuade a CO to go to Vietnam, told him: 'Don't you understand that Vietnam is the *only* game you'll ever be able to play in your *entire* life, where you'll get to put your life on the line?'

In 1914, as Churchill later wrote, 'men were everywhere eager to dare'. Julian Grenfell, who attended Eton and Oxford before joining the Royal Dragoons, wrote to his mother, a fashionable London hostess, in the understated style of his class: 'It is all the most wonderful fun, better fun than one could imagine. I hope it goes on a nice long time. I adore war, it is like a big picnic without the objectlessness of a picnic.' Instead of partridges he listed in his Game Book dead Germans. 'One loves one's fellow man so much more when one is bent on killing him.' After being decorated for bravery he was himself killed in May 1915.

For those who did not share this inclination to fight there was one other weapon that could be used against them which came neither from Northcliffe nor the church: the white feather. The notion of women going up to complete strangers who were wearing civilian clothing and presenting them with a white feather as a mark of cowardice sounds more likely to be myth than reality. However Fenner Brockway, one of the leaders of the anti-conscription movement, described after the war how he collected 'a fan-full of white feathers', which makes them sound like a virility symbol – a battle scar to be proud of – rather than a weapon that would drive a man to war.

Virginia Woolf suggested after the war that only about fifty or sixty feathers were handed out – 'it was more a product of male hysteria than actual practice'. But in fact it is now clear that the white feather was indeed a powerful, sometimes tragic and occasionally laughable recruiting weapon. Much of the evidence for this lies in an unlikely place, the Sound Archives of the Imperial War Museum. To its credit the Museum, which might be expected only to glorify all things military, is one of the key sources on conscientious objectors and it holds the tape-recorded memories of men's encounters with the white feather women – they were always women.

The choice of the white feather as a mark of cowardice comes from the novel *The Four Feathers*, by A.E.W. Mason, first published in 1902. Four white feathers are at the heart of the story. They are given to a young officer, Harry Feversham, by three fellow officers after he resigns his commission rather than be sent to Egypt. His fiancée Ethne adds a fourth feather when she finds out what he has done. From then on Harry's ultimately successful mission is to redeem himself in the eyes of his friends and his fiancée.

At the end of August 1914 Admiral Charles Penrose-Fitzgerald persuaded thirty young women to hand out white feathers to every young 'slacker' on the seafront at Folkestone, to remind those 'deaf or indifferent to their country's needs' that British soldiers were 'fighting and dying across the Channel'.

Before launching his women on the young men of Folkestone the retired admiral warned the slackers: 'there is a danger awaiting them far more terrible than anything they can meet in battle and that is, if they are found idling and loafing tomorrow they will be presented by a lady with a white feather.' From Folkestone, so the *Daily Mail* reported, these women moved on to Deal. But there was some initial confusion; at first the men receiving the feathers thought they were 'favours' presented by attractive women and they put them in their buttonholes or hat bands. Only later did they realise what was going on and took them off.

Age did not seem to worry these women, in spite of the fact that you were supposed to be eighteen before you could join up and nineteen before you could serve abroad. At the outset of the war Frederick Broome, a London lad, had already talked himself into the army at the age of fifteen, taking advantage of the fact that many recruiting sergeants were happy to go along with the convenient fiction that a boy of this age was actually a man of nineteen. He was in France for the retreat from Mons, the battle of the Marne and the first battle of Ypres – experience enough for any man, let alone a fifteen-year-old. Eventually he caught a fever and was returned to England, whereupon his father sent his birth certificate to the army demanding he be discharged.

Broome recalls:

I got a job in civvy street. A few months after I got the job I was walking across Putney Bridge when I was accosted by four girls who gave me three white feathers. I explained to them that I had been in the army and been discharged and I was still only sixteen. Several people had collected around the girls and there was giggling and I felt most uncomfortable and awfully embarrassed and said something about I had a good mind to chuck them into the Thames. I felt very humiliated. I finished the walk over the bridge and there on the other side was the Thirty-seventh London Territorial Association of the Royal Field Artillery. I walked straight in and rejoined the army.

Norman Demuth had just left school and was sixteen when he tried to enlist. He must have been very young-looking because he was turned down. It was soon after this failed attempt that he got his first white feather and decided he had to apply with 'renewed zeal'. This time he managed to enlist as a private in the London Rifle Brigade, and served on the Western Front until he was invalided out, only to get yet more white feathers – in total he says he received about fifteen:

> Some were given to me when I was looking in shop windows, others in buses and others when I was walking along the road, even though I had a limp. At the beginning I got very, very angry. Almost the last feather I received was on a bus. I saw two women looking at me. One leant forward, produced a white feather and said 'Here is a gift for a brave soldier.' I took it and said 'Thank you very much I wanted one of those' and I took my pipe out of my pocket and I put this feather down the pipe and I worked it like I have never worked a pipe cleaner since and then I pulled it out and it was filthy. I said 'We didn't get these in the trenches' and I handed it back to her. She got well and truly barracked by the rest of the people on the bus.'

Sometimes it seems the featherers and the recruiting sergeant were almost in collusion. S.C. Lang was walking down Camden High Street in north London:

> Two young ladies approached me and said 'Why aren't you in the army with the boys?'
>
> 'Well, I am sorry but I am only seventeen.'
>
> 'Oh, we've heard that one before, and I suppose you are also working on work of national importance?'
>
> I said it so happens that I am working at the Camden Loco [then a railway engine shed which meant that he was in a 'reserved' occupation needed for the home front].
>
> 'Well, we've heard that one before.' She put her hand in her bag and

pulled out a feather. I raised my hand thinking she was going to strike me when this feather was pushed up my nose.

Then a sergeant came out of one of the shops. 'Did she call you a coward?'

And I said yes and I felt very indignant at the time. And he said: 'Come across the roadway to the drill hall and we'll soon prove that you are not a coward.'

I got into the drill hall and he said 'How old are you?'

'I am seventeen.'

'What did you say, nineteen?' He weighed me, took my height and I had a medical exam.

Under age he might be, unwilling he might be, but he was in the army.

Most of the feathers appear to have been given out amidst the anonymous protection of the cities and towns rather than in the villages where everybody knew everyone else. Trains, buses and even cinemas were the favoured places for catching a man by surprise. A.H. Wallace was another soldier to come back from the front wounded.

I got on a bus in civvies and a woman sitting opposite me opened her bag, took out a white feather which she gave to me. I was very surprised. 'What is this for?'

'Because you're a coward.'

'Excuse me, I'm not a bloody coward. If you like to have a look at my leg you can find the other piece which is laying on the battlefield.'

A gentleman sitting alongside me said 'Hit the bitch.'

I said, 'I can't do that.' I said, 'The best thing you can do madam is to get off the bus otherwise you might find yourself in trouble.'

She stopped the bus and got off.

Leonard Mundy was also sent home with a wound in his leg: 'a nice little Blighty was one of the things you were always thinking about in the trenches' (a Blighty being a soldier's dream: a wound severe enough to get you back to England but not bad enough to kill or maim you). His mother had said she would take him to a play in Northampton and while they were walking to the theatre they noticed on the other side of the road a bunch of girls.

> One of the girls came straight across and put a white feather in my jacket. I never said anything. I done a grin to myself. I knew what it meant. But my mother, didn't she fly into a temper. She told these girls what had happened. Not only was I in the army, but I was home wounded. Didn't they make a fuss and apologise. My poor old mum was angry.

In the East End of London the 'girls' were not happy with any old white feather: 'they used to get the little white feathers from round a chicken's bum and give 'em that which was adding insult to injury,' says Ted Harrison who was brought up in Hoxton. The recipients 'didn't mind getting a decent-size feather, but when they got that bloody stuff near the chicken's arse they didn't like that'.

Only occasionally did the white feather reach members of the officer class – there were boundaries still to be observed. Mary Brough-Robertson, an overlooker in a munitions factory remembers:

> On one occasion a young man I knew was in a train. He was just recovering from a very bad wound in his lungs and a woman got in and presented him with a white feather after a while and started telling him what he should do and should not do, and ended up saying 'And as for that round your neck I suppose it's an old school tie.'
>
> He had listened very patiently to it all and said nothing until this remark was made and then he said 'The colours of my regiment madam.' She was quiet after that.

Colonel Alfred Irwin won the DSO with the East Surrey Regiment and was invalided home after being shot by a sniper: 'I was sitting in a restaurant with my wife after my wound had recovered and a girl came in with white feathers and I was in civvies.' It was not so much the colonel who was angered by being given a feather but his wife: 'She was so furious about it.'

There was some form of protection if you were working in a 'reserved occupation'. Frederick Sweeting, who worked in Coventry making shells for the navy, never got a white feather because he was prepared. 'I kept a wallet with a leaflet from Lord Kitchener saying my services in the ordnance works were more important than me being in the army. It was stamped quite a few times. I usually wore the ordnance badge on my jacket and everybody knew where you were when you wore that.'

Victor Polhill, who eventually joined up and served as a Lewis gunner 'never wanted to be in the army. I never wanted to have a stripe. I would do the right thing. But I wouldn't do more.' He eventually 'attested' under the Derby Scheme, and the reason for this was simple.

> To avoid the white feather if you cared to join up under the Derby Scheme you had an armlet given to you, a khaki armlet with a crown and you could wear that if you wanted to. If you didn't want to wear it you could keep it in your pocket and to anybody saying 'Why haven't you joined up?' you could say, 'Well, I have already joined up and I am waiting for my call up.'

Although it is relatively easy to find men who were given the white feather, it is much more difficult to find distributors of the feathers – while it might have been the thing to do during the war years, it was not something to admit to after the war had ended and the cost in lives had been added up. Elizabeth Lee, a Red Cross driver, had two brothers killed in the war, and a third brother who worked in an aircraft factory was given a feather. So who gave them out? 'Chiefly what we called flappers in those days. We would call them teenagers nowadays but we were flappers in those days: fourteen, fifteen, sixteen, seventeen. You used to ride on the back of a motorbike and it was sidesaddle on the motorbike, you'd have an arm round a bloke's waist. Those were the people who'd chiefly do it.'

Did she ever give a man a white feather? 'Never, I wouldn't have dreamt of doing such a thing. I felt it was up to people's conscience.' She says that in addition to the flappers some mothers 'whose sons were away' would hand them out as well, and Edward Robinson, at seventeen a junior reporter on the *Northampton Echo* who received three white feathers in a week before deciding to join – under-age – says the women who gave them out were 'mostly middle-aged and a little bit aggressive. It was a rather common thing, I learned afterwards, it was happening pretty much all over the country.'

Linda Sanderson admits to giving out a white feather. She was one of five daughters and her father was part of the family that owned the Donaldson shipping line. 'We gave the white feather to an uncle. He should have enlisted but he didn't.'

What was his reaction? 'Fury.'

Whose idea was it? 'All my sisters and mine. He looked very cross. I think we tied it to his coat when he was in it.'

Was she glad that she had done it? 'Very.' His failure to enlist, she said, 'was disgraceful'.

On occasion the white feather could end in tragedy. John Dorgan's brother Nicol was sent a white feather through the post, probably by a fellow member of the Methodist church in the mining town of Ashington in Northumberland. He went and joined the Durham Light Infantry very soon after receiving it, says John. 'You know he left home and he never spoke. I never saw him no more alive . . . my mother always restrained me from going down to the church.' Nicol was killed on 31 August 1917, most probably by 'friendly fire' from British artillery as his battalion made its way back into the trenches. He was nineteen.

Olive Shapley lived in Peckham, south London, with her parents and two brothers. Her oldest brother, Frank, was out with his scout troop when a woman asked him 'What's a big chap like you out playing, you get out and fight,' and gave him a white feather.

And he went and joined the navy that night. I think he was too young but no one was too bothered at that stage in the war. He went to sea in HMS *Indefatigable* and he was drowned in the battle of Jutland [in May 1916] and I think he was seventeen. There were a lot of white feathers handed out at that time. My mother never really got over it. I remember the waves of the North Sea breaking over my head every night. I can remember when the telegram came from the Admiralty to our house. I can see our breakfast table and this telegram in a green envelope and my mother bursting into tears – and parents didn't show their emotions in those days.

Bert Brocklesby never received a white feather. Perhaps it was the fact that he was a big character in a small town that protected him. People were more direct with him. One former Methodist stopped him in the street and asked directly when he was going to join up. When Bert told him that war was against the Commandments he replied 'Oh bugger the Commandments.' Bert's father suggested later he should have told him 'You may bugger the Commandments, but some day the Commandments will bugger you.'

If his parents tried to put any pressure on him Bert never said anything, but it is unlikely that they did; certainly Phil never pressed him and Harold, his youngest brother, was too much his junior to have much chance of success.

Nevertheless his mother was to receive at least one white feather through the post – anonymously – which seems particularly cruel given that she had two sons fighting for their country and their lives in France.

5

Brothers at War

On 27 August 1915, after six months' training and one failed application to be promoted to officer, Phil was on his way to France. Harold was already in France having gained a commission with the First South Staffords. Like most of his fellow countrymen Phil had never been out of England and after a first uncomfortable night with twelve others in a tent on a plateau above Boulogne he woke up at 6 a.m. the next morning with a sense of wonderment.

> I was in France, grass grew in France, just like it did in England – it was the same colour. I looked down on Boulogne. It was a lovely morning but mist covered most of the town, with church spires and towers sticking through it. As the mist cleared Boulogne revealed itself. Across the town we could see the English Channel and across that – but not to be seen was HOME. I had become a member of the British Expeditionary Force.

Both Phil's diaries and the copies he made of his letters home give a feeling of what a strange mixture of peace and fear France embodied for the soldier in 1915. Gradually the regiment (at this point he was with the Ninth Battalion York and Lancaster Regiment) moved closer to the war. The first hop took them to about 30 miles from the front; able to hear the dull roar of the guns but not to feel their effect. Having successfully secured a billet in a farmer's barn at two o'clock in the morning with the help of his schoolboy French – 'Il y a six soldats qui desirent logement monsieur' – he could write home to his mother 'By Jove this is a jolly fine country. Everything around here speaks of Peace rather than War and if it were not for our own battalion there would be scarcely anything to disturb the even tenor of village life.'

On Sunday morning they watched the villagers go to early church: 'the young girls were in black dresses wearing spotlessly white pinafores, clutching their prayer books sedately.' In the evening their host brought them beer at a penny a bottle and some *vin rouge* and by the third evening they were being invited in for a delicious supper of *haricots verts*. Apart from an unfortunate billet inspection, when the visiting captain ordered them to clean out the cess pit and the delighted farmer told them to put the sewage on his bed of *haricots verts* – 'my interest in *haricots verts* suppers waned' – life in the French countryside in late summer seemed pretty idyllic.

But it was not to last. On 16 September he wrote to his Aunt Bec, who lived with his parents, telling of 'mildly exciting times . . . everything appears to be at peace when Boom Crash a gun speaks and destroys the peaceful rural picture. It almost makes me think that man has obtained too great power and that God should step in and put man in his proper place.'

Four days later he wrote to his aunt again 'This isn't exactly written in the trenches but I am not far away. There are one or two snipers who are doing their best to make life worth living.' Phil's battalion was being moved up in reserve ready for yet another push – this time Loos. Kitchener was determined that the battle had to be fought to take some pressure off the French, but he recognised too that the battle might mean 'very heavy casualties indeed'. Given the disastrous losses the British suffered it was very fortunate for Phil that he was working in battalion headquarters about 1,000 yards from the front. Nevertheless a couple of gun crews were wiped out by German artillery returning fire and 'with Boche shells screaming over us and crashing fifty to eighty yards away, and our own artillery retaliating with an occasional shot just to cheer us up, it wasn't a comfortable day at all'.

A couple of weeks after it was all over he wrote home to his mother in a rather different tone to his previous letters. The battalion's casualties had been very light. One man was repairing sandbags in broad daylight when he got shot by a sniper – 'I had an uncomfortable feeling when I saw his body with the bullet hole in the centre of his forehead.' The death of another, who was killed haphazardly by an 'almost spent' bullet some distance from the trenches, hit home particularly hard because he was a fellow Methodist, who had quickly become a close friend.

Phil was in the army now, there was no way out unless he too got a nice Blighty, but he was beginning to have doubts. 'Oh this war; there are times when my indignation rises to such a pitch that – well I can't explain on paper, but the longer I live the more I agree with Bert's point of view.'

His brother Harold was not only on the battlefield, he was very much in the front line. By the time of Loos he was already a second lieutenant, having just finished his officer training. Like Phil, he had only arrived in France in August, but at eighteen he should not have been there at all. His battalion went into action early on the first morning and suffered some 70 per cent losses before they overran the first German lines. By the evening he was with his men in one of the furthest outposts of the British attack, lying in a shallow trench no more than a foot deep, being intermittently shelled by his own artillery, cut off from the rest of the advance. He sent out two patrols to discover where the British front line had come to a halt and none of the four men came back. When he went out himself he saw in the faint light 'the unmistakable German tin hats' in the nearby quarries which the British had captured only the day before.

'We seemed to be isolated,' he noted dryly. But under cover of an early morning mist they re-established contact with the front line, suffering only one casualty in the process. There, Lieutenant Kenneth Dunlop took him on to the top of the trench facing what he thought was dead ground to show him the lie of the land. 'I could have put my right hand on his left shoulder when I saw a little hole appear in the back of his waist. There was a crack as he fell, and I dropped beside him. With some help he managed to crawl into the trench we had just left.'

Harold made Dunlop as comfortable as he could and went to find a doctor who gave him morphine and said that stretcher bearers would come in the safety of the night to take him away. The last words Harold remembered him saying were 'Don't bother. I'm all right. I've got another job.' A few hours later he was killed by a piece of shrapnel. Three out of the five Dunlop brothers were killed serving with the South Staffords.

This was a battle that the local Conisbrough paper later described as one of a 'series of thrilling experiences' that Harold had been through, although in a later article this was modified to 'a trying experience', which is probably more the way Harold would have described it.

The casualties the South Staffords suffered at Loos give a good indication of the way the war was being fought. They went into the battle with twenty-one officers and 729 other ranks and when they came out their casualties were eighteen officers and 430 other ranks. All the other four officers in Harold's C company were killed. These figures reflect the disaster at Loos. At one point the British were marching into battle as if on parade, with no covering fire. The Germans looked on, amazed that 'a target was offered to us such as had never been seen before, nor even thought possible'. One German regimental history recorded 'Never had machine guns such straightforward work to do, nor done it so effectively.'

In November 1915 Margot Asquith noted the raw figures in her diary: '510,280 killed, missing or wounded. These are terrible figures – will 1916 be just the same?' It was clear that Britain had signed up to a war and a method of fighting which could not continue for much longer. Something had to change. The recruiting posters had already altered in tone. No longer was it simply the bold 'Your Country Needs You' but now there was more than a hint of accusation when posters asked 'Is your conscience clear?' The minimum height needed to join the army had been chopped down a couple of inches to five feet three inches and the age range expanded to forty. There was even a 'Bantam' battalion formed for those between five foot and five foot three inches – on long route marches the men's equipment was put on a lorry rather than carried on their backs – but the ranks being written off in France were still not being replaced and expanded in adequate numbers.

The Derby Scheme had failed, as many had predicted. It had certainly produced more men, but not enough. The romance, the sense of adventure had gone; men now had a clearer idea of what kind of war they were being asked to fight despite the considerable efforts of the government and the army to conceal it. The all-encompassing Defence of the Realm Act passed almost as soon as war was declared allowed heavy censorship, but for the most part the government could rely on the major newspapers to censor themselves. Casualty lists were not published until May 1915 and there was certainly no running total. Reporters were not allowed anywhere near the trenches and Kitchener ordered that any correspondent found in the field should be arrested, have his passport confiscated and be sent home. Instead newspapers had to rely on 'eyewitness' reports which the army itself wrote. Eventually, after much pressure, five war correspondents were attached to the Expeditionary Force. Even then they were under such strict military control, and they identified themselves so uncritically with the army – they were given the honorary status of captain – that their reports did nothing more than hint at the reality of war. Provincial newspapers sometimes carried letters from the front which gave a better idea of conditions. But no amount of censorship could now persuade potential recruits to believe that war was still some kind of enjoyable and short-lived romp.

At the end of October 1915, two months after telling Kitchener that he was 'somewhat doubtful' about conscription, Commander in Chief Sir John French wrote again from France: 'Having regard to the situation at the present moment I have no doubt whatsoever that the time has arrived when compulsory service should be adopted without any delay or limitation. I believe we can never hope to win the war without it.' More men and more arms was his answer to the slaughter at Loos; and although he was forced to resign his command before they arrived, his successor, Douglas Haig, knew they were on their way.

He was joined in the fight for conscription by a key ally: the ambitious Lloyd George. Following the disaster at Aubers Ridge and the bitter recriminations over the lack of high-explosive shells he was put in charge of a new department, the Ministry of Munitions. He was determined for the army's sake – and his own – to make a success of it, and he wanted conscription to ensure that the right men were sent to the front while the skilled workers – who had volunteered in their thousands in the early days – were kept working in the munitions factories.

On the afternoon of Wednesday, 5 January 1916 the Prime Minister rose to speak in the House of Commons. Of the 630 Members of Parliament, 165 were serving in the armed forces and many of them had chosen to wear their uniform for the debate. 'Not since the Cromwellian purges have so many uniformed soldiers been seen on the floor of the chamber' reported *The Times*. It certainly could have been a dramatic occasion – he was introducing a Bill in the middle of a war which transformed the way the British did things – but Asquith, speaking for little less than an hour, deliberately chose a palette scattered with nothing but grey, grey and more grey.

Asquith had set himself a hard task. Only two months earlier he had argued against conscription because it threatened 'the maintenance of national unity', yet here he was introducing conscription. His answer was to claim he was doing nothing of the sort. In attempting to make the Derby Scheme work, he said, he had pledged that married men who had 'attested' would not be asked to serve until all eligible single men had been brought into the army. So now, he argued, by introducing a Bill that forced only single men aged between eighteen and forty-one to join up, he was simply fulfilling his previous pledge. The Bill, he said, 'is one, I think, which can be sincerely supported by those who, either on principle, or, as in my case, on grounds of expediency, are opposed to what is commonly described as conscription'.

It was a ridiculous argument but nonetheless a successful one. He had already lost his Home Secretary, Sir John Simon. 'Poor Simon,' the prime minister wrote later, 'I am so sorry for him in his self-righteousness.' But it was the only resignation he suffered; the three other key Liberal waverers in the Cabinet stayed and only a handful of Liberal MPs had supported Simon. Even more remarkably, Asquith managed to hang on to the three Labour members of his government, including party leader Arthur Henderson, who had all announced they would resign after the party's national executive came out against the Bill. Back in September the trade unions had supported voluntary recruiting at their annual congress but – crucially – had not been committed to action against conscription. By the time the Labour Party conference met at the end of the month and voted against the Bill it was far too late to make any difference. The call of patriotism had won the day and, whatever motions they might pass, the government now had nothing to fear from the unions.

Nevertheless the army was not impressed. On the same day that Asquith introduced the Bill, General Sir William Robertson, newly appointed as Chief of the Imperial General Staff, wrote to Haig who had just taken over from French: 'It is deplorable the way these politicians fight and intrigue against each other. They are my great difficulty here. They have no idea how war must be conducted in order to be given a reasonable chance of success and they will not allow the professionals a free hand.' Four days later he wrote of a 'a great deal of wobbling' among politicians. Wobbling or not, the Bill's passage through the Commons was an easy one. It was passed three weeks after Asquith introduced it by 383 votes to thirty-six and even *The Times* admitted that there had been a 'tumultuously triumphant demonstration' in his favour.

There was at least one clause in the Bill that Sir John Simon had to show for his opposition. The first draft included three categories of exemption: civilian employment in the national interest – the munitions factory for instance – followed by exemptions for men whose dependants could not survive without their breadwinner, and for those who could prove serious ill health. But the second draft – the one that Asquith introduced – had one more category added. When he came to the point in his speech where he announced: 'the fourth ground for exemption is a conscientious objection to undertaking combatant service', it proved too much for many Tories. The *Daily Mail* reported: 'the biggest outburst of incredulous and contemptuous cries came at the news that COs were to be released from combatant service. The laughter was long and loud.' But Asquith was an experienced Commons hand; a little derision was not going to hurt him, and by inserting the conscience clause he ensured that he carried his party with him.

In the Upper House Lord Willoughby De Broke summarised the opposition to the conscience clause: 'A man who conscientiously objected to fighting for himself or for his wife and family, but who was willing that others should be persuaded to lay down their lives for him and his possessions displayed a selfishness, an hypocrisy and an arrogance which were difficult to forgive.' But not everyone felt like this. In Yorkshire the *Mexborough and Swinton Times*, which covered the Conisbrough area, urged the government not to make concessions 'of any kind to the shirker' but still welcomed the conscience clause: 'there is something beautifully English in this courteous concession to genuine scruples and principles.'

Asquith himself managed to paint a rather patrician, rosy view of the conscientious objector to convince both himself and MPs of what the effect of the clause would be.

Those of us who know the real facts of British life know quite well that there are a great many people belonging to various religious denominations or to various schools of thought who are quite prepared to serve their country in the war, but who object on conscientious grounds to the taking of life. They are however quite willing to perform many other military duties. I myself know of many men who hold these ideas and who hold them not only conscientiously but tenaciously who have gone out on minesweepers.

He enthused too about the men who performed duties behind the lines 'with the greatest of bravery and courage'. Asquith was an intelligent and sensitive man; he must have known that his vision of conscientious objectors happily serving on board a minesweeper had little to do with reality, but at this stage the key was to get the Bill passed: sorting out matters of conscience could come later.

As we shall see, the Bill's conscience clause was far from perfect, but again it set Britain apart from both allies and adversaries. On the Continent the idea of the conscientious objector, let alone any right to take such a stand, hardly existed. In Germany an accident of history back in 1868 allowed the Mennonites to gain non-combatant status, although about 400 of them died fighting in the war, but there were no other escape clauses. There were sometimes informal arrangements about whether Jehovah's Witnesses (known in those days as International Bible Students) and Seventh Day Adventists should be allowed non-combatant status, but usually they and anyone else who dared to object were sent to prison or to a psychiatrist and the horrors of the lunatic asylum. (There were very few exceptions, although one fortunate gardener, declared sane after being sent to a psychiatric clinic for refusing to fight, was eventually allowed by the army to go back to the clinic to keep up the garden.) In France conscientious objectors were regarded as deserters and sentenced to long terms of imprisonment or execution. There were no white feathers; they were not needed, for a good chunk of Northern France was now occupied by the Germans and the duty to defend the nation was embedded deep in a French soldier's soul. It was only in 1917 after year on year of horrendous losses that desertions of whole regiments, mass strikes and mutinies occurred – but there was seldom any individual refusal to fight and certainly no right to do so.

After Asquith's speech the *Westminster Gazette* reported that while conscientious objectors might escape combatant duties 'this does not exempt them from other military duties'. It was the commonly held view, but the *Gazette* was actually wrong. While the Bill in its final form stated that any exemption from military service could be conditional or temporary, it also allowed for absolute exemption without conditions. For most people, even those sympathetic to the COs, this was a leap too far and no more than about 200 men were ever given this status.

It was left to local tribunals set up by the 1916 Military Service Act to try to sort out the genuine from the impostors and then decide what to do with them. It was never going to be an easy task. As the Marquis of Lansdowne put it in the House of Lords 'I know of no machinery, judicial, or other, by which you can measure a man's conscience in the same way that you can measure the contents of a vessel, solid or liquid.' The tribunals were given clear and fair advice by Walter Long, President of the Local Government Board, who in the next year was to lose his elder son in the fighting. But it was advice they tended to ignore – and they could, for the most part, get away with it because the mood in the country had hardened: those who could fight should fight.

Lady Helen Pease, daughter of the Liberal MP Josiah Wedgwood, who observed the tribunal at work in Cambridge, said after the war: 'I now feel rather sorry for the tribunals. The chairman of the bench was a very worthy market gardener here, for instance. To have a long argument between the officer of the crown and a very vocal CO on what was the proper interpretation of the New Testament . . . I felt very sorry for them.' An Oxford student remembers a tribunal of 'local bigwigs' who included 'a clerical don from Magdalen who throughout the proceedings sat with his head buried in his hands and didn't say a word'.

Since the tribunals almost never gave men who they considered genuine an absolute exemption, they had two other choices: first, they could send men to join the army as non-combatants once the Non Combatant Corps – soon to be dubbed, inevitably, the No Courage Corps – had been set up. Second, they could exempt men from the army on condition that they did work of 'national importance'. The

Pelham Committee was formed to decide what constituted work of national importance, since this was unclear.

These tribunals had to have a minimum of five members and were usually about nine strong. Their membership can best be described as local worthies, who were often local council members. They elected their own chairman, usually a councillor and sometimes the local mayor, and they often sat in the town hall. There were few women among the membership and in any case one observer reported the women were 'usually fiercer than the men'. The law required at least one representative of the working classes – usually a trade union official – on the tribunal and there were a few Quakers dotted around, but they were a rare breed. However there was one person of key importance who was always to be found at the tribunal and this was the military representative, a post filled usually by officers or retired officers.

Lord Derby put their role succinctly; their duty, he said, was 'to protect the nation by obtaining as many men as possible for the army'. The military representative was in essence counsel for the prosecution although there was no counsel for the defence. But he was more than that; he was an intimidating presence, usually dressed in khaki; he was often a friend of the tribunal members and sometimes sat with them.

In Hyde, Cheshire, for instance, the military representative was the police chief constable and on at least two occasions in the early days when the tribunal members retired to make their decisions he retired with them. 'It is just as if the prosecutor in a criminal case were to retire with the magistrates and take part in deciding their decisions,' Philip Snowden told the House of Commons.

Time was important to the tribunals. Between January and July 1916 750,000 men applied for exemptions – the great majority on grounds other than conscience. In London the Battersea tribunal allowed five minutes for the hearing of each application. Although applicants could be represented by a 'friend' or a lawyer this was discouraged and there was hardly time for legal debate. Adrian Stephen, a legal historian, the brother of Virginia Woolf and later a psychoanalyst, who observed 'several hundred cases' before the London tribunals, wrote afterwards: 'With twenty or thirty cases to be heard between lunch and tea time what kind of nicety of judgement could have been expected of them?' The philosopher Bertrand Russell was rather less inclined to give them any benefit of the doubt. 'The tribunals are monstrous,' he wrote to his lover Lady Ottoline Morrell, 'the law is bad enough, but they disregard it and are much worse. It is simply a madness of persecution.' At forty-four he was frustrated to be too old to be called up: 'I felt horror of the men on the tribunals for their persecuting spirit, but I rather envy the men they persecute.'

There was opposition too from a less predictable source. Asquith had carried his party with him in the House of Commons, but there were still Liberals outside Parliament – many of them members of the nonconformist churches – who opposed conscription. One of them, in all other respects a staunch supporter of the government, was John Brocklesby. Old Brock had been swearing in volunteers from the Conisbrough district since the war began. When the war eventually ended he welcomed the surviving warriors back to their home town in a speech where he recalled 'with glowing pride' the men who had volunteered in their millions and 'absolutely glutted the military machine for weeks and months'.

But conscription was different. Like many members of the Liberal Party, it had taken the German advance into Belgium to persuade Brocklesby to support a declaration of war; but he was convinced that it should be a war fought by men who *chose* to fight. He did not agree with Bert's views, but he did believe that Bert had the right to hold them. If joining up was to be made compulsory he wanted nothing more to do with it. When the Military Service Act was passed not only did he sever his connection with the Liberal Party but he also refused to swear in any more recruits. The Conisbrough recruiting office, next door to the family home, was closed down. By 1916 Old Brock had sworn in close to 1,000 men and sent them off to the army, but now he wanted nothing more to do with the process.

6

'Would You Turn the Other Cheek?'

In France Phil Brocklesby's fortunes had improved since Loos. As the war on the Western Front finally died down for the winter, so his battalion went into reserve. Phil was fortunate enough to be at battalion HQ engaged in tasks like duplicating maps of the trenches rather than being in the trenches themselves. Soon after he joined up Phil had applied to become an officer and was 'crestfallen' when he was turned down – in part he blamed it on the fact that he was unshaven when he was summoned at very short notice to appear for the key interview. He had always suffered at school when teachers made the comparison with his older brother Bert, and now it was Harold, three years younger than him, who was an officer while he had been turned down. But in October he wrote to Harold giving him good news: at last he had been selected as a candidate for a commission and he would soon be coming back to England for officer training.

When he was finally sent on his way Phil was too excited to wait for the official transport; instead he walked 7 miles to catch the train to Boulogne. After a night in the YMCA in London his first duty was to call on the wife of his commanding officer, Colonel Addison, to give her a personal message from her husband and a souvenir of sorts: the fuse cap of the first shell fired at the York and Lancasters. In return he was given wine and biscuits and treated 'very pleasantly'. As always Phil did what he promised to do, for next he was off to Tooting to give another message to the mother of the second-in-command, Major Lewis (within eight months both officers were dead). Then he was off to a comfortable billet in Tynemouth to learn his trade as an officer. He remembers the commandant of the school as 'a decent old dug-out whose capacity for burgundy was enormous. The first night in Mess I saw him drink a quart.' After Christmas he was sent to a training camp on Cannock Chase where over 1,200 newly commissioned subalterns were being trained for the big push on the Somme. 'We were given a place in the camp and told to play at war with each other.' For a time at least his life was going to be easy.

The same could not be said for Bert. The Military Service Act became law on 27 January 1916 and came into force on 10 February. Just nineteen days later, having claimed exemption under the conscience clause inserted by Asquith, Bert Brocklesby appeared before his tribunal, one of the first COs in the country to have his case heard.

His Tuesday morning started in the usual way at the school in Conisbrough where he was still teaching: 'I had a good time in the scripture lesson; subject Christ's Parables in general, i.e. why He spoke in Parables – the Good Samaritan in particular.' Having taken the register and set some sums he left school at 10 a.m. to catch the train to Doncaster. He was joined by Frank Beaumont, a friend whose case was also due to be heard before the tribunal that day. Frank was someone who could enliven any proceedings: when he was secretary of the young mens' club in Conisbrough he had nailed a kipper under the club's table and enjoyed several days of fun while the members tried to locate the smelly drain. Bert also had with him Mrs Wray, a rather more serious friend who was wife of the town's pawnbroker. She was a strong supporter of the No Conscription Fellowship, which had been set up in December 1914 in preparation for exactly this sort of battle.

They reached Doncaster with an hour and a half to spare which gave them time for a good grooming at the local barber. Then they made their way to the offices where the tribunal was sitting. In the waiting room they found a 'motley group of young and old, clean and dirty, rich and poor, sober and – well not drunk, perhaps I ought to say abstainers and boozers. Frank began to get facetious and caused much laughter, but poor old Baker, the greengrocer of Denaby, smiled in a strained sort of way. Poor fellow, the Tribunal had no mercy on his claim on behalf of his two sons.' (He claimed that they were needed for his greengrocer's shop if it was to survive.)

In total about thirty cases were dealt with that morning. One farmer came out of the tribunal triumphantly, telling them: 'You all ought to be farmers.' He had won exemption for his farmhand as long as he stayed on the farm. 'Some men came out smiling, others came out looking depressed, while one man came out and relieved his over-charged feelings with a swear.'

In these early days of the tribunals the press were already present but they did not yet feel confident enough to publish the names of those appearing. However, in the weekly edition of the local newspaper headlined: 'Conscientious objector at Doncaster. "Ready to die for his principles"' it is very clear that the conscientious objector in question is Bert Brocklesby.

The reporter on the *Doncaster Gazette* was in no hurry to get to the story which provided the headline. First he reported on cases where applicants were pleading for exemption on other grounds. 'A Conisbrough father pleaded that his son was really responsible for the management of a fish, fruit and florist business and if he was taken by the military authorities he had no other prospect but to close the business.' He turned down the suggestion that he get a girl to be manager, saying she would not have the money to buy into the business. When told his son would have to serve, the man lamented: 'It will be the ruin of me.'

A failure to find anyone to manage his business – plus defective eyesight – were the reasons given by a Denaby ironmonger for not going to war. The chairman told him 'there are plenty of men serving with glasses now,' but he did get a week's adjournment for an eyesight test. A market gardener who cultivated three acres of land and had a seventy-three-year-old father to look after had his case put back for six weeks. Then it was Bert's turn. The *Doncaster Gazette*'s report on his hearing goes as follows:

A single elementary school teacher at Conisbrough applied for exemption on conscientious grounds to taking part in combatant service. On his appeal form he stated that he felt war was incompatible with Christian principles therefore he could not conscientiously take part therein.

The Clerk stated that he had received a letter from applicant's father stating that though he did not hold his son's views, after very careful conversation with him, he was fully persuaded he was sincere in his conviction. He did not think that he could engage in the operation of war without violating his conscience. Two of his sons held commissions in the army and the third an appointment under the military authorities.

The Chairman: 'I don't think it is any use questioning applicant.'
The Clerk: 'We shall only get a lengthy argument.'
Mr Henry Baker said he thought he had a perfect right to question him [Baker, one of the tribunal's members, was a councillor from Conisbrough, a former police officer and then a brewer's representative who had managed to fall out with many people including his wife]. Applicant entered the room and asked if the public were admitted.
The Clerk: 'The press are here.'
Applicant: 'May I call a witness, please?'
The Clerk: 'Yes.'
Applicant then called in his witness [Mrs Wray] and the Clerk inquired what object he had in calling the witness.
Applicant: 'To make a statement regarding my views as expressed both to her in public and the press.'
The Clerk: 'You have stated that you have nothing more to say than is on our form, so why do you require a witness?'
Applicant: 'I call her to bear witness to what I claim on the form.'

The Chairman: 'We are not disputing it.'

Mr Baker: 'We know what he has stated is quite true.' [At this point after a hurried conversation Mrs Wray tells Bert 'They don't want me here' and he agrees she should leave.]

The Clerk: 'Would your conscience prevent you from taking up arms in defence of yourself and those dear to you, let alone your country?'

Applicant: 'Yes sir.'

'Would it prevent you striking me back if I struck you?'

'According to my principles I could not do such a thing.'

'Give me a straight answer. If I knocked you a tooth out would you knock me two out?'

'No.'

'You would hold the other cheek?'

'I would try to get away. The case is hypothetical.'

'Supposing the enemy were to reach Conisbrough Castle and you and those dear to you were in danger of an aggravated and dastardly attack, would you stand by and see them ripped to pieces?'

'As the case is hypothetical . . .'

'Let us put it really as it has happened in another country and assume for the moment it has really happened. Let us have a straight answer, whether your conscience would prevent you from striking the enemy down?'

'I would certainly not strike them down. No man is justified in taking life.'

'You would stand by and see women and children cut to pieces and not raise a sword in opposition?'

'I would do my best to prevent them, but as the case is hypothetical there might be a chance given them of escaping long before.'

'You would run away?'

'Certainly.'

'Was there a chance in Belgium to run away?'

'In these cases the menfolk in Belgium went away and left the women to the tender mercies of the Germans.'

'What would you do?'

'Take them with me.'

'Have you any objection to non-combatant service?'

'Yes.'

'Supposing you were in a corner with your back to the wall and six men were before you with open sword or fixed bayonet, would you not do something if you had a revolver in your hand?'

'The Sixth Commandment says "Thou shalt not kill". I take it it is better to be killed than kill anyone else.'

'If there were six Germans in front of you and you had a revolver, you would not shoot?'

'No, sir.'

'The odds would be greater against you, but supposing there was only one?'

'I should get away from this miserable world.' (Laughter.)

Mr Baker: 'How long have you been a school teacher?'

'Certified nearly seven years.'

'What is the salary you are getting now?'

'£115 a year.'

'Is it generally known that you belong to a brotherhood [the No Conscription Fellowship] of some fifty or sixty members who agree not to agree to anything the Tribunal advise you or direct?'

'I have never made a secret about the matter. The membership is now 5,000.'

'In this immediate district how many are there of your "club"?'

'About 45.'

'Supposing there was a battle just here and you, amongst five or six others at Conisbrough, could save, say, 500 poor women and children by fighting, would you not help to do your best to save them?'

'I would do my best to save life, but not by taking life.'

'If you could knock one or two down, would not you do it if they were against us?'

'I would not try to take life.'

'You would knock down one or two?'

'Certainly.'

'Is this woman you brought here a member of your brotherhood?'

'Yes.'

'Has she two sons fit to go to the front?'

'Only one of military age.'

'Does he belong to the brotherhood?'

'Yes.'

'You would not assist by going on munitions work.'

'No.'

The Chairman: 'I don't agree. If you would not exert yourself to defend women and children from being murdered I think you are just as responsible for the lives of those women and children as if you had taken lives yourself.' (Hear Hear.)

The Clerk: 'Supposing the government offered you a place as a minesweeper that would be saving life?'

'Minesweepers are only allowed to sweep German mines, they are not allowed to sweep English mines as well.'

'Continually sweeping Germany's mines might stop the sinking of two boats as on Sunday?'

'Other mines are laid to sink other ships.'

'You would be against going minesweeping?'

'Yes.'

'Too much danger?'

'I am ready to die for my principles. I am standing up for freedom of conscience of all Englishmen. You cannot bring evidence to prove conscientious objection. The only way to prove it is to be ready to suffer for it and if necessary die for it. As there are thousands of men who have been ready to sacrifice their lives for their country it would be a pity if some were not prepared to sacrifice them for a higher principle.'

Mr Baker: 'You are a local preacher?'

'Yes.'

'Then I think you had better preach somewhere else.'

> Applicant was exempt from combatant service but recommended for non-combatant service.

And there the hearing ended. But here was where logic and the tribunal collided. Bert was told he was exempt from combatant service, so in essence the tribunal believed him however much they disliked his stand. But – understandably perhaps, given their obvious loathing of all he stood for – they would not take the next step and give him the absolute exemption that he had applied for. Instead they told him he would have to serve in the Non Combatant Corps – the army without rifles – although it was quite clear that there was no hope of him ever agreeing to this.

Mr Baker's anger that the council should still be employing him as a teacher – anger in fact that anyone should be allowed to hold such views – was reflected three pages further on in the editorial page of the *Doncaster Gazette*, which complained that conscientious objectors 'whine like so many spoilt children because the privileges extended to them in regard to military service are not greater than they actually are ... In act, if not in intention, they are friends of the common enemy.' From being the popular local schoolmaster and choir master, suddenly Bert was being condemned as Germany's friend.

This may well have been the first case where this tribunal had heard the CO's case intelligently argued and they seemed genuinely bewildered and angered. It must have been extraordinarily difficult at a time when Britain's army was under genuine threat to understand Bert's argument, let alone accept him. They could perhaps just accept – however much they disliked it – a CO who was prepared to do something for his country as long as it did not involve bearing arms; but a CO who would do nothing at all to support the war effort in any way was beyond their belief. As for Bert, it took both courage and stubbornness to hold the lonely course that he had set himself, but as his hearing showed he was an intelligent, forceful man quite prepared to give as good as he got.

Although Bert's case would appear to be fairly representative of the general level of tribunal hearings it is difficult to tell with any certainty because in 1919 the tribunal records passed to the newly created Ministry of Health and in 1921 the Ministry decided these records were not worth keeping and had them destroyed. It has been suggested that this destruction was part of a conspiracy to cover up the workings of the tribunals; but there is absolutely no evidence to support this and in fact what this destruction leaves us with are the cases which put the tribunals in the worst possible light. A few MPs raised injustices again and again in the House of Commons, leaving a record of the many instances where things were bad enough to reach Parliament rather than the everyday affairs like Bert's hearing.

Philip Snowden MP was careful to praise the 'many tribunals which he knew were at least trying to do the right thing', nevertheless he claimed in the Commons that in 'a great many cases the tribunals are refusing to hear the applicant'. He said that at one such case in Enfield the applicant was brave enough to ask the chairman if he believed him. 'I have no reason to disbelieve you, but I think you are able to go for a soldier,' the chairman replied.

Harold Bing went before his tribunal in Croydon in the summer of 1916 when he reached the age of eighteen. 'The chairman after one or two formal questions asked me how old I was. I said I was eighteen years of age. "Oh in that case you're not old enough to have a conscience. Case dismissed." My father got up to protest at such summary treatment but the chairman called "next case, next case, next case."'

A conscientious objector named Pierce appeared before the Holborn tribunal four days after Bert's hearing in Yorkshire: this is Snowden's account of the hearing:

Tribunal: 'What time do you get up?'
Pierce: 'Between seven and eight in the morning.'
Tribunal: 'What time do you go to bed?'
Pierce: 'Rather late generally.'

Tribunal: 'What exercise do you take?'

Pierce: 'I walk to work and take walks whenever I can.'

Tribunal: 'You take very little exercise.'

Pierce: 'Yes.'

Tribunal: 'You don't walk; you don't cycle. What do you do on Sundays?'

Pierce: 'I go to church and, if there is time, go for a walk.'

Tribunal: 'When do you have a bath?'

Pierce: 'Oh quite often.'

Tribunal: 'Judging by your appearance you don't look as if you did.'

On this evidence he was turned down. 'Can a more serious travesty of justice be imagined?' asked Snowden. The same tribunal turned down another applicant because he was not a Quaker. Evidence of Quaker membership certainly carried some weight, but it did not mean an automatic exemption and it almost never meant an absolute exemption. But if it was difficult to succeed in a claim for exemption based on religious grounds, it was far harder to succeed on political grounds. In Middlesex, for instance, the chairman told the applicant bluntly that since he was a Socialist he could not have a conscience.

A headline in the *Yorkshire Gazette* in June read 'Hanging From A Tree' and beneath it the newspaper outlined a sad story. A sorting clerk at York Post Office, Alexander Henderson, aged twenty-six, 'was found hanging by his braces from the branch of a sycamore tree by the side of the River Ouse, about 3 miles from York'. He was 'very respectably dressed' and his bicycle had been leant against the railing by the tree. A notice to appear before the appeal tribunal on the day he killed himself was in his pocket.

A letter to his mother was also found in his pocket asking her to forgive him. The letter said the reason he did what he did lay between the Creator and himself. 'A Socialist, I cannot conscientiously take part in a war which I feel to be wrong.'

At times the questions and the insults became particularly nasty. Snowden reported that the chairman of the Market Bosworth tribunal declared 'this man put his own skin first. It was the first of the breed he had met and he hoped that there would not be any more.' The same tribunal exempted all the men of the local hunt, presumably on the grounds that they were farmers and needed for the land.

In Hereford an applicant was asked 'What would you do if you saw a nigger assaulting one of your relatives?' The science and maths master at Harrow was told by one member of his tribunal he should be 'put across someone's knee and spanked'. A research scientist appearing before a tribunal near Oldham had everything thrown at him: he was said to be 'exploiting God to save his own skin, a deliberate and rank blasphemer, a coward and a cad, nothing but a disgusting mass of quivering fat'. At Nairn the chairman told an applicant, 'It seems to me that there are two things you possess – cowardice and insolence.' He told another applicant that it was the duty of Christians to fight the Devil, and if the Kaiser 'is not worse than the Devil I am a Dutchman'. When the applicant dared to speak up for himself and say he would 'only be obedient to the Lord' the chairman exploded. 'You are the most awful pack that ever walked on this earth. To think that you would not defend our women and children from the ravages of the Germans. Is that Christianity? It is acting with the Devil in place of Christ.'

It followed that atheists stood no chance; a CO wrote to the No Conscription Fellowship to say he had been turned down on the grounds that an atheist cannot have a conscience. 'I was disappointed at not satisfying the tribunal but not downhearted.'

There was seldom time for a debate on whether war was in all circumstances morally wrong or whether there was such a thing as a Just War – and if so did the invasion of Belgium make this a Just War? There was no time to discuss whether the duty the citizen owes to the state should take precedence over his own principles. On many occasions the debate simply revolved around the question of what an applicant would do if they saw a relative – almost always a woman – being attacked. If the CO said 'I'd do nothing' the assumption was that he was lying; but if he said 'I'd try to save her' this was proof that he would use violence to save his sister/mother/wife and thus there was no reason why he should not be sent off to war.

The NCF and the Quakers had to start organising classes for COs who were ill-equipped for a short, sharp and very public philosophical discussion. These classes were soon described by opponents as a 'school for shirkers'. Those preparing to go before a tribunal were told that the 'right' answer was to try to explain the difference between a policeman and a soldier: just because the CO was against the organised violence of war it did not mean he was against the necessary restraint needed by a policeman to enforce everyday civil law. But the debate seldom got that far.

At times tribunals strayed into wilder grounds with equally absurd effect. At a hearing in London an applicant, when asked his trade, said he was a piano tuner. This reply was not enough for the tribunal. How could he tell what use the piano that he tuned might be put to? It might be used to play military marches and patriotic songs. No piano tuner could be a conscientious objector. Case dismissed. Another applicant said he was a sculptor. He was asked whether he might not some day be offered a commission to produce a war memorial and whether he would accept such a commission. He replied honestly enough that he did not know. This was all the tribunal needed; a man who might possibly sculpt a war memorial could not possibly be a genuine objector. Case dismissed.

If ever there was doubt then the military representative was at hand to stiffen resolve. The military representative in Sheffield was perhaps more extreme than most when he told the tribunal that 'there is only one ground of total exemption before this tribunal and that is death'. But he was run a close second by the military representative at the Stockport tribunal, a Captain Rigby. His questioning of an applicant proceeded as follows:

'What would you do if someone were to knock you down?'
    'I should first of all get up again.'

'Suppose I was to get up from this table and knock you down, I suppose you would get up and run for a policeman and then go home and read your Bible?'

'I am not so sure that I approve of the method you suggest.'

'Well, you had better be careful or it will not take me long to knock you down.'

'Many a time,' wrote Adrian Stephen, 'have I been present when the applicant has stated his case and has been sent from the room. I have known the military representative . . . turn to the tribunal and say "Now I will tell you the truth about this man."'

At Gower the military representative asked one applicant if he had ever been in a lunatic asylum and told another he was a traitor and 'only fit to be on the point of a German bayonet'. In Oxford Herbert Runacres, a theological student preparing to be ordained, was turned down after the military representative read out a letter from someone he refused to identify which read, in part: 'This man is a conscientious objector of an objectionable type. He was stopped by the college authorities last term for addressing Socialist and other meetings, some of workmen, to discourage recruiting. I submit he should receive no quarter.'

The military representative's influence did not end at the tribunal's doorway. If anyone appealed the military representative was allowed to attach his own thoughts to the official documents as they wound their way up to the appeal tribunal. For instance, the Lothian and Peebles Appeal tribunal received this note from the military representative: 'This man would make a splendid soldier. He has a fine physique and just wants the nonsense knocked out of him. When the tribunal's decision was given to him he walked out of the room in a towering rage and slammed the door after him, so I think his Christianity is not very sincere. I think his appeal should be rejected.'

Although it was certainly not easy for Bert to get up and defend himself amidst such universal hostility, in comparison with many of these other cases he appears to have got off relatively lightly – even though he was, in essence, being called a murderer. Adrian Stephen, who observed so much of what went wrong, wrote later:

> I do not know that there is any special indignation against the tribunals. I felt some myself while I watched them, but it would have been asking too much of half a dozen grocers, haberdashers and retired colonels to rise above the general body of mankind to such a height to behave with reasonable forbearance.
>
> The members of the tribunal were for the most part just nice ordinary men. As a matter for fact I often had tea with the tribunals – they always treated me with great respect as a reporter – and it was interesting to watch over their friendly gossip, these men who had just been wrangling with the COs, who had just been conducting trials that would have provoked a storm throughout England had they taken place in an ordinary court in peace time.

The chairman of the Wirral tribunal lamented 'I wish the government had not put this clause about conscientious objectors in the Act at all. I do not agree with it myself.'

But the clause was there and it was not going to go away.

7

Conchies Fight Back

Three weeks after his tribunal hearing Bert Brocklesby was waiting for his appeal to be heard and had time to help organise a '*Conversazione*' in the Methodist schoolroom in Conisbrough. The programme opened with an overture by a string band conducted by Bert and concluded with a sketch 'That Piece of Silk', the characters 'being well sustained' by five women, one of whom was Bert's fiancée Annie. Her brother Gilbert, a dental student, had now volunteered and was serving in the artillery; but she had no trouble accepting a brother who volunteered and a boyfriend who refused to fight. Games were 'afterwards indulged in', followed by a 'choice selection of refreshments'. The proceeds went to the Foreign Mission Society. It was to be one of the last such happy occasions Bert would lead.

He could at least be comforted by the fact that apart from his initial hesitation he had no doubts about the rightness of his cause – whereas brother Phil, now finishing his officer training, was having doubts of a kind that could get him into serious trouble if he allowed them to persist. As always it was to his Aunt Bec that he confided these doubts – his mother usually received a rather more rose-tinted view of life. He wrote from Rugeley Camp:

I have not had much work here, chiefly supervising. To see the men at physical jerks rather gets on my nerves. Some of them don't look physically fit and it is horrible to think that we are training these men to shoot and be shot (some of them look as though it will be a case of the latter).

My feelings begin to revolt against war as they have never done before. Some of the poor beggars make me feel for them more than I were enduring it myself. I wish the war were over, then let me get away from England.

But Phil had made the decision to volunteer and now he had to live with it.

Back at home it was soon Bert's turn to have his appeal heard. One of the tribunal members was Frank Ogley, who had unseated Bert's father in the county council election; a race so bitter that John Brocklesby had refused to congratulate his rival when he learned the result. In addition Ogley had already publicly announced his determination to make Bert go 'as far as he could make him', so he could hardly be called an impartial judge. The family did not think to object to Ogley's presence although Father Brocklesby told him later that if Bert were shot he would blame him. 'Oh I hope it won't come to that,' Ogley replied smoothly.

A headline on a report of the case stated, fairly enough, 'CO says he had rather be killed than kill.' At the time, says Bert, this was considered 'the limit of absurdity as well as the limit of shirking one's duties'. He was asked whether he had ever made any sacrifice for his opinions. 'I answered that for eighteen years I had worked to help missionary enterprise. They looked blank. My gospel was not the same as theirs.'

His appeal changed nothing; again he was ordered to join the Non Combatant Corps. Although some COs were prepared to accept this option, to Bert it was just the army under another name. He refused.

There was only one more temptation to come Bert's way. Soon after his appeal was turned down William Wilson, his class leader in the Methodist Church and owner of a wood mill business, suggested to Bert that he work for him; that way Wilson would acquire a good worker and in turn Bert, as an essential worker, would find a reason other than conscience to satisfy a tribunal. Predictably Bert said no – with thanks. Later Wilson told Bert's father he ought to turn him out of the house. 'Thank heaven,' wrote Bert, 'our family bonds were proof against the shocks of war.' He was fortunate in the father he had; another CO remembers 'Father wanted me to join up. He almost took me by force to a recruiting office. It was one of the saddest things, having to go against his wishes.'

By now the tribunals were coming thick and fast. Harry Stanton, twenty-one and looking rather older than his age, came up before his tribunal in Luton in early March. Stanton had been proud to stay on at school to the age of sixteen – unusual at the time – and to have gone from office boy in the hat trade to clerk in charge of wages. But now his life was about to be turned upside down in a hearing that lasted less than three minutes. The proceedings were marked by a brief exchange about Quakerism because Stanton, like some other Quakers, was uneasy about using his religion as a reason for claiming absolute exemption, feeling it gave him an unfair advantage at the tribunals.

Chairman: 'Are you a member of any religious body?'
Stanton: 'I hope you don't press that question. I don't want to shelter behind any religious body.'
Chairman: 'Give us an answer. Don't waste time.'
Stanton: 'I am a member of the Society of Friends.'
Member of Tribunal: 'Are you willing to do non-combatant work?'
Stanton: 'No. I object to it as much as to combatant service.'
Military Representative: 'But a considerable number of Friends are doing ambulance work.'
Stanton: 'I cannot be governed by their convictions. My conviction is such that I cannot take up any sort of non-combatant work.'
Member of Tribunal: 'Was your father a blacksmith?'
Stanton: 'Yes.'
Chairman: 'Thank you, that will do.'

The tribunal ordered non-combatant service. Like Bert, there was no chance that Stanton would do it. Two weeks later he was given what he called a 'very fair' hearing at appeal; this time he had twenty minutes rather than three.

He was asked if he was prepared to 'take up work' with any public body and he in turn asked if such work would not mean 'a more efficient prosecution of the war'. When the chairman agreed that it would Stanton refused to change his employment and his appeal was lost.

Howard Marten, a Quaker and a clerk in the Piccadilly branch of the Capital and Counties bank, trudged through the snow to his hearing in Stanmore. What he remembers most about this hearing was arguing with the chairman, who was a local Anglican clergyman. They could both agree that 'war was due to the evil tendency in man', but while Marten believed that the 'evil tendency' was surmountable – thus giving logic to his stand – the chairman held out no such hope. The verdict was the same: non-combatant service.

Fred Murfin, a young printer, had his case held in Tottenham town hall ten days later. He is one of the few COs to admit how difficult the hearings could be. 'It was a terrible ordeal to anyone sensitive; I found it very trying. How does one feel when trying, in public, to convince people (who are out to trip up and misconstrue anything one says) that because of one's religious convictions – that no matter what the consequences – no war service is possible?' His memory of his appeal is being asked if he would kill wild beasts. 'The Germans are not wild beasts sir,' he replied. Coming at a time when Britain and France were haemorrhaging men and the German assault on Verdun looked for a time as though it might prove fatal, it was the sort of remark that was not going to win him any supporters.

It had taken two months for the first conscientious objectors to be processed through the newly installed tribunals and appeal tribunals, but now the round-up was ready to begin. Harry Stanton was among the first COs to receive a letter from the recruiting officer commanding him to report ready to join the Non Combatant Corps on Saturday, 8 April. He chose to ignore the order in favour of 'a more interesting engagement' – a two-day emergency meeting of the No Conscription Fellowship at the Quaker headquarters, at that time in Bishopsgate, London.

The No Conscription Fellowship (NCF) was formed three months after the war started by Fenner Brockway, the young editor of the *Labour Leader*, the newspaper of the Independent Labour Party (ILP). This was the party which had suffered such a cruel blow in August 1914 when the workers of Europe marched off relatively happily to war. Although conscription was not a major issue in 1914 when there were so many eager volunteers ready to fight, Brockway was looking to the future. Rather than get into a protracted ideological argument with fellow ILP members over official party policy, Fenner Brockway asked his wife to write a letter to his own newspaper which – unsurprisingly – he decided to publish. It stated: 'It would perhaps be well for men of enlistment age who are not prepared to take the part of a combatant in the war, whatever the penalty for refusing, to band themselves together so we may know our strengths.' Brockway suggested that all men between the age of eighteen and thirty-eight who did not want to fight should notify the *Leader*. Within a day he had 300 replies and the NCF was born.

It received no help from the Labour Party nor from the trade unions. The party was on its way to political power, the unions on their way to economic power and, once war was declared, they were not going to jeopardise their prospects by supporting an unpopular cause like the anti-conscription movement. In the climate of the day any body such as the newly formed Union for Democratic Control that dared question the continuation of the war was labelled as pro-German, or as one Labour MP put it: 'frightened lambs . . . breathing treachery'. The ILP was a weakened force and what support it gave was in the background. The anti-conscription movement had to look for support from the Quakers and the Fellowship of Reconciliation (FoR) which united pacifists from many Christian denominations, rather than any main-stream political party.

The NCF soon had the distinguished philosopher Bertrand Russell on their committee, bringing with him useful if unusual links to the government, and Fenner Brockway was appointed secretary. The key organiser, though, was Catherine Marshall, daughter of a former Harrow housemaster and a veteran worker on the non-violent side of the Suffragette movement. A woman acquaintance who worked as her 'dogsbody' for a fortnight in 1916 described her later as 'tall, imposing-looking and very nice. She was not one of those embittered and hysterical females you did get sometimes.'

Aylmer Rose, secretary of the NCF until he was jailed as a CO, remembers her as 'quite without the aggression and harshness which characterised so many feminists in those days. She was kind and sympathetic, quite without snobbery but always the grand lady.' Others, though, sometimes complained that she found it very difficult to let go of any task, always wanting to interfere.

Marshall certainly had the ability to deal with men outside the NCF. Perhaps the fact that she had been brought up in a boys' boarding school somehow gave her the confidence to take on male politicians at a time when women did not even have the vote. She came from the right class and she treated politicians as equals rather than superiors; for instance after a disappointing meeting with Lloyd George she wrote to him 'I often wish you were an unenfranchised woman instead of being Chancellor of the Exchequer! With what fire you would lead the woman's movement.'

The NCF was always under attack, its leaders either imprisoned as conscientious objectors or, like Russell, charged with one of the many possible offences under the draconian Defence of the Realm Act; copies of its newspaper *The Tribunal* were seized and its printing plant was smashed. But Marshall was always there to organise, and always knew the right person to talk to. Early in 1916, for example, Fenner Brockway arrived red-faced at her flat in Buckingham Gate and admitted he had left his briefcase, with vital emergency plans for what should happen if the government closed down the NCF, in the back of a taxi. She telephoned a friend who was Assistant Commissioner at Scotland Yard and within an hour the case was found at Kennington police station where it had been handed in. Brockway went to collect the case at once and amazingly found all the contents still untouched.

It was difficult being a woman with a key role – albeit unpaid – in what, until its leaders were arrested, was very much a man's organisation. Marshall never quite got the recognition she deserved, despite the fact that for a long time it was she who held the organisation together: visiting COs in prison, working her impressive political contacts, negotiating with the army, and driving herself eventually to the edge of a nervous breakdown. She had a lifelong inclination to push herself too hard – her attention to detail was such that amongst her papers, now all filed safely away, she kept the two lead pellets found in a Suffragist banner in 1914.

The NCF set up an effective joint action committee with the young Quakers and the FoR, and they found a mesmerising chairman. Clifford Allen had gone to Cambridge to study for the ministry and ended up an agnostic. For him Socialism was religion. 'I am a Socialist,' he told the tribunal in Battersea which heard his case, 'and so hold in all sincerity that the life and personality of every man is sacred, and that there is something of divinity in every human being.' Although he was sometimes described as completely humourless it became painfully obvious that Catherine Marshall, nine years his senior, had fallen in love with him – a love that was not reciprocated. Fenner Brockway describes him as 'almost Byronic in appearance', while another supporter of the NCF saw him as 'rather like a pale young curate only a little more vivid . . . he gave one the impression even then of the early Christian martyr.' Many years later both Allen and Brockway were to end up in the House of Lords: if the government had not found a mechanism for releasing Allen from Winchester prison, where his stand against the war eventually led him, he might well have achieved this martyrdom.

It was Allen who was in the chair for the two-day emergency National Convention of the NCF in Bishopsgate in early April 1916 that proved to be the high-water mark of organised opposition to conscription. There was real hope still in the air that, if enough men simply said no, the whole Military Service Act would crumble. So despite the nature of the building with its 'large, ugly circular hall' it was a meeting filled with considerable drama. While the *Daily Express* fulminated about the 'hole and corner peace cranks', Allen warned the police that he expected trouble. Members were intimidated as they arrived at the hall, and there was more intimidation from outside once they were in. But fortunately it turned into a rather wholesome British occasion. Fenner Brockway remembers: 'the building was attacked by sailors in uniform. Some of the sailors got over the iron bars and were just amazed and embarrassed and didn't know what to do and they were received on the other side with handshakes and asked to have a cup of tea.' The *Sunday Herald* saw it rather differently: 'Some of the raiders were thrown out collarless and bleeding. They now have strong views on the subject of non-combatants.' The Manchester *Guardian*, however, reported that 'if the opposition had penetrated into the Friends' Meeting house a riot would have been certain', while noting that no more than three sailors got over the barriers.

In the hall the 2,000 delegates were asked 'to refrain from cheering loudly because we didn't want to exasperate the crowd'. So in place of cheering they were instructed to wave handkerchiefs. It was to this meeting that Stanton came instead of the recruiting office where he was supposed to be. 'It was a thrilling experience,' he wrote, 'to see so many hundreds of men, many of them already awaiting arrest, solemnly pledging themselves to refuse all forms of military service.'

Soon after lunch Bertrand Russell left the hall to bail out from jail a conscientious objector and bring him back to the meeting, to be greeted by much applause – or rather handkerchief waving. Fenner Brockway read out the names of fifteen members who were already in the hands of the military. Many of the men there knew, like Stanton, that they only had days or weeks of freedom left.

There was real tension and excitement in the hall, but the social reformer Beatrice Webb, who was there as an observer, did not share it entirely. Allen, she recorded in her *Diaries*, was a 'monument of Christian patience and lucid speech' but she did not have so much time for the 'would-be martyrs' who were the delegates. She split them into three groups: 'The intellectual pietist, slender in figure, delicate in feature and complexion, benevolent in expression' was the dominant type. Next, 'there were not a few professional rebels out to smash the Military Service Act', and finally, 'here and there' could be found 'pasty-faced furtive boys' who hoped that conscientious objection could 'serve to excuse their refusal to enlist and possibly might save them from the terrors and discomforts of fighting'.

The meeting eventually ended with a carefully crafted resolution, agreed by all but two delegates, which opposed any form of alternative service while still supporting the individual in taking what action he thought right. The language might seem the usual dry assemblage of compromised words that come at the end of any conference, but Bertrand Russell wrote to Lady Ottoline: 'It has been a wonderful two days – the most inspiring and happy thing that I have known since the war began . . . I can't describe to you how happy I am having these men to work with and for . . . I feel they can't be defeated, whatever may be done to them.'

If Russell's euphoria was to last some weeks, Stanton's was to last only a couple of days. The next day he took 'a last long walk into the country which had never before seemed so beautiful'. On Tuesday, 11 April a police inspector arrived on his doorstep. 'My mother and two sisters were fortunately at home and they bade me a brave and cheerful farewell. The inspector by no means liked his job and considerately offered to walk at a distance from me, if I would prefer it. I said I would walk with him; I was not ashamed of my position and people in the town would soon know of my arrest.'

Like most of the pioneers Stanton had led a respectable life; the thought of prison had never entered his mind. He is typical of the majority of COs who came from the upwardly mobile working class or had only just arrived amongst the middle classes. If they were religious, as many of them were, they usually hailed from one of the nonconformist churches such as the Baptists, the Methodists or the Quakers rather than from the Church of England – Fenner Brockway himself was the son of nonconformist missionaries. They were the backbone of industrial Britain, but they were unused to being seen or heard.

A survey carried out by the Quakers in 1917 of 820 imprisoned 'absolutists' – those like Bert who refused to make any sort of compromise over conscription – showed that although 'schoolmasters and lecturers' were the biggest group (49), there was a huge range of trades including bakers and confectioners (8); carmen, chauffeurs and similar professions (15); shopkeepers (20); tailors (8); watchmakers (13); weavers and the like (9); chartered accountants (7); miners (6); pianoforte tuners (3); and merchants and business managers (25). There were even two policemen, who must have found imprisonment particularly hard. Listed under the heading 'University Men' were fifteen graduates and five undergraduates. Of the 329 who indicated their politics the largest number, 195, came from the ILP although there were 85 'unattached'. Among the 252 who gave their religion 106 were Quakers, fourteen Church of England, twenty-one Congregationalists, twenty-one Methodists and nine Jews. (A wider survey of 3,701 COs who were more prepared to make compromises and were not in jail showed that 124 had attended university while 2,870 had not been educated beyond the Elementary stage.)

If this group were unused to standing up for themselves in public, then the idea of going to prison was completely alien to them. Yet Stanton wrote in his diary that when he was deposited in the police cells and the iron door clanged behind him, 'I felt quite cheerful and interested in such a novel situation.' After an unusual 'picnic lunch' provided by well-wishers before he entered the cells he came up before the magistrates for having failed to answer his summons to join the army. At this stage every inch of ground was fought over and his first fight was over his hat – he wanted to keep it on in court, claiming that as a Quaker he was entitled to wear it; the clerk, with equal determination, wanted it off. The clerk's initial request to remove it out of respect to the military representatives in court was guaranteed to fail, but when he appealed to Stanton's better nature off came the hat. Once that was sorted out, the magistrates decided not to fine Stanton and the three other COs up before them because they had made no attempt to avoid arrest. They simply ordered that they should be handed over to the military authorities.

'Our training soon began,' wrote Stanton. 'We had not gone a dozen paces from the police station before the sergeant of the escort was telling us to "to keep step and look like soldiers". I laughingly declined to look like a soldier and strolled along quite independently of the formation, much to the surprise of the sergeant.'

The sergeant, used to a life of unquestioning obedience both in and out of the army, was perplexed by these earnest young men who told him – in the politest terms possible – that they simply would not do what he ordered. He tried a little fatherly advice in the hope that this might shake them out of it, telling Stanton that the army would certainly prove too strong for him so 'we would do well to accept the inevitable without further ado. He earnestly told me that I was just the type of man wanted in the army – that I should be a sergeant in next to no time.'

The four of them were taken by train to Bedford and thence to Kempston Barracks and for the first time Stanton began to have worries – 'As a child I had always felt a strange horror of the Barracks; the huge building seemed a place into which hundreds of men might disappear and never emerge again.' His mood was not helped when he heard the receiving sergeant being ordered to put them in 'the kennels'. The kennels were not much more than that: a room that was pitch dark, cold, smelly and draughty, where 'we groped around and soon located a soldier, lying on a pile of blankets. He was sleeping, but presently woke up and informed us, between hiccups, that he was a deserter.' They had a meal of fruit and chocolate they had brought with them and then lay down on the hard floor and tried to sleep. At about 11 p.m. a drunken soldier in a nearby cell began to shout 'Jacob, ain't I entitled to a blanket?' This continued for most of the night and was echoed by his neighbours. As for Stanton, 'I wrapped my blanket ever more closely around me and waited impatiently for the morning.' When morning came a dim light filtered through one dirty window, but there was no breakfast to be had. They were in the army now.

8

Soldiers Without Rifles

Most units of the British army take particular care to maintain and treasure their often proud histories, which helps sustain and inspire them through victory and defeat even when they are merged and, perhaps, merged again. Victories achieved, medals won, heroes who are not forgotten, defeats made somewhat glorious . . . They all count, even down to the sporting triumphs and the silverware on the table; all part of an ongoing link to past traditions which help turn a group of men into a fighting unit.

There are no such memories of the Non Combatant Corps (NCC). Born of Asquith's best intentions – his vision of conscientious objectors willing to do everything but fight – it was a unit unloved by almost everybody. Harry Stanton once found himself sharing a cell with a 'diminutive, keen-witted Scotsman' who gave him his view of the difference between the likes of Stanton and those who were prepared to serve in the Non Combatant Corps: 'I can admire you; they are cowards, but you are outspoken cowards.' The Scotsman, for all his talk of cowardice, was himself not too eager to get to the front, confiding in Stanton that he 'did not intend to fire another shot for the British army'. However he preferred to achieve his goal in a more traditional way. He used to get drunk and swear at anyone of superior rank, preferably a corporal – so not too senior. He would be duly sentenced and at the end of his detention he would take the first opportunity to get drunk and repeat his offence. He proposed to continue along the same lines until the end of the war. It was much less complicated – and seemingly rather more successful – than relying on the claims of conscience.

As a tool for solving the problem of conscientious objectors the NCC was a failure, or as Liberal MP T.E. Harvey told the Commons, 'a most regrettable mistake'. Only about 3,300 men accepted the tribunals' decision that they had to serve in it. To expect conscientious objectors to wear army uniform, to submit to army discipline and to act like a soldier in every way apart from carrying a gun was to misunderstand the nature of the majority of the men opposed to war. There was confusion among those who did agree to serve in it, considerable scorn from regular soldiers, and outright revulsion from some of the officers and NCOs told they had to run it.

One sergeant major in France loathed the whole idea so much he designed what he thought was a suitable coat of arms and managed to get his design into some newspapers. This included: 'three maggots recumbent proper, baby's bottle rampant, down pillow; supports are two tame rabbits rampant and above this "We Don't Want To Fight" and below "Tis Conscience doth make cowards of us all"'.

The units were attached to reserve battalions whose commanders had the difficult job of deciding what to do with them. The only answer they knew was discipline and more discipline. Arthur Harrison was sent to Richmond Castle to join his unit attached to the West Yorkshire Regiment. Almost as soon he arrived he was given his first route march. It was a 9-mile introduction but fortunately it was at 'slow march pace' which gave him time to spot some 'delightful scenery': 'magnificent halls . . . a huge circular pond . . . plentiful church ruins'. He soon progressed to a route march, this time carrying a fully laden pack where there was no time for church spotting: 'the pack made a tremendous difference, if it hadn't been for the blisters I would have come through all right.'(The captain told him to put a 'darning needle and a piece of worsted through each blister . . . it eased them very much'.)

There were bath parades and he had an hour's saluting practice each day: 'more of a joke than anything'. His routine usually consisted of half an hour's training before breakfast, a three-hour stretch before lunch and two hours before tea. He writes to say how delighted he is to escape a week of sentry duty at the castle gate – 'I look upon it as a farce' – and certainly a sentry without a rifle hardly seems much use to anyone. His whole routine sounds more like punishment than training, particularly since the NCC was only going to do the most basic of army chores. However, after a month of army discipline he was writing home somewhat proudly, 'I don't think the NCC will show a bad example to the world.'

The Times probably painted the most idealised picture of the NCC, with a report from 'Our Special Correspondent' who had been given access to a unit in France two months after the Corps was founded. The story is summed up by one among the several layers of headline above it: 'A Contented Force Doing Useful Work.' The story continues: 'Their conduct is exemplary, an unusually large percentage of them being total abstainers as well as non-smokers. The particular party which was visited is at the moment engaged on railway work, amid very pleasant surroundings, some distance from the front.' The correspondent says they are treated like other soldiers, but with their uniforms they do not wear belts or carry arms.

They use no military titles among themselves, but address each other as Mr or by nicknames. There appears to be no shadow of complaint of any harsh treatment; and if they have been victims of any unusual amount of jeering from their comrades they themselves do not seem to be aware of it.

One man, since they came out here, has found his conscience less obdurate than he supposed, and has asked to be transferred to the combatant ranks. It is by no means unlikely that more will follow.

The best service that can be rendered to them is to forget them, or think of them only as men who are rendering what service they conscientiously can to their country in her need, just like any other patriotic Briton.

Underneath this is a two-paragraph story headlined 'Non-Combatant "Casualties"' which might well have been inserted by a sub-editor who took exception to these non-fighting soldiers. None of them had been killed, wounded or taken prisoner by the enemy, but six had German measles, one had scabies; one had a malady not yet diagnosed and one of the upright abstainers had venéreal disease.

But *The Times*'s picture of general contentment – apart from venereal disease – is not one that comes across from other sources. John Duffield, a padre serving with the Bantam Brigade in France, recalled politely: 'the men didn't like them at all, they disliked them being in uniform.' A private serving with the Rifle Brigade in France was more forthcoming. Asked about the attitude of the soldiers he said: 'They was vile to them. If they got a chance they would knock 'em silly.'

Did he feel they had a case? 'No I didn't. Your country must come first. A great number were malingerers or cowards. They were scared stiff they might get killed themselves.'

Lieutenant James Butlin had left Oxford to volunteer with the First Dorsets as soon as war had started and at just nineteen he had been through horrors in Flanders in 1915 and survived – but only just. For it was, as he wrote home, a time of 'surprise and tragedy for the regiment'. On one occasion, having been ordered to stay in reserve he could only watch while the first two companies started to climb the parapet. 'They were met with such a fire of artillery, machine guns and rifles that any chance of life was hopeless. Of the ten officers of A and B only one got back untouched. Of almost 400 men who set off only sixty men came back.' Eventually he came home on sick leave and remained thus until he was 'pitchforked' into an 'accursed job': that of officer commanding a unit of the NCC in the middle of Salisbury Plain.

For a man who had started the war so full of optimism and spirit and then been shattered into despair by the loss of his friends, his men and his own colonel this was too much. From watching friends die for their country he was now being asked to command men who would not fight for it. He wrote to his good friend, Basil, who had managed somehow to keep out of the war: 'When I heard my fate I swore terrible and cursed every thing within reach. I was wild with anger and am not yet myself again . . . At present I am sinking into a state of nervous depression . . . If I stay here indefinitely suicide is not unthinkable.' It must have been a torrid two months both for him and the men he had to command before he was sent out to France again.

There is no suggestion he took his anger out on his men but others were not so controlled. Norman Thomas, a regular soldier, wrote to his wife Weenie from Seaford in Sussex and in between the usual chat – he mentions that he has no leave coming up but hopes for a weekend soon – he gets on to the subject of the NCC. It is easy to see how frustrating its treatment must have been for him.

There are a great number of conscientious objectors near Seaford. They have been employed for the last four months constructing one of the roads leading to Newhaven. The road is just the same as it was before the operations of the COs.

They have all been allowed home on leave at Easter and Xmas and get real good food. Don't you think it's a bit unfair on us fellows? We often march past them and pass a good deal of comments etc.; sometimes there is a rough house ending with a few COs being badly mauled and a few of us chaps being escorted back to the guardroom and punished. I can see some fun shortly if they continue to keep them here.

Horace Calvert was wounded by a grenade while serving with the Grenadier Guards and was convalescing at the Seaford Camp. Twenty-nine members of the NCC were brought in to the camp after they had refused to load ammunition at the docks. Calvert writes:

As soon as it got round the camp who they were then the people carrying tea in the big canteens to them and giving them food were throwing dirt into the tea and generally upsetting things. Later on all the windows were smashed and they had to put a guard around them.

There was a corporal who borrowed my coat. He said he wanted to borrow it because he had two stripes on his. He took part and of course he couldn't be recognised as an NCO.

Calvert witnessed events from outside the hut, but Arthur Long was inside. Later he wrote to a friend:

We had not been in the hut ten minutes before we were besieged by several hundred soldiers who threatened us with all sorts of horrible things: then the fun commenced, somebody threw a stone and broke a window. I thought the whole camp had gone mad. They laughed and screamed and then attempted to demolish the hut. Think of it, twenty-nine men locked in a hut, a sentry at each end with several hundred soldiers throwing stones and clinkers till every window was smashed, sashes broken, tea-things shattered, fire places torn down. We defended ourselves with tables and forms.

It was the nearest thing I have ever experienced. I thought it was all up, the bugles sounded for assistance, but it developed into a riot – they attempted to break into the hut with large logs. It lasted about three-quarters of an hour, then the Regimental Sergeant-Major arrived.

Calvert thought – in a triumph of understatement – that it was 'rather peculiar' to put men who refused to fight amongst men who had been wounded in the fighting. He wondered, even, if it had been deliberate. He saw the NCC as 'men apart from the normal men', nevertheless he did not like this bullying: 'It was a nasty episode in my mind. I didn't take any active part. I didn't think it was fair. We wouldn't do it to a German prisoner who we had more against.'

Arthur Harrison was careful when writing home not to worry anyone, but he did hint at the problems they sometimes faced: 'We had the usual sally with the combatants up at the barracks when we went to the baths. They have a great contempt for us up there as also some of the townspeople. They all know us now. The little urchins when they see us marching through shout "Here come the conscientious objects". It is rather amusing and helps keep the spirits up.'

The COs themselves were hopelessly unsure whether they were right or wrong to be in the NCC. Was it a stand for peace or had they effectively given in to the army? Thomas Price, a member of the NCC, who also witnessed the events at Seaford, wrote to the anti-conscription organiser Catherine Marshall in the deferential language of the time: 'I must apologise for being a member of the NCC. Had I realised what non-combatant service really was I certainly would not have accepted the position. I readily admit I am extremely grieved for so doing.'

Arthur Harrison wrote from Richmond: 'We now have about fifty NCCs. Did I say that one of us turned his coat and expects to join the Royal Engineers? I mistrusted him from the first. He is a fearful lot of swank. We are all of a non-combatant nature or he would have been ragged.'

Once they were in the NCC there were still confrontations to be had over where the line should be drawn between combatant and non-combatant duty. At times the arguments could get quite ludicrous. In the Commons the case was raised of a Private Mawdsley serving in the NCC who refused an order to sweep out a horse's stall on the grounds that 'it had a distinct bearing on the prosecution of the war'. He was placed under arrest ready for a court martial. But another NCC member wrote from Seaford: 'All we were doing was to pick up big stones, do gardening and roll lawns and cricket pitches. This I felt as a Christian I could not altogether object to.'

Much more seriously, from Newhaven Robert Stott, a Buddhist, wrote to the NCF to say that he was in custody because 'we were ordered to unload trucks containing shells and explosives and I refused. The major portion of the NCC men are prepared to handle anything in order to save their skins, one even said he would load a gun and let another man pull the trigger. The worst offenders are the Plymouth Brethren . . . I feel thoroughly ashamed of myself for having given in at all and feel happier now.' (Being a Buddhist was rare in those days; the survey mentioned earlier, which covered almost 4,000 conscientious objectors, showed eight members of the Peculiar People and three Jewish Christian church members, but only one Buddhist.)

It must have been very difficult for any regular soldier having to deal with these men. Saluting practice, route marches, parade ground drills without rifles and all manner of other tasks could become a point of dispute. What the authorities probably hoped for was that the men would 'turn their coats' and become fighters. Very few did, but when this happened it was considered a triumph. A report in the *Northern Echo* in July 1916, attributed to an 'officer unnamed', concerns a conscientious objector who was 'one of the bravest men I ever struck'. The officer says the man was in a Labour Battalion, but it seems much more likely that he was in the NCC for the Labour Battalions were a regular part of the army and could carry arms.

In the ebb and flow of counter-attacks what is the reserve trench one minute becomes your front line another. It was so with the trench in which this conscientious chap was working. When the Germans got there they found the objector with no other weapon than a spade. The objector never objected so strongly in his life as he did to the idea of the Germans taking him a prisoner. He defended himself with his spade and his example so inspired his comrades they did likewise. They put up a great fight and succeeded in beating back the attack.

It then became necessary to get through to headquarters with a message about the position. The conscience man volunteered to go and he had to pass through a fierce enemy barrage. He was sniped at all the way and was hit four times. He reached headquarters where he delivered his message and came back with a reply. After he had given his reply he asked if he might take a rest as he was feeling a bit queer. That was his way of saying that he had received five very severe wounds. He got his rest and in less than an hour he was dead. I hope he will not be forgotten when the awards are given out.

Another soldier tells of a similar incident: 'There was a batch of about twenty putting in the barbed wire in the front-line trenches. And these Germans came over and we wondered what was happening. We looked over the top and they had picks and shovels and were driving the Germans back to the trenches again.'

It is impossible to know whether these stories are pure fantasy or just embellished – it is certainly hard to believe every last detail of them. But they do at least illustrate the widespread hope that this is what every conscientious objector would do when it came to the crunch.

The reality, however, is provided by George Baker, who was nineteen when the war started: a scholarship boy from Sussex who had gone on from grammar school to become a bank clerk. He called himself a 'freelance pacifist' and put the vivid testimony of all his doubts into a privately printed autobiography called *The Soul of a Skunk* – the title came from a girl who presented him with the first in his collection of white feathers and then called upon her soldier boyfriend 'to give the "pro-German skunk" what for'. (Interestingly the soldier declined, actually encouraging him to 'stick it out'.)

There was only one other pacifist in the area so there was no safety or comfort in numbers when word got out. Soon on the walls in his village he found slogans like 'Baker is a conchy coward' and 'Baker is a Pacifist skunk' and every so often he would get 'rough housed' by a gang – 'I kept these episodes as secret as possible . . . I treated my bruises in my bedroom's privacy.'

He went before his local tribunal, which he considered 'remarkably fair and extraordinarily reasonable'. It believed his argument but, as with other applicants, gave him only non-combatant duty rather than the absolute exemption he had asked for. Having made a half-hearted attempt at suicide by trying to starve himself to death he was finally persuaded by his father to accept the tribunal's decision and join the Non Combatant Corps, which he accurately describes as a 'parody of a combatant regiment' in Shoreham. There he was not sure who was the most difficult to deal with: the corporal ordering him to 'clean them blarsted buttons' or the Plymouth Brethren – fellow conscientious objectors who were 'the thorns in my flesh. One after another they tried to save my benighted, pagan soul. Their earnestness was admirable; their platitudes were not.'

While others saw him as a skunk, Baker saw himself as a Judas in khaki. He was constantly torn between acceptance of life with the NCC, which did at least keep his parents happy, and the guilty feeling that he was a traitor to the cause he believed in. When he was given orders to move to Newhaven where, according to rumour, they were going to be loading ships with 'munitions of war', Baker was ecstatic. It meant that he could honourably refuse to obey an order and so end his time with the NCC. 'It was one thing to dig holes in the Sussex Downs, and to fill them up again after they had been dug – the principal occupation during ten weeks of myself and my NCC comrades.' But this was different. 'Even my father and mother would perceive that I could not, without dishonour, load munitions for other men to use, while I would not use them myself.' But at the docks he had 'one of the bitterest disappointments I have had in my life'. It was not arms but food that they were loading and he could hardly object to that: 'the Tommies had to eat'.

From Newhaven he was sent to Salisbury Plain where he was set 'alternately to make an unmade road, and to unmake with pick and shovel a road already made'. There, having slipped the price of a pint to the guard so that he could fraternise, he managed to make friends with Otto, a German prisoner of war. Otto was obviously a remarkable man who recited Shakespeare, showed Baker the beauties of Galsworthy, introduced him to Nietzsche, described Wells's *New Machiavelli* as one of the six greatest novels in English literature . . . and claimed that 'no man of equal genius had written as much tripe as Dickens'. Ironically it was Otto who eventually spurred Baker into action. '"Be a man," he would urge me, "either fight for your country or fight for L'Internationale."' Finally Baker decided he had had enough and by refusing the next order he was given – to throw some rubbish into a bin – he was soon up before a court martial and then on his way to Wormwood Scrubs to do a year's hard labour. Now at last Judas was banished and the 'miserable loathing of self . . . the wretched knowledge of ideals betrayed' and the 'dishonouring khaki uniform' were behind him. Prison was a relief.

It is hardly surprising that just two months after the NCC had been born the Bishop of Oxford thought it was time to put it out of its misery. Bishop Gore emphasised in the House of Lords how 'profoundly out of sympathy' he was with 'the persons on whose behalf I speak' but went on to say 'the NCC was a great failure from every point of view'. He could hardly conceive of a conscience 'which would refuse to allow a man to bear arms but would allow him to do work which was part and parcel of warfare'.

Yet this was the unit that Bert Brocklesby, Harry Stanton and many others were supposed to join and be thankful for.

9

Prisoners

Late one afternoon in May 1916 a policeman came knocking at the door of the Brocklesby household in Conisbrough. Bert was not there, he was out playing billiards with his brother Harold who was on leave from the South Staffords. So it was his father who had to listen while the constable explained that he had come to arrest Bert and take him before the magistrates for failing to answer the summons to join the Non Combatant Corps. It must have been a very difficult moment for Bert's father, not just fearing for his son's life but knowing too that he would have to face his fellow chapel members, his fellow magistrates and indeed the members of the War Fund Committee. People had already been telling him he should turn Bert out of the house. But he would have none of it. There was something too of the dour Methodist in him; when a neighbour suggested that he should be trying to persuade his son to change his mind, given the likelihood that Bert would be shot for his beliefs, Old Brock told him: 'I would rather Bert be shot for his beliefs than abandon them.'

As for handling the policeman, Bert's father knew exactly what to do. He had a polite word and said that being a magistrate himself he knew that it was already too late for Bert to get to that day's court in time. If the constable would allow Bert to stay in his own house for one more night then in the morning he, John Brocklesby, would guarantee that his son would surrender himself. It was all agreed. The Brocklesby family could have one last supper together.

The next morning Bert duly appeared at Conisbrough police station and from there it was a swift journey through the Doncaster magistrates' court, into the remand cell and on to the guardroom at Pontefract Barracks. These barracks had already seen one Brocklesby; little more than a year earlier his brother Phil had had his first army meal here as a sort of celebration of his voluntary enlistment.

Bert's reception was rather different. 'I still think of my first night "in the army" as the most uncomfortable night of my life,' he wrote.

There were about thirty men in a room designed for fifteen. The stench of humanity and drunks was nothing to the crowning stench of a filthy latrine in the corner, of which the drain was choked and urine was seeping across the guardroom floor. I had to pick a dry patch.

I did not feel happy, nor that I was suffering in a noble cause. I knew that these inconveniences were paltry compared with the sufferings brought to millions by the cursed war, but coming from an ideal home it was bad enough. Two blankets had been doled out, one for mattress and one for cover, but I had no pillow. I had brought my Teachers' Bible, which for many years had given light and strength. This served for a pillow.

The next day, with the help of a few coins, he managed to persuade a bemused guard to put him into a cell. The guard had obviously never before come across anyone willing to bribe their way into solitary confinement but was happy enough to oblige. To Bert it seemed as though he had entered the monastery. 'In that cell was an atmosphere of the peace of heaven, away from the smell of drunks and urine and the filthy small-talk of the guardroom. I drew a deep breath of thankfulness, and felt more at peace than at any time since August 1914.'

The fact that Bert's father disagreed with him did not stop him doing all he could to protect his son. He knew an officer at the Barracks and he sent him a 'discreet' note advising him that Bert was under his 'authority'. Major Ellis, feeling he ought to be as helpful as he could, summonsed Bert to his office to ask if he had yet been paid now that he was in the army. This was rather missing the point, but Bert told him politely that he had not been paid and he wouldn't accept the money anyway.

'Have you a conscientious objection to taking your pay?' the major asked.

'Yes sir.'

'How queer.' The officer then asked if Bert had been before a tribunal and if so what the decision had been.

'Non combatant service.'

'Why, you don't belong here. Off you go in the morning to Richmond Castle' was the major's conclusion. Never had he been more relieved to get rid of anyone.

In the morning Bert was off without any sort of guard or escort; he was a prisoner but a prisoner whom the army thought it could trust – and rightly so. The only small gesture of defiance that Bert committed as he walked through Darlington in his khaki uniform on the way to Richmond was to wear his hat the wrong way round. 'I heard a spluttering noise behind and a decrepit old aristocrat was saying that I ought to be reported to my commanding officer.'

Bert was in no hurry to reach his destination so it wasn't until daylight was slipping away that he arrived outside the imperial walls of the castle and announced himself as a conscientious objector. The NCO pointed to a squad of the Non Combatant Corps who were drilling on the grass within the castle.

'Look, that lot's all of 'em conscientious objectors,' he said.

'Not my idea of conscientious objection,' Bert replied.

'So what are you prepared to do?'

'I'll do anything for the conscientious objectors, but not for anyone else.'

The next morning the NCO brought Bert some potatoes to peel. Bert asked: 'Who are these for?'

'Oh, these are for the Conchies.'

'All right, I'll peel them.'

That evening the potatoes that appeared at dinner for 'the conchies' to eat had their skins on and were none too clean. So when the next morning the NCO brought more potatoes to be peeled Bert had had enough, stating: 'You lied to me yesterday. So I clean no more potatoes for the officers.'

Whether or not Bert peeled potatoes was hardly going to make much difference to the war effort, but now battle had been joined between him and the army and there was almost nothing he would accept without first questioning and then – usually – rejecting it. But it was refusing to appear at drill parade rather than unpeeled potatoes that had him up before his commanding officer. This time it was the captain's turn to try to persuade Bert of the error of his ways. His questioning began.

'Why are you a conscientious objector?'

'War is breaking the command "Thou shalt not kill".'

'Do you not think that those commands apply to individuals but not to the state?'

'They apply to both.'

'Are you a Christian?'

'Yes.'

'There are thousands of Christians in the war.'

'It's not my idea of being a Christian.'

When the captain realised he was getting nowhere he sentenced Bert to three days' bread and water in the cells.

The main block of eight cells at Richmond was built in the nineteenth century, but they look as though they date from medieval times. In addition the guardroom opposite and possibly a dungeon in the castle keep were used. The dungeon has been cemented over for some years but it is probable that a young Jehovah's Witness from Leeds, who arrived a few days before Bert, was put in here. The floor was covered in two to three inches of debris and the only light came through a narrow slit in the walls. He was so terrified he very soon had to be moved. Herbert Senior, another Jehovah's Witness, volunteered to take his place: 'It certainly was queer,' he says. 'I hadn't been there long when a noise like an old rusty windlass and a clanking thick chain started up. I have never been afraid of evil spirits and now I went down on my knees in all the dirt and told Jehovah about it. I then lay down on a board, went straight off to sleep and never woke up until morning.'

But it was to the block of eight cells that Bert and the other absolutists were sent as punishment when they refused to obey the orders that were supposed to transform them into happy members of the Non Combatant Corps. They were dark, lonely places with just a narrow window for each cell. On the first floor these gave some light, but on the ground floor almost none filtered through. Heavy wooden doors, with a communication hole set into each one, were there to prevent the escape that was never going to happen – Bert had walked into the castle, he was not about to walk out again. These cubicles measured about six feet wide by nine feet long, and the most important thing in them for Bert was not the window, nor the door, but a hole just off the ground where pipes for an old hot water system used to run through the cells. The pipes had gone but the hole remained. At once his solitary confinement was solitary no more.

Bert soon discovered that by lying on the flagstones he could peep through this hole to the next cell 'and there was the bright smiling face of Norman Gaudie' who was also on a punishment diet of bread and water. Bert had managed to hide some bacon fat in his trousers before being pushed into the cell, but perhaps more importantly, he had also hidden a pocket chess board which was to make innumerable journeys through the hole. A friend, chess, bacon, Bible study: all that was missing was music . . . but not for long.

Gaudie wrote in his diary: 'In the evening we enjoyed a sing of the hymns. Our gem piece was "Nearer my God to Thee". I took melody, Alfred Myers [another CO] took tenor – I beat on my cell floor to keep Alf right – J.H.B. the bass. We were able to provide harmony for those unfortunate outsiders.' The day before Gaudie noted: 'Chess – Bible study with J.H.B. Bath at barracks. Delightful time joking and laughing.'

The castle, a forbidding fortress erected by a nephew of William the Conqueror, was designed to intimidate and even in its present-day, much reduced state it still does. The cells were designed to have the same effect but Brocklesby and Gaudie, helped in part by an army still not sure how to deal with these unusual creatures, were, if anything, to thrive on this intimidation.

The summons into the army had come for Norman Gaudie just as he was beginning to do well for himself. He had left school at thirteen and started off in the ticket office of the railway company in Newcastle and now, at twenty-nine, he had risen to be an accountant for the company. He was a good cricketer and an even better footballer: good enough to be a reserve centre forward for Sunderland and outside right for Darlington. When he argued his case before a tribunal the local newspaper headlined its story 'Footballer With A Conscience.'

Norman Gaudie was the baby in the family from the mining village of East Boldon in County Durham, the youngest of seven children. He had lost his father when he was six months old. His four older brothers had all managed to escape conscription for reasons that had nothing to do with conscience. Age excused the oldest brother; the next successfully pleaded health problems although somehow he remained a very good fast bowler with the local cricket team; the third landed in the army pay corps, and the fourth was excused because he was doing vital transport work.

Norman was a non-smoker and a non-drinker and his son says that even in his cricket team they thought him a bit different. One friend recalls 'his entrance to the dressing room was a signal for the bad language to stop.' Norman's religion mattered enormously to him and his Congregational Minister, who lived next door, wrote to his tribunal telling them 'I believe him to be perfectly sincere in his conviction.' His prison diary is full of devotions completed, the Bible read and even sometimes memorised, and sermons sent in by his Minister to read.

He held a fierce attachment to his mother and he wrote to her soon after he arrived at Richmond Castle: 'I often think of you and try to bring your dear face into my room; the strongest impression I have is my last look before leaving that morning and how I treasure that beautiful picture of my dear mother waving so bravely from the familiar doorstep.'

In the developing battle over conscience both sides were making it up as they went along. Should potatoes be peeled, should a horse's stall be cleaned – sometimes the lines being drawn in the sand seemed absurd. But men like Gaudie and Brocklesby were having to stand alone, holding firm in their convictions, making ad hoc decisions without the support of any of the assortment of groups that exist today. On the army side there was puzzlement and outright hostility. These men were not being asked to fight, they were simply being told to join a Corps set up not to fight. What could be the objection to that?

It could get very personal. In Seaford Camp in Sussex Fred Murfin, who had taken exactly the same stand as Bert Brocklesby, was questioned by a lieutenant who only had one arm. 'He told me he had lost his arm defending me. I replied "You lost your arm whilst you were trying to destroy someone else." This made him mad.' Understandably so.

When Norman Gaudie was first arrested and taken under army escort to St Peters Hall in Sunderland he saw challenges where Bert had seen none. The army wanted his clothes off for a medical inspection; Gaudie refused and it was left to his escort to take them off. They got as far as his expanded chest measurement – thirty-seven and a half inches, 'poor for a footballer' – but there was no way they could force him to read the letters on the wall for his sight test. The medical was abandoned. An officer watching all this told him what many soldiers in the hall may have thought: 'If I had my way I would do what the Germans do – shoot you.' Instead he was ordered off to the barracks at Newcastle.

There he refused to put on uniform, but having seen that he was well outnumbered he allowed his escort to dress him. Not only did they dress him but they also hung his kit around his neck before packing him off to the cells – 'I was very much humiliated.' The uniform did not worry Bert Brocklesby, turning his cap backwards was enough defiance for him; but as soon as Gaudie was left alone in his cell off came his uniform and he stripped to 'waistcoat, pants and socks'. At his tribunal the chairman had suggested to him that his objection to war might be nothing more than 'nervousness' but he showed no 'nervousness' now when his guards decided to put his uniform back on. In retrospect the scene is almost comical. A fit, strong Gaudie showed no signs of pacifist intentions as he took on his guards and, as his son later said, started throwing people about. It required reinforcements before he was 'badly handicapped and forced to submit'. After this he too was sent to Richmond where he was welcomed by a 'good deal of taunting' in the forlorn hope that he would co-operate and join the Non Combatant Corps now being assembled there.

For most people today the memory of conscientious objectors in the First World War is understandably vague or non-existent. If they remember any names or incidents they are usually either Siegfried Sassoon or the cast of characters from the Bloomsbury set. But Sassoon had enlisted as soon as he saw the war coming and when he issued his public statement in protest against the war in June 1917 it was, as he said, as 'a soldier, convinced that I am acting on behalf of soldiers'. The Bloomsbury set were to follow the likes of Bert Brocklesby and Norman Gaudie, but they did not carve out the way.

The conscientious objectors who were corralled in Richmond in the spring of 1916 and who would not join other COs in the Non Combatant Corps soon grew to sixteen. They were far apart in distance but also in class from both Sassoon and the Bloomsbury set, who despite the unpopularity of their views remained very much part of the establishment. Their religion was almost always nonconformist in one shape or another. At the time of writing it is not possible to determine the religious beliefs of all sixteen men – some of them had none, but it appears that there were five Jehovah's Witnesses, three Methodists, one Quaker, one Congregationalist and one from the Church of Christ. For some their protest was purely political, for some it was religious and for others there was a strong element of religion in their socialism.

Amongst the Richmond group – and they soon found strength in numbers – there were a couple of ironstone miners, a decorator whose mother was an early suffragette, a shopkeeper and a clerk who worked amidst a stronghold of Quakerism: the Rowntree's chocolate factory in York. Intelligent and often god-fearing in the most literal sense of the phrase, today many if not all of them would have gone to university; but in 1916 none had – Bert's teacher training in London set him slightly apart.

Life at the castle was a mixture of threats, punishments and blandishments. Horace Eaton, who was stationed at the castle having agreed to join the Non Combatant Corps, witnessed it all: 'The methods adopted to try and make these young fellows into non-combatants or soldiers often made one's blood boil with indignation.'

And over it all hung the threat of being sent to France. Gaudie was told by one soldier that a unit of the Non Combatant Corps already sent thither had been told their job was to lay barbed wire between the British and German trenches: they decided to take up arms instead. Another version of this story – equally untrue – was told to new NCC recruits in camp at Weymouth. This time, so the story went, 107 men of the corps had been sent to France and seventy had already been shot when sent out in front of the advance trenches to mend the barbed wire. Rather more plausibly, Gaudie was told by a sergeant that the army would either kill or cure him. 'Don't think you will be allowed to serve your time in gaol – you will be taken to France and out there, those of you who refuse will be accidentally shot so that your friends won't know the worst.'

To their guards the COs must often have seemed intensely irritating as every order was examined, dissected and fought over. Thus Gaudie was told his sister was outside the castle waiting to come in and have tea with him, but he could only see her if he put on his puttees (a part of the army uniform protecting the lower leg). He acquiesced, allowed the puttees to be put on him and so was allowed to have a 'nice tea' with his sister – although by his terms this was a defeat. Similarly, he was told he could only learn what had happened to his civilian clothes and missing twenty shillings if he stood to attention in his cell while the captain was talking to him. Gaudie refused and was told nothing about his belongings – victory, albeit at a cost – he wrote in his diary: 'This day I felt very lonely.' When told to carry planks for whitewashing, Gaudie thought they were going to be used for military purposes. He refused so he was given forty-eight hours' bread and water, his letters stopped and his books confiscated – victory of sorts. A few days later a sergeant who had 'a very nice manner' assured him that in doing the whitewashing he 'could conscientiously say that it was not assisting the war' and claimed he was asking for the task as a personal favour. So he went out on whitewashing duty and he got 'more freedom and better rations'. Defeat? At times temptation was thrust under his nose. He was allowed a visit from his Congregational Minister, Dr Cadoux. But the visit came with an unusual condition attached: 'he had some eatables but was under promise not to give me any – so I had to imagine the good things – I much enjoyed his visit.' Victory?

Attempts at conversion came from all quarters. One of Gaudie's guards told him he had got it all wrong. Gaudie might think he was being asked to fight for King and country but the guard knew it was for the poor women and children of Belgium and France. The guard had fought in France and he recounted 'how a Belgian girl, about seventeen, naked, had found shelter between him and another man, and to his honour, he said it might have been man or woman for all he knew. I, of course, must take the man's word for it.'

A few days later he had a rather more detailed argument with the captain of the guard, who told Gaudie that the tribunal did not believe that his claim was genuine. But this is where the tribunals and indeed the army ran into trouble. For by sending him to the Non Combatant

Corps, as Gaudie argued, the tribunal was showing that it *did* believe him. The argument was not about whether or not his beliefs were genuinely held, but over what those beliefs would allow him to do. (At this stage the idea of a genuinely alternative form of service was only just beginning to be thought out.)

A week later the men were stopped in the middle of their exercise for an attempt at an even more curious form of propaganda. They had 'to listen to an address by a cripple for twenty years. He made out that because he bore his sufferings, then we ought to bear our part by helping our country in face of danger.' Gaudie's verdict on his argument: 'very weak'.

Gaudie, who was not by nature a complainer, calls the colonel who sentenced him to fourteen days' detention for disobedience a 'gentleman'. But he was a gentleman somewhat out of his depth. He tried on one occasion to force Bert and others to drill – ensuring only a ludicrous spectacle. An NCO first forced Bert's arms in and out then pushed him towards the ground for a double knees bend, at which point Bert lay inert, thinking 'They shoved me down, they can hoist me up.' It was soon decided it was useless and they were marched back to their cells 'feeling we had won that hurdle'.

Another CO, a schoolmaster from York who refused all orders, was knocked down by the NCO giving the orders, then carried forcibly to the parade ground where he was put up against a wall in very public view and stripped of everything but his shirt. The incident would never have been known about but for the fact that a civilian who had come to the castle to say goodbye to his brother – a soldier about to leave for France – was so incensed by what he saw he lifted his hat to the CO as he was being forced back into the cells and told him to 'stick it out'. He was promptly arrested and kept in custody for twenty-four hours. As the MP who raised the case in the Commons said, 'He went to Richmond as a supporter of the war but I am quite sure he returned in a very different frame of mind.'

On another occasion Norman Gaudie and Bert were exercising

together in the castle yard when Gaudie laughed but Bert was blamed for it and was sent off to the cells again. In many ways this proved to be a fortunate mistake. For, although he was never to know it, the drawings he made on the limewashed walls of his cell as he sat there alone are now preserved as carefully as any medieval wall paintings. English Heritage has produced a book, *Our Painted Past*, displaying the most important wall paintings – from Roman times to the twentieth century – to be found amidst the 400-plus properties that it cares for. Among many others there is *The Last Judgement* painted on the ceiling of the Westminster Abbey Chapter House and the extraordinary fresco commissioned by Prince Albert, painted somewhat inappropriately on the nursery landing of Osborne House in the Isle of Wight. And there on the back cover, looking as though she is not quite certain whether she should be keeping such exalted company, sits Bert's fiancée, Annie Wainwright.

Bert drew her on the wall, her hair brushed back, looking like a pilgrim who has just stopped by to check out prison conditions before setting off across the Atlantic in the *Mayflower*. He claimed her as his own with the words 'Annie Wainwright' above her and rather more properly 'Miss Annie Wainwright' at the bottom. But at some time after Bert left his cell poor Annie had her name crossed out and she was claimed by another prisoner who renamed her 'My Kathleen', so this is the name she still has scrawled across her – rather unfairly – today. Apart from Bert's confident touch, what also stands out as unusual, perhaps unique, amongst graffiti artists anywhere is the precise way Bert signs his work: 'J.H. Brocklesby fecit 22.5.16.' There cannot be many graffiti artists who employ Latin to sign off.

Indeed, the standard of graffiti on the walls of these cells maintained a pretty elevated level. Fortunately the soldiers imprisoned here during the Second World War for offences such as drunkenness and being late on parade appear to have been so overawed by them that, apart from claiming Annie as Kathleen, they wrote around their earnest predecessors' drawings rather than on them. The conscientious objectors' graffiti vary between the religious and the political: 'If you take a sword and use it to run a fellow through then God will send a bill to you,' wrote one. 'Brought up from Pontefract and put into this cell for refusing to be made into a soldier' wrote another. Even the painters in Cell One, cleaning off their brushes, left alone the advice: 'Stand firm let the nation see that men should brothers be.' There is the occasional wholly political tract: 'The only war which is worth fighting is the class war. The working class of this country have no quarrel with the working class of Germany or any other country. Socialism stands for inter-nationalism. If the workers of all countries united and refused to fight there would be no war.' But going from cell to cell what strikes you most is how much God there is on the walls. Bert drew a man lying on the ground struggling with the load of a heavy cross; he captioned it: 'Every cross grows light Lord beneath / The shadow Lord of Thine.' And he again added a touch of Latin: 'Jesus Hominum Salvator' (Jesus the Saviour of Mankind).

Brocklesby was a busy artist. He also attempted a portrait of Gaudie's mother, using a picture that Gaudie had managed to hide in the secret pockets sewn for him by his mother inside his trousers. Beside the portrait, so that there was not any doubt, he wrote 'N. Gaudie's mother' and someone else added 'To mother with love.' Norman Gaudie's son says 'It is an amazing likeness.' But at the time Gaudie himself was not so sure. He wrote home to his mother, 'Brocklesby is quite an accomplished chap and he has drawn your photo on the wall, so that I close my eyes partly and imagine it is really you; he has made a good attempt, but it is not quite a likeness.'

The most chilling line comes in Cell Six on the first floor. It is dated 29 May and signed by Clarence Hall, a Jehovah's Witness from Leeds: 'Sent to France with seventeen.' He appears to have got his numbers wrong – sixteen men went to France. But he had certainly got his destination right.

Why France? Other members of the Non Combatant Corps were being sent there from Richmond and the army argued that it was simply an administrative decision. But in fact it was very obvious that Bert and others were not suddenly going to become happy members of the NCC as soon as they crossed the Channel. No, they were being sent abroad because the threats and punishments had, so far, all failed. But when they were in France things would be very different. There they would be part of a force either engaged in operations against the enemy, or taking part in operations in a country wholly or partly occupied by the enemy. In other words they would be on active service; if they disobeyed an order – any order – they would then face a field general court martial. They could have gone before a court martial in Britain but one with only limited sentencing powers. In France, under the field general court martial, the penalty for disobedience could be death.

10

'We Tame Lions Here'

In mid-April 1916 at the Capital and Counties Bank's Piccadilly branch in London, a quaint little ceremony took place. Howard Marten, one of the clerks in the bank, a Quaker all his life and chairman of the Harrow branch of the No Conscription Fellowship, was leaving the bank. Everyone knew where he was going – and it was not to a better job. He had already received a notice telling him to report to the Harrow recruiting office and had politely informed the officer in command that he would have to ignore it; the police would soon be round to his house. So the staff at the bank wanted to make him a little leaving presentation. 'The only one who was later a little stuffy about it was the manager. But my own colleagues who knew me were quite understanding about the whole issue.' There were no leaving cards in those days but he received a formal letter from eight of his colleagues, asking him to 'accept the accompanying pipe as a small souvenir of your labours in our midst and as a token of our regret at losing you'.

Bert Brocklesby was among the very first conscientious objectors to go before a tribunal, but it was in the south of England that the round-up gathered pace. Howard Marten makes his arrest sound like one of the weekend rambles he used to take. Nevertheless it meant much more than that to him and his family. He was an only son and he admits he had led 'a particularly sheltered life'. He adds, 'I hadn't even been to boarding school', which he obviously thought would have been the best preparation for the course he had embarked on. A policeman first came calling on Saturday, 15 April 1916 but Marten and three friends were out cutting the grass and tidying up the local Quaker burial ground in Uxbridge. The policeman returned again on Sunday and they agreed together that Marten could have two more days of liberty.

On the Tuesday, Marten 'was arrested with Corney Barritt [another CO] at Pinner and, accompanied by a few relatives, taken to the picturesque police station, which in summertime nestles amid a profusion of roses'. From there it was swiftly through Wealdstone police court – where he was given a £2 fine for refusing to answer the call-up notice – and on to Mill Hill Barracks. Barritt was asked by the first officer he met: 'How long are you going to keep this up? You belong to your King and country now and must do as you're told.' As for Marten, the officer in charge told him he was 'sick of conscientious objectors' and sentenced him to seven days' detention for refusal to obey army orders.

Fred Murfin, whose case had been heard at Tottenham town hall, had been at a Sunday Tottenham Friends meeting when the policeman came for him. His landlord told the constable where and when to find him so he came back the next evening. After a polite chat the policemen questioned Murfin.

'Well, you know what I have come for?'

'Yes.'

'Will you meet me in the police station tomorrow, or would you like a few days to arrange matters?'

'If it's all right for you I would like to have a few days.'

They were both happy with this arrangement and Murfin had time to go into work for a couple more days. He thought about going to say goodbye to his parents in Lincolnshire but 'this experience seemed unreal to me and I carried on as usual, which seemed the right thing to do at the time.' He wrote to them instead before presenting himself at the police station on Thursday morning.

Jack Foister, a stocky, cheerful-looking fellow, was another CO who was out when the policemen came calling. So he took himself off to the police station to be arrested. 'I was rather amused that the young policeman who admitted me had played in orchestras in the two missions in which I had taken part. We were both indifferent violinists; I'm sure he was the better.' Although Foister had just finished at Cambridge, where he had won a scholarship to St Catharine's College, his father was a boat builder and he came from the same sort of social background as the policeman. At twenty-two he was a regular attendee at his Primitive Methodist Church but his views against the war were based more on his socialism than his churchgoing. One of his teachers remembered him as 'the most obstinate boy in the school'; once he had made up his mind there was little anyone could do to change it.

He might easily have had trouble at home; his father who was in the Territorials was called up almost as soon as the war started to serve in the equivalent of the Home Guard. His mother, who was very anti-war, used to tell him: 'Don't bother your father too much about things like this.' But perhaps she underestimated her husband, for on the first night in prison the violinist policeman unlocked the cell door and allowed in his father, just home on a short leave, bearing a magnificent meal. They were allowed to spend an hour together.

Foister had hoped to join the Indian Civil Service but the exams had been put off by the war so instead he ended up teaching at King's School, Peterborough. The headmaster was rather more concerned with keeping his teachers than the rights and wrongs of the war and he knew that an objection on conscience grounds was a hopeless cause. So he prevailed upon Foister to have a chat with his father-in-law, a retired colonel. The colonel was a realist: if Foister confined his case to the educational needs of the school and the fact that his eyesight was genuinely poor, the chances were that he would be exempt from service. The school would get to keep a good teacher and Foister would not have to fight – everyone would be a winner. But the colonel, rather like the government, had completely misjudged, or perhaps misunderstood his man; the last thing Foister wanted was some sort of grubby compromise.

His first steps along this unknown road were comparatively friendly, although he did have some trouble with a 'cheerful cockney' named Cole who shared one cell with him. 'Learning the reason for my incarceration he was forthright in condemning me. So I asked why he was there – it was for desertion – the third time!'

His treatment was a complete contrast to that of Alfred Evans. Evans was a Catholic – unusual amongst this group of mainly low church objectors – but it was socialism rather than religion that drove him on. He did not apply for absolute exemption: instead he told his tribunal he was prepared to serve in the Royal Army Medical Corps because 'I was prepared to take the risks of war without inflicting death on other people.' Unusually the tribunal granted him exemption provided he joined the corps. This understanding attitude might well have had something to do with the fact that the tribunal's chairman was in the same branch of the National Union of Railwaymen as his father.

Armed with this certificate, Evans reported on the appointed date to the recruiting office on Ealing Broadway where he was handed over to a lieutenant. 'He asked for my exemption certificate and promptly tore it up. He then set an official document before me, saying that I was to be put in the Non Combatant Corps and that I was to sign this paper – I was not even to read it. I refused to sign it so he called two men with fixed bayonets and he said "Take this man to Hounslow Barracks."' The RAMC lost their man and the army gained a problem.

The pressure points for most of these men were much the same, although the way they dealt with them was often different. First came the inevitable medical exam and the donning of khaki. Evans had no problem with this, nor did Foister. Marten took a stand that was a sort of halfway house. Once in solitary confinement in his cell in Mill Hill he realised that the uniform was to be his first test.

You'd either got to accept uniform and take it, or you had to sort of sit on or lay on the floor and kick. Well, I wasn't prepared to do undignified things. I said to the NCOs in charge, 'Look here. I suppose you've got orders to dress me forcibly. I've no objections to putting on

The four Brocklesby brothers, Phil, George, Bert and, seated, Harold, photographed in 1915. George – who could not fight on medical grounds – was the local recruiting officer who signed up Phil, while Harold had joined the Officer Training Corps at University. Although Bert refused to fight, the four brothers remained close. *(University of Leeds, Liddle Collection)*

The thriving Methodist church in Conisbrough in May 1915 with Bert, both organist and choirmaster, standing proudly in front of the organ. His mother is seated on the far right, with his fiancée, Annie Wainwright, next to her. Bert's opposition to the war horrified many of the congregation. *(Mary Brocklesby)*

Phil Brocklesby's wedding day, Conisbrough, 6 July 1921. Bert Brocklesby stands fourth from left; Phil stands on the right of his bride, Doris, and next to Harold, their father John and Aunt Bec. Their mother, Hannah, sits in front of her husband; the fourth brother, George, sits in front of her. *(Mary Brocklesby)*

The Brocklesby family photographed in Conisbrough in Spring 1915, shortly before the two brothers in uniform were posted to France. Standing from left to right: Harold, George, his wife Alice, Bert and Phil. Sitting: their mother Hannah, father John and Aunt Bec. *(University of Leeds, Liddle Collection)*

Bert's fiancée Annie Wainwright in 1924 aged 25. Annie supported Bert's position, even visiting him in prison, although her own brother, Gilbert, would be killed in action in 1918. Their engagement ended when Bert went on an aid mission to Austria just after the war; Annie accused him of feeding the people who killed her brother. *(Shirley Bracewell)*

Phil and Harold Brocklesby on leave, photographed by their brother George in May 1916. Phil had taken a few hours unauthorised absence, but most of the time was spent posing for George's camera under gas light. Although the brothers look exhausted they were simply tired of remaining immobile – the last exposure taking 35 minutes. *(Malcolm Brocklesby)*

Dear Mr E A Brookes
Seeing that you cannot
be a man not to Join
the army we offer you
an invitation to Join our
Girl Scouts as washer up.
BATH GIRL
SCOUTS   Scoutmistress

In an attempt to persuade men to volunteer for the army women used to present a white feather to men of the right age in civilian clothes who looked likely candidates. But sometimes, as this anonymous note shows, they used other weapons in their efforts to shame men into joining. This letter reads: 'Dear Mr E A Brookes, seeing that you cannot be a man not to join the army we offer you an invitation to join our Girl Scouts as washer up'. *(Imperial War Museum)*

WE DON'T WANT TO. FIGHT

LEM ON ADE

'TIS CONSCIENCE DOTH MAKE COWARDS OF US ALL

COs were sometimes sent to the Non Combatant Corps where they would undertake routine army tasks but would not have to fight. Soldiers soon dubbed it the No Courage Corps and one angry Sergeant Major serving in France designed his own scathing 'coat of arms' which he sent home to be published in English newspapers. His crude design included 'baby's bottle rampant and three maggots recumbent' and the motto 'tis conscience doth make cowards of us all'. *(With the kind permission of Wilfred Hayler)*

THE PLACE FOR THE PEACE CRANK—THE LUNATIC ASYLUM.

DAILY SKETCH.

GUARANTEED DAILY NETT SALE MORE THAN 1,000,000 COPIES.

No. 2,089.　　　LONDON, TUESDAY, NOVEMBER 30, 1915.　　[Registered as a Newspaper.]　ONE HALFPENNY.

PEACE BANNERS TORN TO PIECES.

WOUNDED CANADIANS, AUSTRALIANS, NEW ZEALANDERS, AND SOUTH AFRICANS SHOW LONDON THE WAY TO DEAL WITH PEACE TRAITORS.

Some newspapers enjoyed baiting the COs. *The Daily Sketch* celebrates the victory of a group of 'Colonial' soldiers convalescing in London who had broken up a peace meeting in Farringdon Street, stolen the meeting's banner and taken their prize to Trafalgar Square to conduct their own recruiting meeting. The newspaper's banner reads 'The Place for the Peace Crank – The Lunatic Asylum'. *(Wilfred Hayler)*

"FETCHED": THE OBJECTORS' SAD FATE

Two impeccably dressed 'conchies' are handed over to a military escort in May 1916. Of the 16,300 Conscientious Objectors, 6,000 served some form of prison sentence. This proved a considerable shock to men from respectable backgrounds, who had never been in trouble before. *(Wilfred Hayler)*

The famous graffiti on the cell walls of Richmond Castle from May 1916 which inspired this book. Both these examples are drawn by Bert Brocklesby who signed them very precisely. Although the second drawing is of his fiancée Annie Wainwright, an unknown prisoner later scribbled out the main reference to Annie and claimed her as his own Kathleen. *(English Heritage)*

One of the cells in Richmond Castle where the COs were held before being shipped to France. In the left hand corner is a bricked up hole where an old heating pipe once ran through to the next cell. Bert Brocklesby played chess with a fellow prisoner, passing the board through this hole.
(English Heritage)

Conscientious Objectors, with Bert far right, third row, at Dyce Quarry near Aberdeen, where they had been sent in the Autumn of 1916 to do work of 'national importance' as an alternative to prison. This photograph included nearly all those who had been sentenced to death in France. The camp was closed after three months.

Bert Brocklesby remained true to his convictions throughout his life. In August 1962 he was photographed in front of the war memorial in Scunthorpe, where he then lived, conducting a lonely vigil for peace to remember those who had died at Hiroshima. He told a reporter: 'I think it is an idea that will grow'.

A family reunion at Phil's house in Lincolnshire in August 1961. From left to right: Phil's wife Doris, George's wife Evelyn, Bert's wife Olive, Bert and Phil. It was during his retirement in Lincolnshire that Phil, with the help of a sand model of the trenches, relived the Battle of the Somme time after time. *(Malcolm Brocklesby)*

Phil Brocklesby photographed at the Thiepval Memorial Arch on 1 July 1966, fifty years to the day since he had taken part in the opening attack of the Battle of the Somme. He had returned to what he called a land of 'nightmare dreams' with 'memories crowding around me' to commemorate the battle. Phil could never really understand why he had survived.

uniform, but it won't alter my attitude.' And I compromised in that way . . . it's what you would do, not what you would wear which was much more important.

Murfin, who was held at the same barracks, had much the same experience. 'The officer said, "Now, my lads, we want you to put khaki on." We all refused and we each had a soldier to dress us and undress us. My attendant suggested that as my feet smelled so badly I'd better see to my own socks! I did and we both enjoyed the joke. He was a nice fellow – we found, as a rule, that if the officer was decent, the men were.'

In contrast, in Kempston Barracks Stanton was having none of it. He paints a vivid picture of the scene in the barracks' medical room where he and three others COs were taken for their examination. In the room were three sergeants and several of 'their underlings'. The staff sergeant came up to them and asked 'How many of you are conscientious objectors?'

'All of us,' replied Stanton. 'I can only speak for myself but you may as well know at once that I do not intend to be medically examined, or to obey any military orders.' The staff sergeant's first reaction was blank astonishment followed by 'vehement denunciation'. When Stanton refused to be measured or weighed he was grabbed and put on the weighing machine; all this accompanied by 'a chorus of curses and choice remarks about COs in general and me in particular'.

He refused to strip when ordered to do so. 'The whole place was filled with the sound of wrathful curses.'

'Shall we turn the hose pipe on him?'

'Let's drop him in the horse-trough. He'll strip soon enough then.'

The staff sergeant had other ideas. 'We'll take you out the back and shoot you straight off, like we did that fellow last week.'

Stanton, guessing that the sergeant had to be bluffing, suggested that he needed a court martial first. 'Court martial be damned, fetch that gun.' One of his men soon returned with a rifle.

'Now, for the last time are you going to strip?'

'No.'

'Then I'll send you to the colonel. He'll throw you out of the window . . . we tame lions in the army.'

But being sent to the colonel is hardly the same as being shot on the spot – Stanton had won this round.

This, of course, is Stanton's version of events but, however differently the staff sergeant might tell it, he would surely agree that he was exasperated almost beyond measure by the likes of Stanton and the growing numbers of COs. What made it worse for him was that he had no weapons to fight with other than huff and puff. A CO imprisoned in Cowley Barracks, Oxford, only a short distance from his previous home at Balliol College, got rather more: 'the quartermaster dared to strike me with his stick and one of his subordinates followed this up with his boot'.

The colonel whom Stanton was sent to had a much easier task than his sergeant. He was not about to throw anyone out of the window and in fact had quite a long talk with Stanton, telling him – correctly – that there were several Quakers who supported the war.

'No convinced Friend can support the war,' replied Stanton.

'Well, perhaps that is so,' said the colonel. 'Anyway I am not in a position to argue with you. I am afraid I shall have to send you down to the Non Combatant Corps.' Thus the colonel was quickly off the hook. Stanton had to wait an hour in the guardroom before Bernard Bonner, one of his fellow COs, rejoined him and told him that the sergeant had had considerable success: he had cajoled the other two into giving in. As for Stanton and Bonner, they were bound for the Eastern Non Combatant Corps attached to the Bedfordshire Regiment at Landguard Camp in Felixstowe, where they would soon find themselves under much greater pressure.

It is hard to believe it was pure coincidence that of the two key places where the most stubborn of the COs were sent in these early days, one was a medieval castle with prison cells to match and the other was Landguard. Here, the original fort – greatly expanded in later years – had been built by order of Henry VIII.

Landguard, spread across one side of the entrance to Harwich Harbour, does not have the same intimidating presence as Richmond Castle. However, it was only a short boat ride across the harbour entrance to Harwich where the army had at its disposal another fort, smaller but just as threatening as Richmond. The Harwich Redoubt is a remarkable circular fort sunk into a hill. Completed in 1810 to protect both town and harbour from Napoleon, it has three-foot, granite-lined walls, its own water well to enable the occupants to withstand a siege, a twenty-foot deep moat, a drawbridge providing the only way in or out, and a set of three dark, dank cells which rival those at Richmond.

Getting the COs to Felixstowe was no trouble because these were men who, despite being called cowards, were not about to run away. As Marten says, 'We weren't people like the Irish who tried to stir up trouble. We were the last people in the world to want to be violent. We shouldn't have been there if we did.' Marten remembers starting off on their journey being kicked and harassed by their escorts on the way to Mill Hill Station, with the added humiliation of having their kit bags, which they had refused to pick up, being tied around their necks. But as the journey progressed so the three 'elderly' NCOs who accompanied them started to warm to them, eventually ending up showering them with cigarettes amidst expressions of regret that they had not shown more consideration earlier.

Foister simply gave his word that he would report to Felixstowe and was allowed on his journey without an escort. In fact it was the loneliness more than anything else that was his problem. These were the days when men were hardly allowed to express their feelings and certainly not encouraged to do so, but in his diary he does hint – however formally – at what he felt as his train left for Ipswich.

If Father could not read my feelings as the train left Cambridge it may have been because like feelings had dimmed his eyes. In former days I might have scorned a sentimental weakness, but now I would have counted it shame if I had not experienced misery at the thought of separation from all friends and all kin, a separation perhaps for ever.

I buried myself behind a newspaper to protect me from any train journey chatter. I swallowed my grief, a grief spoiled though not made less poignant by an undercurrent of self-pity . . . In order to reduce the distress at my home-leaving I had made a half-promise that if taken to France I might reconsider my position – I had not thought it likely but Father did. I thought this over and before Ipswich was reached I had made a firm decision that come what may nothing would make me become a soldier, nor an indirect supporter of the war. Was there something of vanity in these thoughts? Anyway I felt the decision revived my spirits.

Although Foister had no guards to deal with, his problems started as soon as he arrived at Landguard: 'I had not anticipated that getting arrested would be as difficult as it turned out to be.' It is hardly fair to say it, given that here was a man who did not know whether the next few days and weeks would bring life or death, but Foister's arrival in the orderly room at Landguard has a hint of comedy about it. First he tried the sergeant of the guard and made it clear to him that he intended to reject all orders – the sergeant made it equally clear he wanted nothing to do with him and suggested another NCO to try, who turned out to be just as unhelpful. He then spotted some conchies who were willing members of the Non Combatant Corps sitting down to their dinner. Despite disagreeing with them he saw no damage to his principles in joining them for what might be his last meal for quite a time.

It was only after dinner that he finally found a sergeant prepared to listen to him – up to a point. 'He put on an air of mingled anger and pity, but most of all boredom. He emphasised that in any case I should soon find myself in France where I should be shot.' Finally a lance corporal was detached to take him before yet another sergeant. 'This sergeant seemed kindly. He wasted some of his time trying persuasion on me. Failing in this he called a corporal to act as a witness, gave me an order to join some men on parade and on my refusing formally arrested me.' Success at last, someone had arrested him! He was given three blankets and the floor of the detention room to sleep on and the next morning he was sentenced to twenty-eight days in the cells across the water at Harwich.

Alfred Evans arrived at much the same time as Foister; like him, he had been trusted to take himself off without an escort to Landguard. Even though his arrival coincided with a Zeppelin raid, he did have a slightly easier time of getting arrested once there. Again, like Bert Brocklesby in Richmond, potatoes played a key part in his arrest. He was ordered to peel potatoes for the Non Combatant Corps. 'I didn't mind peeling potatoes but I wasn't going to do it as a military order,' was how Evans saw it, although the corporal who gave the order saw it rather differently: 'The bloody sod won't even peel spuds for his own lot.' He too got twenty-eight days in Harwich.

Back in the guardroom for the night Evans made an important discovery: he was not alone. 'There was a schoolmaster J. Foister BA; a civil engineer A. Priestley; a felt company's clerk H. Stanton; a bank official Cornelius Barritt; a bank clerk Howard Marten (the last three were Quakers), a Co-op manager J. Ring; a watchmaker B. Bonner and a student missionary named Bromberger.'

Stanton, who was one of the first to arrive at Landguard, had learned from his experience at Kempston Barracks which orders were worth fighting over and which were best just to accept. So now although he would not put on his uniform himself he did not object if others did it for him – 'they were surprisingly gentle with us under such trying circumstances.' On his first morning he refused to parade; the sergeant who gave the order took his decision 'quite philosophically' and he was rapidly passed up the line to Colonel Croft, the commanding officer. 'He listened to me with an air of incredulity and without further ado sentenced me, in the tone of a quack doctor prescribing an infallible remedy, to 168 hours detention at Harwich Redoubt.' His guard had enough time to warn him that before long he should be 'pushing the daisies up' and then he was off by the ferry to Harwich.

The Redoubt was ruled over by Sergeant Chalkey, 'a man of enormous girth with voice to match'. Some COs called him a 'brute' but at his first meeting Foister didn't think the tag fitted: 'for he laughed and he joked as he promised me a hard life if I didn't behave myself and only a bit less hard if I did.'

When Stanton arrived he was met by a group of about thirty prisoners, soldiers who had committed a variety of crimes, 'as fine a collection of blackguards as one was likely to meet', curious to see and hear a conscientious objector. He must have been just as curious about them too for they lived in a world way beyond his experience where 'men laughed at the mention of crime and boasted of what they had done and would do again when released'. One man had spent fifteen of the last seventeen years in prison and 'many had deliberately committed minor offences in order to be sent to prison and so escape further service at the front'.

He had no time to explore this new world much further because after a brief spell cleaning the brass handle of the well in the centre of the courtyard – which even Stanton could not object to – he refused to do drill and soon found himself in the punishment cells. In Stanton's day there was just one small window which had to serve all three cells and when he entered he could see nothing. Soon, much to his surprise, he heard a voice softly calling hello. It turned out that a fellow CO was in the next cell so at least he had company. He needed it: 'moisture trickled down the cell walls and the floor was rotten and broken through here and there. I found it almost impossible to sleep, so bitter was the cold . . . one of the ordinary prisoners thinking that my need was greater than his, had given me a small Bible, but the light was insufficient for reading.' All this on bread and water.

Small wonder then that when the pair of them were let out and a friendly warder gave them the job of washing jam jars they found no military significance attached to the task. But even Stanton could not be washing jam jars forever and he was soon back in the punishment cells. (In a similar manner Foister was later given the task of washing the flagstones that ringed the fort's courtyard. As he washed away on hands and knees – 'à la pinafore'- he was told by his fellow washers to slow down and wash and re-wash the stones, in the same style as the jam jars, as otherwise they would run out of acceptable work.)

Nearly all the COs who kept diaries or have written memoirs talk of how ordinary soldiers who were initially appalled by their stand soon began to sympathise with them once they listened to their side of the story. It is difficult to tell how much of this is accurate and how much is wishful thinking. Stanton himself realises just how difficult he could be as he questioned each and every order – he tells the tale of his battle over the amount of exercise he had to take and then ends, 'We were not quite as objectionable as we might appear from the bold narration of such an incident.' But Stanton does provide hard evidence of the fact that even his guards could warm to him: the warder who locked him in the cells came back after a few minutes with writing paper and an envelope and offered to post a letter for him. 'I was astonished. I had so often been told that any soldier back from the front line would be glad of the chance to shoot me out of hand; yet here was one offering to do me a service at the risk of losing a safe and comfortable job.' A letter was soon going off to his mother.

War was proving a wearying business. Although Britain had not been involved in major battles on the Western Front, it had been a miserable winter: German gas attacks were repelled, raiding parties launched and casualties recovered as well as the troops enduring the more everyday list of misery – rats, lice and trench foot. One journalist wrote (albeit after waiting until the war was over): 'Our men were never dry. They were wet in their trenches and wet in their dugouts. They slept in soaking clothes, with boots full of water, and they drank rain with their tea, and ate mud with their "bully" and endured it all with the philosophy of "grin and bear it".'

It is this background which helps explain how some, but by no means all, of the guards could side with the conchies. Foister says, 'It was probably less a matter of sympathy with us than hatred of their own bonds that prompted so many of them to encourage us to stick to our guns. On the other hand, there were those who urged us to accept the inevitable, as they saw it, from a genuine concern for us. I well remember one very young fellow who broke in: "But they'll shoot you" in quite a horrified tone.'

Their guards were threatening that they would soon be taken to France and shot, but Adam Priestley had already been to France once. Before arriving at Felixstowe he had been working with the Friends Ambulance Unit (FAU) near the front, but when conscription was introduced he came to believe that staying in the unit only ensured that someone else was sent to the trenches in his place. Foister called him 'the most sensible one in our group, anything he said was well thought out'. Stanton too was 'always impressed by him' and by the 'firm foundation for the line he was taking'. Priestley had resigned from the unit, come back to England, lost his argument for absolute exemption before his tribunal and was now being held in Felixstowe – of no help to anyone.

The Friends Ambulance Unit was an attempt, as one writer put it after the war, 'to go to war and be a pacifist . . . it was the sincere expression of two overmastering and wholesome impulses, the will to share in the common ordeal and the will to make some kind of protest against the common folly.' As described earlier, it began with about forty volunteers and ended with more than 1,000; nine were killed by shellfire or in air raids; ninety-six were awarded the Croix de Guerre or other similar honours. A few followed the same line as Priestley and resigned to go before the tribunals. But many others felt like David Blelloch, an Oxford scholar, who looked back on his three years in the FAU with 'pleasure and gratitude'. He adds:

> It would be absurd of course to compare the dangers and minor hardships that most of us had to undergo with those which the soldiers had to face. However we did occasionally come under shellfire, a good

many bombs were dropped all around us and one bomb destroyed our headquarters (I was not in it at the time). So I didn't spend the war entirely shielded from all danger, I should be a strange sort of creature if I didn't feel glad to be able to say that.

Corder Catchpool, however, was beginning to have the same doubts as Priestley. The early excitement of the FAU had, inevitably, turned into routine. He had been promoted to become the unit's Adjutant (it was organised on semi-military lines and Noel Baker's successor as commander was given an honorary commission in the army). This meant he had time to buy himself a hairbrush and a pair of pyjamas, but he was an administrator now, out of the danger zone: the adrenalin had gone and with it the sense of being able to give immediate help and comfort to men in real need. 'I feel more and more that we who have been spared are only justified in going on living if our future lives manifest, at every point and at all times, a heroism at least equal to that of the soldier killed in battle.'

In January 1916 the Quakers had held a special meeting at their headquarters in Bishopsgate where the great majority of the 450 men of military age in the hall pledged to refuse any form of service that would help the war effort. Catchpool happened to be home on leave, so he was able to attend and was more than impressed by the determination of his fellow young Quakers. Back in France, he wrote home: 'Ours is and has been good pure testimony for peace. But it is a side show.' For the first time he began to question this work – was he helping the war effort instead of opposing it?

Nevertheless he felt a considerable sense of responsibility for the unit. He wrote home in March: 'A good many of my boys are getting restless, being afraid that Conscientious Objectors will be forced either into the Non Combatant Corps or into prison and that if so they must resign the Unit and take their share of the hardships,' adding 'I think at the moment such action would be hasty.'

By mid-May he had changed his mind: the unit, he believed, had become 'in effect a conscript unit' with men being given exemption by the tribunals on condition they joined it. Like Priestley he too resigned from the FAU and like Priestley he would now have to face a tribunal. While Priestley was already held at Landguard, Catchpool would have another eight months of freedom before he was even called before a tribunal.

In many ways the FAU appeared to be the ideal place for a conscientious objector – someone not prepared to fight, but ready to risk his life for those who were fighting. Catchpool himself is the best man to explain his decision. 'We went out to the Ypres front sector when the fate of Flanders still hung in the balance. I little expected ever to return, and asked only the privilege of serving, for a few weeks at least, in saving life.' But in his nineteen months of service, he claimed that:

> ... voluntary units were either dispensed with or practically absorbed into the regular armies. Men displaced from the services taken over by the Unit, of which I had become adjutant, were often drafted to the firing line, and complained bitterly that I and my colleagues had sent them there.
>
> I was baffled more and more by the consciousness that, under military control, the primary object of our work was the refitting of men to take their place again in the trenches.

Yet the view of Priestley and Catchpool was the minority view; the great bulk of men in the unit were convinced that their work was worthwhile – they treated 12,000 cases in the FAU's Dunkirk hospital, one of twelve run by the organisation, while the unit's hospital ships transported 33,000 patients. Blelloch, who stayed with the unit, says he was willing and in fact eager to undertake some kind of war work 'provided its aim was not to contribute towards winning the war'.

11

The Real Battleground

Among the conscientious objectors now being warned that their days were numbered was one man who was slightly different from all the rest and whose presence was to prove crucial. Rendel Wyatt had the handsome looks of an old-time movie star and in his letters home there were no Biblical quotations or tales of early morning devotions. Indeed, at one point he talked of every man in the guardroom except him reading Bibles, 'including the agnostic Socialist'. At twenty-three he had been a teacher until he ended up in Landguard, and he remembered his pupils very fondly. In one letter home he wrote that he spent his free moments in Harwich Redoubt sitting on his folded blankets, his overcoat around his head as it hung above him, talking to the boys at school 'as they come and nestle all round me and quietly show their sympathy. I can tell they are thinking of me.' In the evenings when possible he was giving classes to the other prisoners.

Like others, he found some soldiers 'full of real admiration and sympathy which makes me feel we are doing the right thing'. The fort was getting so crowded that he had to spend one night with men who had accepted their posting to the Non Combatant Corps. 'We are under canvas tonight and it's raining cats and dogs . . . nine others, such a crowd, but a top-hole crowd. They are a ripping lot. Socialists, young Wesleyan ministers, Huntingdon farmers, teetotaller keeping a pub. Salvation army lad full of peace fight, says he won't arrest me if he's told to, bless him.'

His letters use language fractionally foreign to that of his fellow COs, and Stanton describes him in slightly guarded terms: 'He wasn't a Quaker. He had been a teacher in a Quaker school and he was a very nice fellow though he wasn't quite so firm, if I can put it that way, as Howard Marten and that group.' When some German prisoners at Harwich who had been captured off a submarine shouted 'Guten Morgen' from behind their barred windows it was inevitably Wyatt who climbed on the shoulders of another CO to talk back to them in German. Having exchanged pleasantries he had to explain to what must have been a rather puzzled audience of German submariners that he was sharing the same prison for refusing to fight them. (In a surreal scene, some of them shouted back that they approved, they were Socialists against the war and 'that's what we shall do the next time'.)

Coming from a slightly different social class, Rendel Wyatt – or rather his parents – had connections. When he refused to parade at Landguard Fort he was sentenced to eight days in the punishment cells, while Marten and Barritt, who also refused to parade, got twenty-eight days each. Wyatt was at a loss to explain the difference in the length of sentence: 'I suppose the Colonel thought I could not stand it, or that I should give way quicker. Or else because he "was Cambridge too", as he put it.'

Not only was Wyatt 'Cambridge' but his father was a distinguished professor there and his parents very rapidly set up a connection with Gilbert Murray, the Regius Professor of Greek at Oxford who was sympathetic to the COs' cause and already a considerable public figure. Asquith himself had a First in Greats from Oxford and when, in 1908, he appointed Murray to the professorship, Murray replied thanking him for an appointment 'greatly enhanced' by the knowledge that it was made by 'a scholar and a President of the Classical Association as well as a Prime Minister'. These were the days when both Oxford and Cambridge really mattered.

Murray was not on the side of the conscientious objector in the wholly committed way of someone like Bertrand Russell – while he saw the military acting like 'rampant griffins' he acknowledged too that some COs were 'obstinate mules'. But by the middle of April 1916 he was already writing to the Home Secretary to arrange a meeting to discuss their treatment and by the end of April he was lunching with the Prime Minister, pressing for better treatment.

The fact that the COs were beginning to get noticed was just what the government did not need. Quite apart from having a war to fight, Asquith had other problems. Returning to London from his Easter weekend he was told of rebellion in Ireland. 'Well, that's something' was his only response before going off to bed. The rebels had lost patience with the endless round of constitutional talks. They seized key buildings in the centre of Dublin, including the imposing Post Office where Patrick Pearse read out the proclamation declaring a republic. For six days the Easter Rebellion flamed viciously before the army's artillery forced the rebels into submission. In all some 560 people including rebels, military and civilians lost their lives and, with martial law proclaimed, the military had to decide whether to execute the rebel leaders who had surrendered.

In March General Sir William Robertson, Chief of the Imperial General Staff, had written again to Haig arguing that 'the present Military Service Act is a farce and a failure. It was a regular political dodge and of course political dodges will not stand the stress of war with Germany. We want men.' By early April things had changed: Asquith had come back from a relatively leisurely trip to Italy to find the conscriptionists within the coalition cabinet, led by Lloyd George, in full cry. At the same time as he was facing rebellion in Ireland, Asquith was being forced to bring in a Bill to conscript married men which, in effect, meant universal male conscription. Sir John Simon, Asquith's former Home Secretary, who led the opposition against the original Bill, had then asked: 'Does anyone really suppose that once the principle of compulsion is conceded you are going to stop here?' It took just four months for Simon to be proved right and Asquith hated it.

The House of Commons was in no mood for compromise and nor was the Northcliffe Press. Asquith came perilously close to resigning –

he wrote of 'preparing to order my frock-coat to visit the sovereign this afternoon' – but eventually chose to introduce a measure that he had genuinely but mistakenly thought would never be needed. The second Military Service Bill, which extended conscription to everyone, married or unmarried, between the ages of eighteen and forty-one, went swiftly through the Commons on 25 May 1916 with the Prime Minister getting little thanks for it.

Robertson now wrote to Lloyd George: 'For this Bill the Empire's thanks are due to you – alone.' In turn Haig could write to Robertson: 'I do congratulate you most heartily in the success of your efforts to bring about universal service . . . You have done well.'

Naturally enough Asquith's wife Margot did not see it quite that way. In her diary she noted it was 'Henry's patience and skill' in keeping Labour in the government while at same time introducing conscription that was amazing. 'The change in England has stunned everyone. The betting was 100 to one against these islands ever adopting conscription.'

But the Cabinet Secretary, Sir Maurice Hankey, was more realistic. He observed later: 'The people who wanted compulsory service did not want Asquith, and those who wanted Asquith did not want compulsory service.'

The *Cologne Gazette*, watching from afar as the battle over conscription unfolded, said it just proved how difficult it was for England to swap horses from volunteers to conscripts in mid-stream. The paper quoted an editorial from an English newspaper which, in arguing against conscription, said there was no more reason for a man with no calling for soldiering to become a soldier than for a man with no calling for the church to become a priest: 'The English point of view cannot be better or more characteristically rendered than is done here by this representative of private English selfishness in its purest form.'

The *Gazette* was right only on one point: it was proving extremely difficult to move from a volunteer army to conscription in the middle of the war. In Parliament some MPs still argued 'we shall never defeat Prussianism and militarism in this great War by adopting Prussianism itself. We shall never be able to Prussianise half as well as the Germans can.' But the army had no time for the luxury of liberal doubts. Its main concern was to show that conscience was no easy option; it had to dissuade as many people as possible from trying their luck as COs.

The two key officers responsible for dealing with the difficult legal problems caused by COs were the Adjutant General (the army's most senior administrative officer), Sir Nevil Macready, and the man he had appointed as both Director of Personal Services and director of the new unit – AG3(CO) – set up to deal with them, Major General Wyndham Childs. Their friendship went back to the beginning of the century when Macready had been impressed by the way Childs had put down a troop mutiny in South Africa, and their bond was sufficiently close that they could call each other 'My beloved chief' and 'Fido'.

But Fido was not as cuddly as his nickname suggests. Mrs Margaret Hobhouse, a very well-connected, formidable operator who was determined to get her son Stephen, a conscientious objector, out of prison, wrote to a supporter: 'General Childs with whom I have had two interviews of more than an hour each is a man clever, narrow, like an Inquisitor of old, determined at all costs to get the better of the COs.' He was soon complaining that his new unit was being 'inundated with letters of every kind and description from irresponsible people' alleging ill treatment of COs. He also complained of the 'insubordinate attitude' of the COs who were refusing to obey orders and setting 'a most dangerous example to other soldiers'.

In mid-May Kitchener submitted a confidential memo to the Cabinet from Macready that put Macready's and Childs' worries clearly: 'There is reason to believe that if men find that objection on religious or other grounds has the effect of removing them from danger, a very large number will endeavour to take advantage of this means of escaping, especially when operations become more arduous and the casualty lists heavier.'

There is absolutely no proof that this would have happened and in fact Britain's remarkable record of volunteering – 2.4 million men in total – would suggest otherwise. But it is against this background of the army's anger at this challenge to its previously unquestioned authority, as well as its desperation for more men, that the treatment of COs has to be seen. When Frank Beaumont, who had gone before his tribunal in Doncaster on the same day as Bert Brocklesby, refused to serve in the NCC, an officer had impressed upon him the absolute insignificance of one individual in a modern army: 'He told me having been handed over by the country to the Army authorities, they could do just as they liked with me.' But a few absolutists – men who would not help the war effort in any shape or form – were challenging this assumption. They had to be broken.

Despite the first questions being asked in Parliament about them, their treatment had grown worse. Rendel Wyatt had managed to get a note out to his parents from Harwich on a scrap of paper, telling them: 'There are eleven of us in dark cells. We were put in irons tonight for refusing to drill and we shall get eight hours tomorrow morning for the same reason.' But harsher treatment did not appear to have any effect on them; indeed, as they discovered there were others like them they grew more, rather than less, intransigent.

Bertrand Russell was one of the first to see which road the army might go down. Early in May the *Herald* published a letter from him headlined 'Will they be Shot?' in which he pointed out that there was nothing to stop the army taking these men over to France where they could meet this fate. For in France they might be stationed well to the rear but as members – however unwillingly – of the Non Combatant Corps they were undoubtedly on active service. A conscientious objector could not be shot for refusing to become a soldier, but once forced into the army then army rules applied.

Russell and the army were thinking along similar lines. On a Saturday evening in early May Stanton, who was awaiting court martial at Landguard for his persistent refusal to obey orders, was summoned before Colonel Croft who was surrounded by a group of lesser officers.

'I am sorry to tell you,' the colonel said slowly, as if to emphasise the drama of the occasion 'that I am instructed by the war office to cancel the order for your court-martial and to send you to France.'

Stanton was honest enough to admit 'the news came as a shock although the decision was not entirely unexpected. Our guards had repeatedly told us that we should "soon be pushing up the daisies".' Evans and the others still at Harwich were brought back to Landguard and told they would be 'taken in irons to France'. Howard Marten was warned that once across the Channel, acts of disobedience 'would meet with the extreme penalty of death by shooting' and that their 'friends in Parliament' would be unable to do anything for them. It was Foister who admits 'it was a trying time for all of us, for now it really did seem that we had but a few days before we should "shuffle off this mortal coil" '.

What the army had actually done was what it has always been best at doing: turn this group of nervous individuals into a unit where they all drew strength from each other. The men being held in Harwich were brought back, making a total of seventeen absolutists, and Foister remembers with delight the first meal they all had together in the guardroom in Felixstowe. They were allowed to hold a Friends' Meeting on Sunday afternoon – Foister, now a determined Socialist, found no inspiration in the meeting although he enjoyed the hymn singing and recitations that followed later, but it gave many of the others the spiritual support they needed.

A sergeant was detailed to make a list of their next of kin so that they could be informed 'if anything happened to us'. Then it was time for arguing – something they were nearly all very good at. Should they refuse to carry their packs? Refuse to march? Start a hunger strike? Harry Willson from St Albans proposed they should compel the army to transport them forcibly so that it could never be said that they went willingly. 'We turned this down,' wrote Foister, 'for it could have imputed cowardice.' Nevertheless when the call came for them to get up at three the next morning Willson stuck firmly to his bed and his principles. Two military policemen had to drag him out and dress him.

Then the seventeen were given breakfast, placed at the head of 100 members of the Non Combatant Corps and, with a line of military policemen on either side of them, marched off to Felixstowe Station. Their escort, says Stanton, 'proved to be sympathetic, but all foretold an unhappy ending to our career when we reached France'. There had been rumours in London that they might be on their way and a Quaker chaplain was hurried down to Felixstowe to find out what was going on. In addition a father of one of the COs had travelled there in search of his son. But the army was one step ahead of them both: they arrived to find all seventeen had vanished. The father wrote: 'I have had a very sad and fruitless journey today . . . This trouble seems almost more than I can bear.'

Before leaving Felixstowe they had been given permission to write letters home, but none of these were posted until some time after they had left. However they were determined to get the word out; somewhere on the train's curious route from the east coast to the south coast, two letters were hastily written and posted. A porter at a stop on the outskirts of London posted one envelope addressed to the No Conscription Fellowship and a friendly guard posted the other during a stop at Basingstoke.

So when the group reached Southampton they felt secure that their supporters would at least know they were off to France, even if they did not know exactly where. And they were right, for three days later the Quaker MP Arnold Rowntree asked in the Commons about the whereabouts of Rendel Wyatt and was told by the Prime Minister that he was looking into the case, although he was 'not yet able to ascertain whether Rendel Wyatt has been sent to France'.

At Southampton the army had a considerable problem. One of the Non Combatant Corps with whom they were travelling had developed a case of measles. No one wanted an army defeated by measles so it was decided that the NCC would be held in quarantine in Southampton. The measles exposed the army's case for the sham it was: the absolutists were supposedly going to France simply because they were part of the

Non Combatant Corps that had been ordered there. But when measles struck and it was decided not to send the NCC, the seventeen were swiftly detached from everyone else and sent on their way regardless. They would not fight; they would not assist and they might be carrying measles, but still they were shipped over.

The group was taken on board SS *Viper*, which was packed with troops returning to the battlefield. Howard Marten writes movingly about them: 'Never shall I forget the spectacle of a huddled mass of humanity occupying every available corner; and a heartrending sight it was. The circumstances of our own position were forgotten for a moment before the manifestation of the appalling tragedy being enacted on the battlefields of France.' They were warned 'to keep our own company, for many of the troops were the worse for drink and might entertain hard thoughts for us'. But as heavy rain can take the sting out of a potentially violent demonstration, so a heavy swell soon reduced both willing and unwilling soldiers down to the same level: weak, miserable, very seasick human beings. Whatever fears France might hold, everyone was grateful to reach Le Havre and dry land.

As soon as they arrived in France it was clear that no one had any better idea about what to do with them than in England. They were marched 4 miles one way with the only relief being provided by the 'never bashful' Rendel Wyatt – inevitably – who persuaded a farmer's wife he spotted quietly doing her knitting to part with some of her cider. 'Prisoners and guards alike gulped down the cider; there were many who forgot they were teetotallers.' When they reached camp they were assigned tents and told not to move. This presented Foister with a problem: the cider meant he desperately needed to urinate – but he had been ordered not to move. 'I know it sounds ridiculous, but I had got it into my head that once in France officers and NCOs had absolute powers and, if defied, the offender could be shot offhand.' In the end, he says 'the cider won', and he managed the trip to the latrine without being shot.

From the camp – in time-honoured army fashion – they were soon marched the 4 miles back the other way to Le Havre; the pessimists feared they were to be sent straight to the front, the optimists hoped they were being sent back to England. Neither view was right; it turned out that their next stop was 'Cinder City' outside Le Havre, a large camp full mainly of those who for one reason or another were no longer fit for combatant duties but who could work in the nearby engineering shops or the railways or the docks.

The first mistake the army made here was to put them all in one hut where they could debate what to do next. Stanton writes: 'It was agreed that we must refuse to do any of the work on which the soldiers of the camp were engaged, otherwise we should tend to be involved in more and more compromising acts. Also it was necessary to keep the issues clear-cut or we might lose the opportunity for a striking demonstration of the power of the pacifist against military domination.'

The next morning the bugle call went for parade and the corporal in charge expected them to be out of the hut instantly, but, wrote Foister, 'he was nonplussed at our declining the invitation'. The company sergeant major, however, appeared to be more of a diplomat, agreeing at once to take them to the commandant's office. All they had to do was 'fall in behind the corporal and march directly behind him'. Foolishly enough they believed him. They loosely approximated a march – out-of-step – to what they thought was going to be the colonel's office. In fact it turned out to be the parade ground. Colonel Congdon was there but so were about 1,000 men waiting on parade. Rather than being allowed to stand as one group they were pushed and shoved into different gaps in the assembled ranks. Then came the first of their tests in France: 'Right turn, Quick March' was the order.

Stanton describes best what happened next:

Visualise a large parade ground covered with rank upon rank of soldiers and the same ground half a minute later, empty save for seventeen conscientious objectors standing at irregular intervals over it. For some moments we stood there, striving to suppress feelings of unholy mirth, until those in command realised what had happened. The commandant took in a deep breath and then proceeded to expend it in his most lurid language. The parties of soldiers were halted and men sent back to bring us into line.

The seventeen were later fined five days' pay for refusing to parade, a wonderfully useless punishment since they were all already refusing to accept any army pay.

Having lost that confrontation the commandant did at least learn something: he separated the COs into different huts and they were given different jobs to do. 'During the day,' says Evans, 'officers came round and told each man separately that the others had given in. It was not easy to face this sort of thing alone.' They appeared to focus on Evans in particular, trying to convince him of the error of his ways. 'One army chap, I don't know who it was because it was dark, spent all night trying to persuade me against it.' At one point he told Evans 'You won't be sentenced to death, you will be sent to a tough military camp out here where you will die with no questions asked.' He was later followed by two priests, who were, said Evans 'worst of all. They came and tried to persuade me against it and wanted me to lodge an appeal with the Pope, to which I replied, "Well, no minister of religion is greater than his master". Of course they took the line that I was obdurate. Always if you defeat people in argument and they don't like it, to them you are obdurate.'

The new tactics did have some effect; Evans and Howard Marten were taken to a foundry together to cast the 'railway chairs' that hold the tracks to the sleepers. 'The chaps there were having a rough time of it so we gave them a hand.' Officers were quickly summoned to see the COs at work, at which point both of them downed tools.

But Frank Shackleton relented and agreed to do work in the camp. In his very thinly disguised autobiographical novel, the main character writes of agreeing to undertake this endeavour 'provided I am not asked to do anything connected with the war'. But as soon as he is alone again he begins to worry: 'What would my comrades think of me? Could I dare to face my friends and relations after so abject a surrender?' For a time the hero considers cleaning broom handles, sweeping the barrack yard, distributing blankets to his fellow COs and dusting down his hut sufficiently unwarlike. But after a couple of COs have 'a talk with him' he decides the torment of the easy life is too much, and he is very soon refusing orders again.

For three or four days the army and the seventeen absolutists from Harwich were involved in a test of wills similar to the opening skirmishes of a battle, with each side probing for any signs of weakness that could be exploited. One sergeant major was 'begging us to give in and do the work. His special point was that he had never put any man in the camp on a charge and it would hurt him to lose that record.' If begging was one way, threats were another. Foister was brought before the camp commandant on his own. 'He made an eloquent little speech, the main burden of which was that he was dealing leniently with us this time, but that if I persisted in my folly the end was inescapable: "You will be stood against a wall and shot".'

Eventually the army had had enough. In the guardroom the COs were told they were to be 'sent up the line' where, if they persisted in their course of action, they would be shot. Officers and NCOs used to their every order being obeyed instantly had been made to look like fools – and this in the shadow of a war that seemed unending. It was not often that an officer put his frustrations on paper but Lieutenant Colonel Reginald Brooke, who was in charge of the military detention barracks at Wandsworth, made his thoughts very clear. He had to censor a letter a wife had sent to her soldier husband in the barracks, mentioning 'scandalous cases like that of Rendel Wyatt who was handcuffed in a dark cell and sent to France'. The letter was returned to her and Brooke had written at the foot of it: 'Not of a sort I will pass. If your news as to Private Rendel Wyatt is true, I am delighted to hear it and sincerely hope the whole lot of them will be treated in the same way.'

On the night the absolutists were told they were being moved on,

Evans along with Marten, Wyatt and another CO, Bert Lief, all brought back together in one hut, had something of a party. It was a party that lent credence to the COs' assertion that if they had a chance to explain their case to regular soldiers then their sympathies would often change somewhat. The sergeant of the guard – an Irish Guardsman – looked in and asked them for any money they had. 'They've gone into Havre tonight both officers and men and I thought you boys would like a bit of a do, you've got a tough time ahead.' Evans says 'He was a grand lad who did us proud,' buying much more from the canteen – cakes, fruit, chocolate – than their own funds could have paid for. 'Bearing in mind the threat we were under it was a very good party.' The sergeant joined in when he was not doing other guard duties, singing 'She is far from the land' with a fine tenor voice. When the four of them had finally divided up the floor space and rolled up in their blankets, the sergeant even came in with a nightcap of freshly brewed tea.

Marten too wrote how the atmosphere in the camp turned from 'threatening' to 'large-heartedness'. Most of the men there were soldiers who had been marked PU (Permanently Unfit), in other words not strong enough to fight, not weak enough to be sent home. They were working in the docks, the railways and the engineering shops, keeping the army on the move. For the most part Marten found them friendly and his complaints about them are of an entertainingly disapproving nature: 'one outstanding fault was the remarkable way in which unconsidered trifles disappeared – of those of us who brought safety razors to Havre, not one remained in our possession by the time we left Cinder City. Gambling, mostly with cards, was all too common and occasioned much feverish excitement in the huts at night.' Foister talks of the low level of knowledge that the ordinary soldier had about them: 'Strangely few of them realised that conscription was in force. Time after time we were asked why we had joined up with views such as we held.' Wyatt was true to form: 'The men are without exception ripping. Many of them have suffered a good deal and on the whole they don't want others to.'

The next night they were on their way, not to the front but to Boulogne in the usual French railway truck of the time, marked '40 hommes – 8 Chevaux'. The railways of Northern France were so clogged by the preparations for the imminent Somme campaign that it took thirty-six hours to cover the distance of some 150 miles. The train was slow enough that children could at some points outpace it, shouting 'bullee biff' and 'biskeet', and the embankment 'was strewn with derelict meat and jam tins and fragments of biscuit'. Although the COs had nothing to give the civilians the soldiers on the train were generous. France was not starving; conditions for civilians in Germany were much worse, but army food was free, and the story went that on certain sections of the track entire French families gave up work and instead concentrated on extracting what they could from the slow-travelling Tommy.

A batch of COs who followed soon afterwards found that they could get off the train and pick some wild flowers, yet still have no trouble getting back on again. It was their escort, off picking apples, who had trouble getting back on to the wagon and needed help from one of the conchies he was escorting. 'He passed his gun up to me and without thinking (it all seemed so unreal) I took the gun and then helped him up. But I wiped my hands afterwards!'

The COs sound almost like tourists enjoying the 'charming hills and valleys and the rich woodlands' of their journey. Yet there was something more going on in at least one wagon, where Howard Marten and three other conchies, including Wyatt, were guarded by a three-man escort. After they had finished their rations for the night, 'we expanded into song. We had two copies of the Fellowship Hymn Book and went steadily through all our old favourites. Our Welshman [one of the guards] was in great form and his companions also chose the hymns they liked best. For a change I gave them Longfellow's "King Robert of Sicily". In spite of an unknown future it was an evening of happiness and promise.'

They spent most of one day stopped at Rouen and had another stop in Etaples where they were visited by a couple of army chaplains: 'One of them was particularly kind and sympathetic. He gave us each some Oxo cubes and left us with many good wishes.' Finally they reached Boulogne and having waited an hour or two beside base headquarters, where they were allowed in in twos and threes to wash, they were marched up past the railway station for another half a mile before turning down a narrow side street where they stopped outside an old low building. It looked nothing like a prison, which was hardly surprising because it used to be the town's fish market; but now a small board on the wall by the entrance announced 'Field Punishment Barracks'. They had arrived. The first thing they faced was a very thorough search and, while Stanton's Bible and his 'religious-looking' copy of *Tom Brown's Schooldays* survived, the Oxo cubes did not; only a couple of COs who were quick enough to swallow them as 'pills' got any benefit from the chaplain's gift.

Soon after they had come off the boat in Le Havre one officer had told them: 'I had heard there were such queer people as conscientious objectors but I didn't believe it. Well, you've got your convictions and I don't blame you for sticking to them, but I've got a conviction too that I can make you work.' He failed like the others had. Now it was up to military police to show what they could do. Foister called it 'the real battleground' and he was right. Coming to join them soon on this battleground were the sixteen men from Richmond, including Bert Brocklesby and an additional eight men from Seaford in Sussex.

12

The Price of Disobedience

Anyone arriving at Darlington Station on the evening of Monday, 29 May 1916 would have come across an odd sight. There on the platform was a group of sixteen absolutists from Richmond Castle dressed – roughly – in army uniform, plus a rather more correctly turned-out squad of the Non Combatant Corps of which they were an unwilling part. The sixteen were cordoned off in a square marked by platform seats and they were all singing their hearts out. For three hours they sang all the hymns they could remember – and this was a group of men who could remember quite a few. The other NCC members joined in 'with zest' and the captain of their escort even suggested a hymn himself. Another officer who dared criticise their singing was rebuked by a porter who demanded to shake hands with each one of the COs, telling them 'There's some spirit there.' Not quite everyone agreed with the porter; Gaudie says rather curiously there was 'only a slight evidence of derision being manifest', which hints that there might have been rather more opposition than he cared to mention. They eventually left Darlington just after midnight – on their way to London, Southampton and then France, following closely behind the men from Felixstowe.

Just as in Felixstowe, the officers in Richmond were glad to get rid of them although they had had more trouble doing so. Eight men in the guardroom had refused to go – they did not fight, but they certainly resisted, clinging to anything they could find: the table, chairs, door-frames. One witness said they were 'very badly handled'. Gaudie said there was 'an unfortunate scene. I saw the quartermaster-general kick one of the chaps in the ribs while on the ground. Further, the captain asked if we were going quietly for if we did not we should be prodded with bayonets from behind and he would order it.'

At this point Bert Brocklesby, who was in the cells with seven others, asked to see the captain. 'I begged him to let me speak to the guardroom lads, saying I hoped I could persuade them to give no more trouble.' The surprised captain not only gave him permission but also came to hear whether Bert could succeed where the army was failing.

'Look here, chaps,' said Bert, 'it's no use offering resistance to these orders. If you use force to resist, I can tell you the Army knows all about force and you don't stand a chance. We must rely on spiritual force. For my part, they can take me where they will, even into the front-line trenches, but they will never get me to raise my hand against my fellow men.' His speech was successful. They went to the station willingly, prepared to fight their battle on a wider canvas than the guardroom of Richmond Castle. Norman Gaudie wrote home to his mother 'If the worst should happen I am thankful to say I am quite calm and peaceful, and I hope that God in his great mercy will give you similar peace to mine.'

A cousin of the Quaker MP Arnold Rowntree who visited the castle a day or two earlier had picked up the news that they were likely to be sent to France, but by the time Rowntree could raise the matter in the Commons it was too late. What was far more disturbing was the fact that not only had the men gone but it seemed very clear that the government had lost control of events. The Under Secretary for War, Harold Tennant, admitted that he had made an attempt to stop the men from Richmond and a further eight absolutists from Kinmel Park in North Wales from being sent to France, but he had failed totally. He read out telegrams from the War Office addressed to the commanding officers at the two camps: 'Take steps to ensure that they do not go to France. If they have already gone, take steps to recall if still in this country or state whereabouts as far as is known.' He then revealed the replies received from the two camps, which admitted that the men had already left bound first for Southampton. The reply from Richmond sounded as though the commanding officer was almost enjoying himself: 'The sixteen men are probably now in France.' Tennant went on to argue that it did not matter where they were – France or England – but for Rowntree and other MPs sympathetic to the COs' case it must have been a frightening moment, for the minister was virtually admitting that he had tried his best but he could not control his own army.

At Southampton the absolutists joined up on board the *St Tudno* with other Non Combatant Corps units, including the party from Kinmel Park Camp and a small band of eight absolutists from Seaford Camp in Sussex. (In total forty-nine COs were sent over to France at this time, fourteen were sentenced separately from the thirty-five our story covers.)

The men at Seaford had gone through much the same battles, fighting them in slightly different ways. They had not needed to be dragged out of the guardroom but each man had been assigned an escort as they started off on the way to the train station. They tried to draw a thin if slightly comical line between going willingly and being forced to go. Thus Fred Murfin told his escort, 'Give me a push or I won't walk.'

'All right, mate,' the escort answered and, with a gentle push, off they set. When they reached the train the officer in charge had asked if they would agree to have their handcuffs off – they refused. Before the train started they refused again. At the first stop he tried again: would they take their handcuffs off as a favour to him? In this theatre of the absurd, where the prisoners were asking for harsher treatment from their guards, the COs accepted, but only if the captain agreed that the handcuffs would be put back on again before they left the train. And when they reached Southampton and their handcuffs were duly put on again they said they would not board the ship until they had an escort. Everyone's honour was satisfied: no one could accuse them of going willingly to France and no one could accuse the officer of treating them inhumanely.

As for the men from Richmond, they were prodigious hymn singers. They had begun on Darlington Station, continued 'much to the surprise of Londoners' after they were shipped across London by bus to Waterloo, and they were still singing on the boat. 'Simply trusting every day' appears to have been their favourite hymn and Gaudie says it did not matter whether they were 'agnostics, artists or Christians of different sects' – everyone joined in. This boat taking troops to the front even had a destroyer for an escort – and as had happened with the first shipment of COs, they were only allowed on deck for an hour for fear there might be problems. Gaudie describes their reception in somewhat Biblical language. Their hour, he wrote, was enough to prove 'a most valuable utility to the CO cause and also Christianity, Bert Brocklesby being a living testimony for both causes'. They returned to their cabin feeling that 'though our host were encamped against us, yet we would hold erect our heads'.

They were fortunate to have a much smoother crossing than the first group, and witnessed a spectacular sunset over the Isle of Wight. When they reached Le Havre the army did not even bother with Cinder City; they were simply put on the slow train to Boulogne. It was, says Bert, 'a grand tour of Picardy and Normandy, leisurely and lovely through miles of orchards rich with the blossoms of May'. Happily for them there was no room left at the punishment barracks so they were marched up the hill to a much bigger barracks at Henriville, just outside the centre of town.

So now, despite the government's attempts to stop them, the army had in its hands, in two separate but close camps in Boulogne, its first collection of absolutists from around the country. Friendly persuasion and unfriendly persuasion had both failed. What next?

Murfin and the other men from Seaford who were allowed to wander within the boundaries of the Henriville camp were soon accosted by some curious soldiers. Murfin writes:

They said a lot of COs had been shot the week before at this camp. We knew there had been about sixteen COs ahead of us and asked these men if they knew the names. 'The names were posted there,' they said, pointing to a hut. We went to see but found no names posted, and we ran after the soldiers to tell them so. 'Oh well,' they said, 'they must have been taken down – they were there earlier today.'

Although Murfin says it did nothing to make him change his mind, nevertheless it must have been a frightening introduction to France. Indeed, a few days later one of the Seaford men, known as Billy, gave up his fight to remain an absolutist and agreed to help around the camp. It was hard for him; he was bitter at himself for giving in and to make it worse he now had to bring his former cellmates their rations. He told them: 'You have your religions, I have nothing.'

Bert Brocklesby and the men from Richmond were given freedom not just of the camp but of the town too. Bert remembers: 'The commanding officer told us that as we were now on active service: the penalty for refusing to obey orders was death; he would give us twenty-four hours to think it over.' The officer finished with a warning and a plea: 'You won't be considered as martyrs, it will be very quietly done. No one will know. It won't be in the papers. For God's sake consider what you do; think if it is worthwhile.' It seems as though these men were forever being threatened with the death sentence, but this time the threat seemed real.

'We were set at liberty and walked around the town,' wrote Bert. 'We went and bathed on the shore, our first bath for many days.' There was even a game of pick-up football on the beach. Then they behaved like true Englishmen: 'We pooled all our pocket money and went and had a nice tea in a cafe.'

As they walked up the hill back to the camp towards the end of a wonderful day, a day which had given them such a tempting taste of freedom, Bert turned to the others: 'Well, chaps, we're up against it now. It looks as if the first lot sent out here had given in, else they would never have brought another lot out.' He describes what happened next.

'"How far are you prepared to go?" I asked Leonard Renton, an International Bible Student from Leeds. "To the last ditch!" said he, and one by one they all said the same. It was the most thrilling experience of my life.'

There was something about the Northerners from Richmond that conformed to all the north–south stereotypes. Some of them had to be moved for a time to the field punishment barracks, where Harry Stanton was captured by their unbounded enthusiasm. The Felixstowe men, he admitted, had been 'lacking in humour or, at least, gaiety, since Wyatt had departed' (he had been moved to a camp in Calais). But the Northerners 'seemed to liven us up. They were less reserved in manner than we, with perhaps a different sort of reaction to the daily rubs of Fortune if the military machine might be so termed . . . One of them, named Brocklesby, who was still at Henriville, had made himself immensely popular among the casual drunks who drifted in and out of the guardroom, by getting them to blow bubbles.'

The Felixstowe group needed some laughter, for they had heard exactly what could happen to them if they refused to yield. One Sunday after lunch, all the prisoners in the punishment barracks, not just the conscientious objectors, were assembled in the courtyard. There, they had to listen in silence while an officer read out the sentence of a court martial on driver John William Hasemore. The case had been chosen very deliberately. Hasemore, aged twenty-three, had been charged with disobeying a lawful order while on active service – exactly what the conchies, now listening to the verdict, knew they would face. Hasemore had not been conscripted; he had joined the Royal Field Artillery in 1915 as a volunteer – and he had kept out of trouble until April the following year.

According to reports his work had always been 'satisfactory' and then something seemed to snap. He was given twenty-eight days' punishment for disobeying a lawful command of his superior officer. But while in the middle of that punishment he got into more trouble: he refused to continue his task of carrying horse rugs and instead went into the guardroom, lay down and refused to get up when ordered. So when his battery started to move out of the front line into the reserve – there was no suggestion of cowardice here – Hasemore was under guard at the rear of the column.

Second Lieutenant Steven was later to tell Hasemore's inevitable court martial that because Hasemore was not marching properly he had ended up three-quarters of a mile behind the front of the column. When Steven gave him a direct order, he said 'I will not fucking well march.' The lieutenant halted the column and had Hasemore tied with a rope around his waist to a gun limber. Hasemore then told the lieutenant: 'You are having a fine game with me. I will not fucking soldier in France. I have finished soldiering.'

The section moved forward again, but after about 100 yards Hasemore cut the rope and said 'Fuck you.' He then asked to be allowed to march without being tied and Lieutenant Steven agreed. This time they got about 200 yards before Hasemore began to drop behind again and once again he was tied up. This time Hasemore was even more forthright: 'You dog, you pig, you sod, you rotten fucking bastard. It is men like you who spoil the British Army. Call yourself a British officer?' The only way to keep him moving was to lift him on to the gun limber and tie him up there. It took just six weeks for his words to catch up with him.

At the Public Record office at Kew in London, you can find the file on Hasemore's court martial – and pretty unimpressive it is too, even allowing for the fact that his trial was held in the middle of a war. Apart from the charge sheet and other details the record of the actual court martial takes up only nine pages, and is written entirely in pencil. A note explaining the month-long delay in holding the court martial explains that the case is a 'very complicated one', but it is hard from this record to see what is complicated about it.

Hasemore pleaded not guilty to four charges: two of using insubordinate language to his superior officer, one of using threatening language, and lastly the key one – that while on active service he had disobeyed a lawful command. The evidence of Sergeant Eager, detailing Hasemore's refusal to leave the guardroom when ordered, takes one page, including three lines for cross-examination. Hasemore, whose knowledge of the law must have been nil, defended himself without the help of the prisoner's 'friend', as a defending officer was called, while Lieutenant Steven gave his evidence without any cross-examination. In all there were six witnesses and only one was – briefly – cross-examined.

Hasemore's only explanation for his conduct appeared to be that while he was being punished for minor offences, the bombardier responsible for him had 'kept nagging at me', and when he dropped a couple of horse rugs had demanded: 'What are you dropping them for, you silly fucker?' At this Hasemore had demanded to see the sergeant major and when no sergeant major appeared, he said 'I won't do any more work until I have seen him.' Of his refusal to march, he said 'I lost my head and really can't say what happened.' Evidence as to his character was short. The sergeant who made the case against him stated that Hasemore had been in his sub-section for about six weeks 'and his work had been proved satisfactory'.

The papers give the accused's rather sad defence of his own character: 'I have been at sea all my life and can speak German, Spanish and Italian.' And that was the case in full. It has to be remembered that Hasemore was not being ordered to advance into battle: he and his battery were moving from the front line into reserve. He was not charged with desertion but with disobedience. Nevertheless, having been found guilty, he was sentenced to be shot at dawn. The file spiralled upwards through Major General Hickie, commander of the Sixteenth (Irish) Division, who recommended that the sentence be carried out because the crimes were deliberate, repeated and took place in public on the line of march. Then it continued on its way through the line of command to General Sir Charles Monro, commander of the First Army, who agreed: 'this driver appears to possess no sense of discipline'. The charge sheet was confirmed at the highest level by Sir Douglas Haig on 8 May and Hasemore was shot at dawn in an abattoir at Mazingarbe at 4.25 a.m. on 12 May 1916. He is buried in a peaceful corner of a cemetery in France with a second lieutenant of the Royal Dublin Fusiliers on one side and a sapper of the Royal Engineers on the other – in death the Commonwealth War Graves Commission makes no distinction between how men were killed.

Although the army nearly always circulated the news of any execution, reading out Hasemore's sentence like this was very unusual. It confirmed to the conchies that the army was prepared to carry out the death sentence. The army had chosen its case well. Out of all 306 men shot at dawn during the First World War – usually for desertion and cowardice – only five were shot for disobedience, and Hasemore was one of those five. This was a message to the conscientious objectors that they could be shot for the same reason. If the COs needed any further reminder of the army's power then they had only to look to Ireland where the army had been given a free hand to deal with the Easter rebels which they had no hesitation in using. Fifteen leaders of the rebellion were executed after summary secret trials by courts martial – martyrs for the generations to come.

In 2006 the British government pardoned all 306 soldiers. The Defence Secretary said in essence that the evidence no longer existed to assess all the cases individually and it was best to acknowledge that injustices were done in some cases, even if he could not say which, by granting a posthumous pardon to all. So ninety years after his death Hasemore won a pardon, but in the spring of 1916 the lesson for the absolutist COs was very clear.

This attempt to frighten them into submission was typical of the field punishment barracks at Boulogne, which the conchies soon found lived up to its reputation as the prison with the toughest regime of any of the British army prisons in France. Among the military police there, Harry Stanton said bitterly, 'a lack of humaneness is almost a qualification for the job'. His bitterness was echoed by the ordinary soldier who 'hated and despised them and said they only took the job as a means of avoiding service at the front'.

The Felixstowe COs had been in these barracks for less than a day when they were confronted with the inevitable order to drill. Just as inevitably they refused. But this time the army was ready for them – each one of them was ordered to be made ready for Field Punishment Number One or what was commonly known as 'crucifixion'. Crucifixion had been introduced into the army as a substitute for flogging and while it certainly was more humane, it was both harsh and degrading. Some of the COs had already experienced it for a couple of days soon after their arrival at Le Havre when they had been shipped off to a punishment barracks at Harfleur, but now fourteen men from Felixstowe were forced to endure it. (Two others had been taken to Calais with Wyatt.)

Reading the various accounts of crucifixion, with its medieval undertones, it becomes more and more difficult to decide just how brutal it was. The basic facts are these: originally the offender would be attached to a wagon or gun wheel and sometimes this still happened. But as spare guns or wagons were in short supply they were now usually substituted by a beam, a piece of rope stretched out between posts about five and half feet high, or – on at least one occasion – a handy barbed wire fence. The offender had his arms fully stretched out and tied to the wheel/beam/rope/wire; in addition his feet were tied closely together. He had to stand there for two hours every day. Every fourth day he was given a day off from crucifixion although he would still be subjected to a permutation of solitary confinement, handcuffs, bread and water and hard labour. The punishment could last for a maximum of twenty-eight days. Stanton, who did not usually overstate his case, said: 'Especially in the case of the shorter men, who were virtually hanging by the wrists, we found it an exquisite torture. One or two almost fainted under the strain.'

Stanton in fact became something of a veteran of Field Punishment. At Harfleur he had been given the full treatment, including a bread and water diet and solitary confinement. He was usually tied to a beam but on one occasion it was a barbed wire fence: 'I found myself drawn so closely to the fence that when I wished to turn my head I had to do so very slowly and cautiously to avoid my face being torn by the barbs. To make matters less comfortable it began to rain and a cold wind blew straight across the top of the hill.' When he had had his two hours of crucifixion he was brought back to the tent where his hands were handcuffed behind him to the tent pole. (His attempt to lie flat on the floor and read his beloved *Tom Brown's Schooldays* failed at the point where he had to turn the page. Eventually a warder came by, took pity on him, and handcuffed his hands in front of him so that page turning was now much easier.)

But Foister, who also first experienced crucifixion in Harfleur, painted a completely different picture. First the handcuffs which kept him bound to his tent pole were shown to be almost worthless by an 'ordinary' prisoner – an ex-convict – who crawled into his tent, removed Foister's handcuffs, put them on himself and then removed them 'almost effortlessly'. After this demonstration, Foister says, 'we had to consider handcuffs as a joke, even though a bad joke'. As for being tied to the barbed wire: 'we noticed that the ordinary prisoners knew a trick or two, for their bonds seemed loose, and when the corporal called time they just walked away without waiting to be untied. They passed the trick on to us.' One senior officer claimed at the time that Field Punishment Number One 'involved a certain amount of discomfort and a considerable amount of disgrace'. But he was wrong: field punishment involved a huge amount of discomfort and – for the COs – no disgrace, for it became almost a badge of honour.

As an author puzzled by Stanton and Foister's conflicting reports, I decided in the end to try crucifixion myself. An unwilling helper tied my arms at full stretch against a builder's metal fence at a height of six foot and then tied my feet together. The moment he left me, I wanted to be released. The very idea of two hours standing there with nothing else in my world seemed impossible. My arms very rapidly began to ache and I had only been going two minutes. Tying my feet together was the torturer's touch; the whole thing would have been easy if I could have kept moving. There was one moment – probably about halfway through – when it was only shame that prevented me calling for help. But eventually after the allotted two hours I was set free. It certainly was not torture, but it was very unpleasant indeed. I felt stiff, exhausted and humiliated. And when I finished I had a proper lunch to come instead of a punishment diet and a punishment cell, and I didn't face the depressing prospect of doing the same thing again the next day.

The regime the COs had to endure in Boulogne was certainly a harsh one, whether they were being crucified or just existing for the remaining twenty-two hours of the day. They were squashed into the three cells that the barracks possessed and given three days' bread and water when being punished. (Because bread was in short supply they received four biscuits a day instead, except on one occasion when Foister asked politely if there was a double ration to celebrate the King's birthday and the amazed guard gave him the whole tin.)

The cells, in the darkest corner of the barracks, were about eleven foot square. They were made of wooden planks and, since there were no windows, the only light came through gaps in the planks. There was just one bucket for them to share as a latrine and their hands were kept in handcuffs behind their backs during the day and at the front during the night. There were no beds, only blankets, and no exercise. The army, said Stanton, had 'certainly found a way of making life almost unendurable'. By the second night their guards relented a little and a warder came in to undo their handcuffs for the night. One of them actually slept through this whole process and awoke to discover his hands were free – unsurprisingly, he thought there had been some sort of overnight miracle.

If the army hoped they might be sitting in their cells debating whether to give in, they were comically mistaken. With nothing at all to do, they started the first in a series of debates. Stanton remembers some of the topics: 'Marxism, the Tolstoyan philosophy, Esperanto, vaccination and the existence of a personal devil.' (This pretty much sums up the disparate beliefs that had been brought together in

Boulogne: Utopia, pacifism, the brotherhood of man, personal liberty and God.)

After three days of solitary confinement – or as solitary as the prison could provide – they were let out to see if anyone had changed their minds.

Two relented a little. Shackleton, who in Le Havre had already compromised once, again said he was ready to do odd jobs around the camp and this time he was joined by Frederick Bromberger, a student missionary with the Plymouth Brethren. Now the twelve left were asked by an officer: 'What's the harm in doing this? You won't win the war by standing to attention. You don't help to kill anyone while you keep in step.' But again they held fast. They had decided that it was better to refuse to obey any order, however trivial, 'for that way we should keep the issue clear. Had we obeyed such orders we should undoubtedly have gradually found ourselves up against more serious ones.'

So the twelve were returned to the cells – but this time they were all forced into one cell, where they had to divide up the floor space so that taller men slept opposite shorter men. It was, as Stanton says in his understated way, a 'tight fit'. They celebrated their return to the normal prison diet with 'a feast' of bully beef and tea and waited to see what the army had in store for them next. In the meantime they managed to sneak back some of the books that had been taken from them, so they could share their own unusual prison library which included the Fellowship Hymn Book, the inevitable *Tom Brown's Schooldays*, *Childe Harold*, *Bees in Amber*, a 'little book of thoughtful verse' which became a surprise best-seller, and Jack London's *The Iron Heel*.

In Henriville, where the newly arrived Richmond and Seaford groups remained, Bert Brocklesby's concern was not with punishment cells or punishment diets but whether or not anyone in England knew where they were. He could be certain that their supporters were aware they were being sent to France – Gaudie's brother and sister had been there to say goodbye to them at Darlington Station, and Herbert Senior was met by three fellow Jehovah's Witnesses at Kings Cross – but he could not be sure if anyone knew where exactly in France they were being sent to. And given that the army appeared to be able to do pretty much what it wanted, this could prove crucial.

Very soon after Bert arrived in France he got hold of a card that the army gave out to men sent overseas. These cards served two purposes; they took the pain out of the business of letter writing and they made the life of the censor considerably easier.

There were several statements on the postcard that could be crossed out by the sender, so a soldier could happily get away with nothing more to write than his signature. (It was stated very clearly that if anything else was added the card would be destroyed.) The early sentences would be of vital importance to most relatives: the soldier had a choice between: 'I am quite well,' or 'I have been admitted into hospital' with a few additional small options. But Bert concentrated on two sentences further down the card. They read: 'I am being sent down to the base. I have received no letter from you for a long time.'

He went to work on a careful set of deletions so that the card he eventually was allowed to post looked like this: 'I am being sent ~~down~~ to ~~the~~ b ~~ase I have received no letter from y~~ou ~~for a~~ long ~~time.~~' Anyone combining the two sentences would see: 'I am being sent to b ou long.'

It was hardly the work of a sophisticated code-maker and as Bert says, 'I made my cancellings look as haphazard as possible but thought it looked blatantly clear.' Yet his card 'evaded an overworked censor and told the folk at home'. Bert sent one of these cards to his family in Conisbrough and the No Conscription Fellowship also received one, although it remains unclear whether this card was simply passed on by his anxious parents or whether Bert managed to get a second card through the censor.

Phil Brocklesby had been on officer training for six months but he knew his time away from the front was soon to end. At the beginning of June he took a test for those being sent overseas. It was quite difficult to fail – he had to do some written work and show that he could drill a squad of men. Having passed the test he was then sent on a bombing course. But he had only just started the course when he was told that he was bound for France. He could have forty-eight hours' leave to say his goodbyes at home.

Phil arrived back in Conisbrough to say goodbye to his parents at the same time as the postcard arrived. He promised his mother and father that he would do everything he could on his way to the front to find Bert. He could only hope that the ship taking him across the Channel would dock in Boulogne; even if it did he would have to move fast.

For in France events had already started to move on. The twelve men from Felixstowe in the punishment barracks continued to be confined to their one cell. There was only room for exercise to be conducted in batches of four men at a time. On cold days when they needed to get warm they would march round and round the cell until they became giddy and then they turned round and unwound themselves. But the worst part was the latrine bucket all twelve had to use. Only on Mondays were they taken through the streets of Boulogne to 'les bains' for their weekly bath. Inevitably they started to get ill and Alfred Evans was taken to hospital with dysentery. They could not be kept like this indefinitely.

After three weeks Howard Marten was singled out as a ringleader and put in a separate cell. This was no hardship: it gave him much more room and created a space in the overcrowded cell. That night they all decided to hold a Friends Meeting, 'a time of great strengthening in which we became aware of our unity' wrote Stanton. Since the cells were only divided by wooden planks Marten could join in too. The next day three more 'ringleaders' were sent to join Marten and all four were then summoned to appear before the commandant of the Boulogne base.

Foister recalls the scene: 'I was brought from the cell to the office and stood at attention in front of a table at which three officers were seated. The one in the centre lectured me quietly but firmly on the sin of disobeying orders on active service, said he was going to give me an

THE PRICE OF DISOBEDIENCE

order and, if I did not obey, I should be court-martialled for disobedience, the punishment for which could be sentence of death.'

An ordinary soldier was standing to attention in the same office. 'The order given me was to fall in behind this soldier for drill. "Right turn, quick march" came the order. There was no response.'

'It was all water off a duck's back,' says Marten when he went through the same process after Foister. Instead of obeying the order he told the officer, 'While I did not wish to show him any personal discourtesy, I could not recognise any military authority and must refuse to obey such an order.' Marten recalled later: 'I hardly knew what they were talking about most of the time. And of course, what must have galled them was that while we were reasonably civil, we were never prepared to do things in a military way. We never saluted anybody; we never stood to attention.'

But Foister was much more tense. He says that at this point he remembered all too clearly listening to Hasemore's death sentence being read out a few days earlier:

> The greatest strain that I ever experienced was when that order was given because I knew it was the final point and I was the first one to be given the order and my mind went quickly round. Will the others do what I am going to do? But it was all in a flash you see. I didn't have minutes to think about it . . . a couple of seconds. I was not going to fall in. I was ready to do whatever happened.

One by one these first four went through the same procedure. They all refused the order and they were then separated and each told they had five minutes to reconsider their decision. Since the group had come this far with such growing determination, the army could have held out only the faintest of hopes that they would change their minds even if they had been given five days, let alone five minutes. They did not recant, and were told they would now face a court martial.

While the Public Record Office at Kew holds the proceedings of some courts martial, no records of the key trials of these conscientious objectors have yet been found other than a leather-bound volume which notes, with painstaking penmanship, the name, the regiment, the charge, the date and the sentence of these men and that of many others – but gives no further details.

Even if the records do show up they are unlikely to contribute much, for there was little or no dispute over the evidence of the men's wrongdoing; they had clearly refused to obey the orders given to them by a whole assortment of superior officers. The dispute was over whether they should ever have been in the army in the first place, which was not something that any court martial was going to sort out.

The trials of these first four were held in a shed which joined a YMCA store, and Marten describes the process as 'necessarily long and tedious' as the evidence was taken down in writing by the president of the court. (All the cases were heard by three officers with the president being the senior officer.) Marten did not bother to cross-examine the witnesses who gave formal evidence of his disobedience. The court, he says, gave an 'attentive hearing' to the statement in his defence that he read out. The whole trial, with a possible sentence of death waiting at the end of it, took about an hour and a half; but no one complained that the hearing had not been fair.

Ironically it was the army that discovered that, however fair the hearing, there was a technically significant fault in the way it had been held: the officer who had convened it was of junior rank to one of the witnesses. A week later all four cases had to be heard all over again. At the first court martial it had been Foister who was tried first, but this time he could stand outside and listen to Marten's defence through the wooden planks: 'I rank it as very much better than mine.' A major from the South Staffords, waiting there because one of his men was to be court-martialled after the four COs, was also listening with Foister: 'The major said to his companion, "It would be monstrous to shoot these men." An ominous comment it seemed to me.'

The courts martial over for the second time, now all the four could do was wait and try to guess what the verdict might be. At least it meant they were allowed out to exercise twice a day, and from the limited punishment diet they switched to the so-called 'full rations' which they shared with their grateful friends who were still on punishment diet.

Now the courts martial began to come faster – and to take less time. While the first cases had taken an hour and a half they were soon taking little more than fifteen minutes. Just how thoroughly they were in the grip of the army is shown by the legal representation they were provided with: 'The sergeant major in charge of the barracks was the only adviser provided for us, although he was also the chief witness against us,' says Stanton. 'He gave us information as to what was and what was not permissible to say, but this seemed of no great value.' As Foister says, if they wanted a 'prisoner's friend' to help with their case 'we would have to go back to England to find one'. But Marten had been refused permission to telegraph back to England asking for legal representation. Instead of proper representation or even just a 'friend', Foister says, 'we were just given a large sheet of paper and told to prepare a defence.'

Stanton refused to plead because he did not recognise the right of any military officer to command him, nor of any court martial to judge him, so the president entered a plea of 'not guilty'. He listened to two military policemen give evidence of his refusal to obey an order and then he read his own statement of defence. The three officers sat in complete silence while Stanton told them that 'all war was contrary to the spirit and teaching of Christ'. He added that in cases where the claims of the state were in conflict with those of God, 'I must obey the higher authority.' With that the court martial was over; there was not the slightest hint of any common ground.

The men from Richmond and Seaford had had it slightly easier than those from Felixstowe. Their camp up the hill at Henriville was not run by the military police and there were no punishment cells. Having been given twenty-four hours to make up their minds, the next morning they were ordered on parade by a NCO who assumed they were ordinary prisoners who had simply committed one of the routine sins of army life. He was therefore very surprised when no one responded to his order.

'Who are you chaps?' he asked.

'We are conchies,' replied Bert Brocklesby.

'Get back to your hut. I'm not going to be witness to get all you chaps shot.'

So they had another twenty-four hours' reprieve before it was their turn to go through a similar ritual to the Felixstowe men. They were ordered out of the guardroom and told they had to make their way down to the docks. Here they found Sergeant Foster, who had last encountered Bert Brocklesby when he had tried – unsuccessfully – to make him do Swedish drill exercises in Richmond Castle. This time he had a rather easier job because he only had to collect evidence for a court martial rather than seriously trying to make Bert or anyone else do something. Bert says:

> We were lined out in a dock shed and there was a case of bully beef on
> the floor. Foster went along the line and asked each man individually:
> 'If I tell you to pick that case up, will you do it?' I was the last on the line.
> I saw Foster getting redder and redder as each man refused, and when
> I said 'I am sorry . . .' he burst out with 'Sorry be damned!' and relieved
> his feelings with a round of oaths.

Back up the hill they went. There they were taken before an officer who asked them one by one if they intended to still disobey orders. No one had changed his mind.

They were then sent back to the guardroom where the conditions were considerably better than at the punishment barracks. They were usually joined by a nightly assortment of drunks; one man, 'a huge fellow', learned that they would not take part in the war and wanted to pick a fight with Bert. But Bert simply held out his hand to shake and peace was restored. From then on life at Henriville became a question of waiting: first for the court martial and then for the verdict.

Norman Gaudie's diary records what was important to him in terse notes.

> Saturday: Able to take exercise in the shape of a football match with some Frenchmen which I greatly enjoyed.
> Tuesday: Court-Martialled. Three witnesses called.
> Thursday: Amusing experience – being taken to the fumigator to have the chats [lice] executed and also bathed in formalin.
> Sunday: Bible class in afternoon. Singing at night 'Trusting Jesus' . . . eight times.

For their actual court martial they were taken down to the field punishment barracks, where they were all held in an army hut. Waiting proved a difficult time: 'The only exercise we could think of was Leap Frog,' writes Murfin. 'Very soon we found the asbestos lining [of the hut] smashed up by our play, so we used the bits as marbles for a game. If this sounds silly or frivolous, think of a lot of healthy young men shut within four walls for a long time, waiting for we knew not what.'

The courts martial were following a pattern but as usual Bert Brocklesby was not going to let his court appearance happen without using the opportunity to argue his case. He wrote:

> The president was clearly at a loss to understand my line of defence, which was to show that I had consistently disobeyed all military orders from the start. He said 'You seem to be making your case twice as bad as it need be.' This struck me as being really funny and I almost laughed out; as though the penalty would be to be shot twice. Then he too seemed to see the logical absurdity for he smiled in a sheepish sort of way.

Now all Bert and the others could do was sit and wait for the verdict.

Murfin says that in the night after their cases were over 'when the rest of the men were asleep Stuart [Beavis] and I lay awake discussing what we thought might happen to us. At the time we thought the first sixteen COs had been shot and it seemed to us probable that one or two of us might be shot and the rest given another trial.'

Stanton was just not sure what to believe. On the one hand they had had a visit from a senior Baptist minister, accompanied by a Quaker who was later to go to jail himself as a CO, which showed at least that the outside world knew where they were. But the warders were still telling them that they were going to be shot, and Stanton writes that they were more convincing than they ever had been:

Before our trial we considered such talk mainly as a form of intimidation, but we were surprised to find the statement made even more persistently when the supposed motive for it could no longer exist. That it was not simply malicious was indicated by the fact that our most friendly warder now repeated the assertion, with a good deal of emotion.

13

Sentenced to Death

There was no doubt that this small band of conscientious objectors – in the army against their will, in France against their will – was unquestionably guilty of disobeying an order, many orders in fact. The only question open to doubt was what the sentence would be: life or death?

By an extraordinary coincidence Phil Brocklesby reached Boulogne just in time to hear the answer. He had arrived with a group of about 100 raw young lieutenants, all being shipped to France at the very last minute in preparation for the biggest British offensive of the war: the battle of the Somme (how many of this batch ever survived the Somme it is impossible to know). While the other subalterns went on their way Phil quietly disappeared and set off to try to fulfil his promise to his parents.

He had no clues other than Bert's postcard. So Phil went first to the camp which had been his introduction to France almost a year earlier. There was no Bert there but Phil was an officer now, he had a bit of clout, and he was eventually told he might have more luck in Henriville on the outskirts of the town. Late in the afternoon he arrived at the Orderly Room at Henriville where the guards confirmed that they were holding Bert: he was still alive but Phil would have to wait for him to come back from being deloused.

Delousing had its humorous side. Gaudie says, 'We felt this day our former respectable habits were conspicuous by their absence.' Fred Murfin remembers: 'We sat one in each end of a bath flavoured with strong disinfectant while our clothes were fumigated. After the bath, a pretty picture we looked in dressing jackets and any old thing until our clothes were ready. The exercise too was very welcome. We were taken on the hills and we could see the white cliffs of Dover. We ran and jumped and played leap frog . . . we made the best of it.'

It was an impressive setting for the two brothers to meet. The camp was perched on a cliff high above Boulogne. Ahead was the sea, England and safety. Below and to the right was the port where Bert had refused to pick up the case of bully beef. Phil remembers: 'I sat on the top of a grass hummock about four foot high at the top of the hill. About 4 p.m. some forty men came marching up the hill and I saw Bert in the centre ranks. I shall never forget how his face lighted up when he saw me.' Bert himself wrote: 'Phil's visit was a real joy to us all. We knew we were not cut off entirely from our friends.'

As soon as they were in the guardroom, Phil presented himself and asked for Bert. 'I saw him for about half an hour alone. He was very cheerful and seemed to be enjoying himself under the circumstances. He told me that his court martial had taken place the previous Monday. Also he told me that there was to be a promulgation of sentence of the first four conscientious objectors who had been tried if I could stay and hear it.' Phil knew he had to wait and just hoped that for a few hours he would not be missed.

At about 4.45 p.m. somewhere between 600 and 1,000 men, members of the Non Combatant Corps and the Labour Battalions, were marched on to the parade ground at Henriville and posted to form three sides of a square with a collection of curious spectators in the background. By this time Bert was back in the guardroom, but Phil was among these spectators. The whole scene was staged with theatrical precision. The adjutant came out and stood firmly in the middle of the 'empty' side, his back to the sea. The first four conscientious objectors, who had waited just over a week for this verdict, had been brought up from the field punishment barracks. Howard Marten, Harry Scullard, Jack

Foister and Jonathan Ring were shepherded to one side with a guard for each man and two officers in charge. They must have looked a forlorn party standing there amidst the imposing might of the British army.

Finally, the moment had arrived; Marten was the first name to be called out and he had to march towards the centre of the square. Given that there was usually a battle over every order did he march or walk at this point? 'I wouldn't say I marched. I never did march. I just walked ordinarily. I did keep in step but it wasn't intentional.'

The adjutant read out his name. Phil remembers the scene vividly: '"When on active service refusal to obey an order. Tried by court martial and found guilty." A very deliberate pause. "Sentenced to death by shooting".'

'Well, that's that,' thought Marten.

Jonathan Ring, whose objection was, unlike Marten's, political and not religious turned quickly to Foister and, preserving a remarkable sense of black humour, told him: 'If they shoot Quakers you and I will be burnt at the stake.' He was instantly told to shut up by the guard, for there was more to come.

There was a long, dramatic and intentional pause, more than enough time for all four men to realise that the sentence really was a death sentence, before the officer continued: 'This sentence has been confirmed by the Commander in Chief' –'that's double-sealed it now,' thought Marten – 'but afterwards commuted by him to one of penal servitude for ten years.'

Both in his diary and in later interviews, Marten had difficulty answering the inevitable question about exactly how he felt at that moment. As he stood there waiting for verdict he said he had 'a feeling of a sinking in the stomach, wondering what was going to turn up'. The verdict took him somehow beyond himself: 'On that parade ground I felt that I was a different personality. I was part of something much bigger outside myself. I was part of something that I couldn't explain. There was something mystical about it. It was very strange.'

Marten says he had visions of Dartmoor prison, 'cells, bolts, bars and gangs of stone-breakers', but at least he knew he was going to live. Phil Brocklesby, standing on the parade ground to hear this verdict, says 'my heart relaxed, my tension disappeared'.

Bert heard of the verdict sitting in the guardroom. 'The corporal of the guard came rushing in, bursting with the news. "My gosh! You chaps ain't harf for it. They've just read out four conchies from the field punishment barracks. They all got the death sentence with commutation to ten years." Well, we felt relieved and very hopeful we should get the same. "Ten years" held no terrors for us.'

At the field punishment barracks they waited for the four to return. Stanton wrote:

> At last they came back and were locked up in our cell. We lost no time in asking what had happened. 'Sentenced to death!' came the answer. For a brief moment we were silent, thinking of all that the decision meant for us, for our dear ones, for the cause. Then a chuckle from Scullard broke the tenseness, and the others began to smile. 'It's true,' said Ring 'but the sentence has been commuted to ten years' penal servitude.'
>
> There was a gasp, whether of relief or incredulity. Ten years' imprisonment. Did the government really mean it or was it yet another stage in the game of bluff?
>
> Slowly we came to realise that a great, perhaps a decisive victory had been gained. Once and for all, we hoped, the government had been brought to face the question of its ultimate treatment of COs and had decided not to shoot them.

Phil Brocklesby left Boulogne with a 'lighter heart' but with no time to spare. He managed to slip his brother a little money he had with him as a parting gift – a fellow CO says somehow this got turned into sweets, 'the first for a long time and the last we had for three years'. Then he was off. For by now he should have been at the base depot at Etaples, twenty-five kilometres south of Boulogne. Eventually he found a train and arrived at the camp at midnight. He was too late to report officially so instead he was given blankets and a tent and left to himself. In the morning he went in search of breakfast. 'I found an *estaminet* and got coffee and omelette. It was food for the Gods for I hadn't had a proper meal since landing. When I reported I was annoyed to find that the most objectionable subaltern in the group that I came over with – a twerp who was not responsible for me – had reported my absence, but I never heard anything more about it.'

Now Phil had four days of peace, interrupted by a little revolver practice (twelve rounds) and rifle practice (fifteen rounds). He was undoubtedly an uncomplaining sort who got on with life as best he could. Where he had found food for the Gods, Siegfried Sassoon, who had arrived in Etaples seven months earlier, had found only a 'rotten café'. While Phil had nothing bad to say about the camp, other officers found it 'a hellish dump without a single redeeming feature'.

He had time to write to his father telling him the news of Bert, but he seems to have been unsure about what he was allowed to say for his letter is very formal. 'What Bert's sentence will be I cannot say but I was present at the promulgation of sentence of five COs [actually four] and I thought it was stiff. I may say that up to the present the extreme penalty has not been carried out and I don't think it will be in Bert's case.' The Brocklesby family, particularly the eldest brother George, used to enjoy conjuring tricks and Phil wrote a second, secret message using George's method of waxed paper and carbon. In this he was more explicit: 'Sentenced to death by shooting. Sentence confirmed but commuted to ten years' penal servitude.' But whether it ever got through or anyone ever managed to read it, he admitted later, was 'doubtful'.

He also wrote to Bert. Phil was heading for the front and a battle for each inch of Flanders mud where death hung over every trench, but there was not a hint of disapproval of his brother's very different fight. He asked Bert if possible to let him know the result of his own case, 'for I shan't be able to settle down until I know. I wish I had your faith, Bert, but your example even before the War has helped me tremendously. Adieu Bert, God guard and protect you. I pray God will open his mouth and stop these puny strivings of men. Love Phil.'

Four days later it was the turn of another seven COs to have their sentences read out. The form was exactly the same: a death sentence, confirmed by General Sir Douglas Haig and commuted to ten years' penal servitude. Stanton was number three on the list. He heard the first two sentences read out and assumed he would get the same treatment; but as he stepped forward he caught a glimpse of his papers as they were handed to the adjutant. Printed at the top in large red letters, and doubly underlined, was the word 'DEATH'. He later wrote in his diary:

> I had faced the possibility of a death sentence before, and now accepted the fact almost without concern, whilst my mind was occupied mechanically and dispassionately with considering the immediate practical effects. It would be a great trial for my mother. My sister would have to leave school. People in England would make a great fuss. The thought of why I should receive a different sentence from the others did not occur to me. I simply accepted it as a fact.

And then, once again, the key words followed: 'and commuted to ten years' penal servitude'. Instantly his feelings changed – to joy, triumph and pride at being 'one of that small company of COs testifying to a truth which the world had not yet grasped, but which it would one day treasure as a most precious inheritance'.

But whatever Stanton's hopes and dreams, at this moment the world still had no grasp at all of what was being played out in Boulogne. On 20 June 1916, the day after Stanton heard his death sentence read out, the Under Secretary for War Harold Tennant told the House that judging by the information he had, which he admitted was a little old, the COs in France 'were getting on very well and doing admirably and helping their country . . . those for whom my Hon. Friends are apprehensive are not really declining to obey orders but are obeying orders – I think that is going on happily.'

It is impossible to believe that a minister could lie so blatantly when the chance that he would be found out was overwhelming. What becomes clear from Tennant's replies to further questions over the next few days is that he appeared to have very little idea of what the army was doing in his name.

In Boulogne it was now Bert's turn to hear his fate. Bert remembers the captain who read out the sentences telling a Quaker visitor later: 'he thought we were very brave men. It is, I think, a long-standing tradition in the army to acknowledge the courage of the enemy.' Bert's sentence was the same as the others – death commuted to ten years' penal servitude. By this time the whole ceremony had become part of army routine. Gaudie's diary, so full on some days, is as laconic as it could possibly be about such a sentence:

Tuesday: Adult school at night. Subject, prejudice. Opened by J.H. Brocklesby – good time.
Wednesday: Talk on materialism by A. Martlew.
Thursday: Beavis on elections.
Friday: Heavy rain.
Saturday: Sentenced to be shot. Commuted to ten years' penal servitude.

By 22 June all thirty-five men had been court-martialled, apart from Evans who was sick. (He was court-martialled very soon afterwards and given exactly the same sentence.) All those from Felixstowe had heard their death sentences read out and on 24 June the Richmond men and the men from Seaford had heard their sentence too. Yet back in England a completely different picture was being painted.

On 22 June, in a late-night adjournment debate in the Commons, George Barnes, a Labour MP for a Glasgow constituency, asked the unfortunate Tennant about a report 'current in the lobbies tonight that four men in France have been sentenced to death. These men are stated to be conscientious objectors . . . I cannot believe this report is true, and I merely raise the question now to give the Right Hon. Gentleman an opportunity of assuring the House that this particular report is not true.'

Tennant rose to tell the House that the great majority of rumours about conscientious objectors were untrue and this, he assumed, was another unfounded rumour. 'I can assure my Right Hon. Friend who has put the question that there is no intention of dealing with them in any way harshly and that there will be no question of their being sentenced to death.' Again, it must have been ignorance rather than deceit that sculpted his answer, for had he been lying he was bound to have been found out.

Indeed, four days later, when the Commons resumed after the weekend, Tennant had to rewrite his own history. Faced with a barrage of questioners he admitted that thirty-four conscientious objectors in France had been sentenced to death. Despite suggestions that he had misled the House there was not even a hint of an apology. Three days later the Prime Minister himself was emphatic about what was to happen in the future: 'As far as I am concerned, and as far as the War Office is concerned, no soldier will be sent to France who we have good reason to believe is a conscientious objector.' So now, in the space of a week the government had admitted what it had at first denied and then accepted that it should not be allowed to happen again. But it had been a very close-run thing.

As for the men who had supposedly never been sentenced to death, they were now on their way by stages back to England . . . and their ten-year sentences in civil prisons. The reason for this was that at the end of May 1916 the government had faced an unlikely combination of conchie supporters campaigning for better conditions and army commanders who did not want conchies held in army jails 'contaminating' ordinary soldiers if there was no hope of making them fight. In response the government issued Army Order X which stated that if a court martial sentenced a CO to imprisonment, his sentence should be served in the nearest civil prison.

Howard Marten and the other three COs who had been sentenced with him were the first to go, shunted down the line to a hard labour camp at Rouen where they were no more than 'birds of passage'. Then they travelled on a ferry which in happier days used to ply the Dover to Ostend run, down the idyllic last few miles of the Seine as it found its way to the sea out past Le Havre, and, protected again by destroyers, on to Southampton and a homecoming of sorts at Winchester prison.

The next batch of prisoners, including Stanton, had five days in Rouen, where the commandant had worked out a way of making their life as unpleasant as he possibly could. Since they refused to do any work connected with the war he made them dig a big refuse pit. It was 'very disagreeable but we could not object to doing work just because it was very unpleasant', says Stanton. This was followed by enforced weeding with a table fork, stamping down loose stones which made up the road to the prison, a day at the laundry and then back to the refuse pit.

At Rouen they met up again with Rendel Wyatt and the two other prisoners who had been separated from them mysteriously at Boulogne. It turned out they had been taken to Calais where their sentences were much less severe: no death penalty and two years' hard labour commuted to one year, which would mean a slightly softer regime in prison. Quite why they had been separated remains unclear. By chance in the first days of their arrival at Le Havre they had not been charged with any offences in the way the other Felixstowe men had been – Wyatt, for one, had been sick. Illness provides one explanation; but it seems much more likely, although impossible to prove at the time of writing, that Wyatt was spared the death sentence and the ten years' penal servitude because of the pressure brought to bear by his influential parents back at home.

When it was the turn of the Richmond and Seaford men to move to Rouen they were treated to a lecture, Bert says, by the 'aristocratic governor. He said he didn't know what we were sentenced for (strange!) and he didn't care (not strange!) but whether we had obeyed orders or not (he seemed to know!) we were going to obey orders there. Any questions?'

But life was not quite as simple as the governor imagined. The next day, a Sunday, they were ordered to dig a hole and all refused – gaining three days' bread and water as punishment.

Since it was a Sunday they were also visited by the sort of army chaplain who gave religion a bad name. 'The cell smelt awful,' wrote Murfin. 'The following dialogue is word for word – parson holding his nose':

'What is your name?'
'Bert Brocklesby.'
'What is your religion?'
'I'm a Methodist.'
'Oh, I'm sorry I can't help you – I'm Church of England.'

The conversation was repeated with Norman Gaudie, who the chaplain could not help because he was a Congregationalist, and Fred Murfin himself, who was rejected because he was a Quaker. At last he reached John Routledge, who was the genuine article. 'You're Church of England are you? Church of England. If you'll give me the name and address of your vicar I'll write and ask him to pray for you.'

'I can pray for myself, thank you,' replied Routledge.

They never got to complete their three days' bread and water, for at the beginning of the third day they too were ordered down to the docks. Again it is not possible to know exactly what happened there, for the COs who survived France were soon to take on mythic status, with all their actions seen by their supporters through a somewhat golden light. A pamphlet issued after the war entitled 'The Courage that Brings Peace' tells of how the COs were waiting on the dock beside a hospital ship when a sizeable crowd gathered around them. This crowd was aroused by an orator who praised the brave men of England who had come to France's aid and who now lay wounded and perhaps dying on the hospital ship, comparing them with the 'despicable cowards' who had come from England but, in the face of the enemy, had refused to fight. The orator claimed they should have been shot, but instead were on their way home. The pamphlet paints a dramatic picture:

> The crowd grew angry, dangerous, and jostled and pushed until they were almost thrown into the water. There was only one of the group who spoke French [Bert Brocklesby]. He said to a small boy near him 'We are trying to follow the Good Saviour.' The boy's face suddenly changed and an old man near him asked what had been said. The words were repeated and repeated again, and behold slowly and silently the crowd moved away.

Compare this with Bert Brocklesby's own much more modest version of events. He says there was a crowd of about 100 or more. 'Among them were some ordinary British Tommies who asked our guard about us. When they knew we were conchies on our way back to England instead of being shot, they became very indignant and one man who could speak French tried to incite the crowd to throw us in the river, but he had no success and we got safely aboard.' His own involvement does not even get a mention.

Having navigated the Seine, Bert eventually felt the 'unmistakable heave that told us we were at sea. We hugged each other and rejoiced at leaving that land of death behind; how much of a land of death we were to learn later; about the time we were in Rouen military prison one of the bloodiest battles of all history, the battle of the Somme, was being fought.'

And brother Phil was in the middle of it.

14

Over the Top

Phil, of course, had little concept of what was in store for him: his two months in France the year before had been a mere taster of what was to come. He wrote home to his Aunt Bec on 20 June: 'After a twenty-two-hour train journey I have arrived at Mailly Maillet and reported to my new battalion, washed myself and had a good tuck in and at present feel at peace with the whole world . . . It's very mild sport this, comparatively speaking, everybody seems to be in good spirits. I hope it is a happy augury of the end of the war. A band is playing in the distance and it is quite cheering to listen to it.'

Phil was usually rather more honest when writing to his aunt than to his mother, who he was careful not to worry too much, so his optimism was almost certainly genuine. His first command as a fresh-faced second lieutenant was with D company, Thirteenth Battalion York and Lancaster – the Barnsley Pals who had volunteered with such overwhelming enthusiasm back in 1914. Their innocence was still pretty much intact, they had not yet been tested in any major fight; their training had turned them from miners into soldiers and now they were about to join the battle with the same optimism with which they had joined the army some twenty-two months earlier. Phil's letter reflected that optimism – as later letters reflected the despair that followed.

In December 1915, at a conference at the French Commander in Chief's headquarters in Chantilly, the Allies had agreed that in 1916 they would commit armies to a war on three fronts – the West, East and Italy. It was hoped that these co-ordinated offensives would turn the war, although the generals who met at Chantilly knew victory would come at considerable cost. By the spring of 1916 the British army had expanded tenfold since the beginning of the war and there were now seventy divisions under arms. The army had a new Commander in Chief, Sir Douglas Haig, a Presbyterian who, ironically, was just as deeply religious as any conscientious objector and who, towards the end of the war, became convinced that God had somehow chosen him as 'an instrument for the triumph of the allies'.

He was a meticulous planner. On the Western Front the chosen battlefield was the Somme, and Haig, having decided that the attack would be launched at the end of June, had three broad-gauge railways built, two million shells stock-piled, and new roads constructed – a huge military encampment was established for 400,000 men and 100,000 horses. What he had not planned for was that the Germans would launch their great attack on the French at Verdun in February, which meant that the Somme would have to be a predominantly British-led attack. And while he knew that the German defenders were well dug in he did not comprehend just how impregnable their defences had become.

The conscripts who started to be sucked into the army early in 1916 did not fight at the Somme – without the training and discipline they would have been worse than useless. Instead it was the battle in which Kitchener's volunteers were given the chance to prove their worth. Nevertheless it was conscription that made the battle of the Somme and the campaigns that followed possible. When Haig was given an estimate of 40,000 British casualties on the first day of the battle (an under-estimate: it turned out to be closer to 60,000, including 19,420 dead), he noted in his diary, 'This cannot be considered severe in view of the numbers involved and the length of line attacked.' He did not have to rethink the way he fought because he now knew he had the men being trained to replace those being lost in such profligate numbers. But the cost in both men and money was devastating. Indeed, the American military analyst Hanson Baldwin suggests in his book on the First

World War that the decision to commit to a mass army and adopt conscription meant 'the beginning of the end of Britain's long preponderance as a world power'.

On 27 June Phil wrote his last letter home to his mother before the battle began.

> I have had a letter from Harold with the glorious news that he has been left out of attack which is shortly to take place.
>
> Did I tell you I have been given charge of No 13 platoon? Ain't I lucky: Thirteenth Battalion, Thirteenth platoon. We are about six miles from the trenches here but I went up to the trenches yesterday to have a look round. The men seem to be confident that the war will be over before long. I hope they are right.
>
> I wish you could have seen Bert when I saw him; his eyebrows went up and his face beamed; God bless him, I'm right proud of him. I shall be glad when we can all be together again.

Although his letters now stop he still kept notes which trace his life over the next week. He reported first to his commanding officer Lieutenant Colonel 'Bullfrog' Wilford, who had served with the cavalry in India. It was easy to see how he earned his nickname: 'he was a largely built man with a florid face, a loud voice and a red silk handkerchief, the flourishing of which remains with me as being one of his characteristics.' Under him were Captain John Normansell and Captain George De Ville Smith, the vicar who had so enthusiastically given up his church for the army back in 1914.

Mailly Maillet was a hive of activity but it was none too safe. 'The first casualty I saw was an artillery man who stood near our billet when a shell burst forty yards away. A flying piece of shell cut his throat and ended his service for king and country.'

From there Phil was moved up to Warnimont Wood to begin a mere two days' training for an attack due to begin on 29 June. For the infantry the attack required more nerve than skill; when the whistle was blown they had to rise up out of the comparative safety of the trench, move forward in line slowly and steadily up a slope and put the Germans to flight. They were all issued with the steel helmets the army had been introducing.

It was in the artillery where the skill was required. For a week before the attack, they were to pulverise the enemy front line. The expectation was that this bombardment would devastate the German defenders, destroy most of their artillery, and seriously damage their trenches and the lines of barbed wire that protected these trenches. Once the artillery had done its work the infantrymen could move forward while the artillery crept slightly further ahead to concentrate on new targets.

Haig wrote to his wife before the battle: 'You must know that I feel that every step in my plan has been taken with the Divine help.' With God and the artillery on their side it is easy to understand why one brigadier general told his men they could 'slope arms, light up your pipes and cigarettes and march all the way to Pozières before meeting any Germans'.

The attack was planned with nineteen British divisions and three French divisions. The main front stretched out over some 14 miles from just beyond Serre in the north to Maricourt in the south. Phil was one of 2,600 men of the Ninety-fourth Brigade, who were to attack across a front 650 yards long. Leading the attack were the Pals from Accrington, the Eleventh East Lancashire Regiment and the Pals from Sheffield, the Twelfth York and Lancaster Regiment. The Thirteenth and Fourteenth York and Lancasters were right behind them.

Phil was taken through the details of the attack, using a mock-up of the German trenches marked out with tape (but understandably not dug) by the Royal Engineers. 'I never really got the hang from this layout,' said Phil many years later. 'I was supposed to move forward and I took my two platoons off and my commanding officer said "Where is that bloody white-faced bugger who calls himself an officer taking those men?" and I pointed in the direction. He said "Right, carry on" and that was all the training I had.'

What was Phil's target to be? 'The only instruction I got was to be taken to the trenches and, from an observation post, Serre, 1,400 yards to the east, the objective of the Brigade, was pointed out to me.'

It was during this 'training' that he met a fellow Conisbrough lad, Lieutenant Stephen Sharp. 'He was the only one in the Battalion I knew. I had a four-minute chat with him and never saw him again, for he was killed on 1 July.'

There was time for Phil to have his first taste of whisky and discover he didn't like it – 'at a suitable moment I left the tent and emptied my glass on the ground' – and there was time too for several pep talks, the first of which came from Major General Wanless O'Gowan, the divisional commander. Phil neatly summed this up:

> The local German reserves have already come up, owing to the bombardment, but unfortunately for them they have run into a lot of deadly gas, which we have been letting off. Never before have we had such a preponderance of all arms as we have on the divisional front. We have 596 guns, such a concentration has never been known. We have superiority in numbers also. The village of Serre will be taken.

It was the same story in the attack on the next village along, Beaumont Hamel; an NCO serving with the Second Battalion Lancashire Fusiliers recalls the general addressing them: 'There would be no Germans left to combat us because the barrage would be so terrific – it was a walkover the way he was talking.'

Continuous rain meant the attack had to be postponed for two days but everyone, including the Germans, knew it was coming. It was the moment for men to write letters home in case they never came back themselves. If Phil wrote such a letter it no longer exists. But Second Lieutenant Frank Potter, with the Fourteenth Battalion, wrote a moving three-page letter home, reprinted in Jon Cooksey's book on the Barnsley Pals, which captured the spirit of the men and their country at the time. It emphasises just how isolated the conscientious objectors, now on their way back to England, must have felt.

> For my part I am content and happy to give my services and life to my country, but it is not my sacrifice, Mother and Dad, it is yours. The one great thing of this war is that it has taught us to appreciate our homes, and to realise our duty to you more, and also the enormity of your sacrifice in giving your sons to our country. At a time like this I couldn't be anywhere else but here. We have all been brought up at home, in school and church to a creed which places our duty to our country next to our religion, and I should not have been a true son if I had stayed at home instead of coming out here.

Lieutenant Potter received a fatal head wound on the first day of the battle; his body was never recovered.

The next pep talk came from an even more senior officer – this time the Corps Commander Sir Aylmer Hunter-Weston, 'Hunter Bunter' as he was sometimes known, who, according to one member of the Barnsley Pals, 'looked like he'd just stepped out of a band box, all polished up and with red tabs'. The brigadier general commanding the brigade describes his speech as 'magnificent', saying it 'obviously strongly impressed the men'. But Phil was not so impressed: 'He was florid of speech, and gave us a lot of hot air about the honour that had been given us.' Hunter-Weston told them that two nearby divisions had performed glorious feats – one at Gallipoli, the other in the Great Retreat from Mons. ' "The deeds of these divisions will never be forgotten as long as the world endures. You are Englishmen, even as they, and you now have the chance to shine. You must stick it. I salute each officer, NCO and man." Whereon we were saluted.'

If Phil was sceptical about Hunter-Weston so too, at the other end of the chain of command, was Haig. The night before the attack he wrote in his diary: 'I have seen personally all the Corps commanders and one and all are full of confidence. The only doubt I have is regarding the Eighth Corps (Hunter-Weston) which has had no experience of fighting in France and has not carried out one successful raid.'

But it was far too late to start changing things at this stage. The night before the attack Phil had a little time to try to get to know the platoon that he was about to lead into battle. 'My Wesleyan upbringing was very strong within me and I remember, that after introducing myself, saying a prayer for the coming day in which we surrendered ourselves to the Almighty and his wish.' At 7.30 p.m. on 30 June 1916 – a glorious evening – the battalion, now equipped with newly issued steel helmets, left the wood where they had been camped for a 7-mile march to the front line trenches. The padre watched them go. 'Cheer oh! Padre,' Phil shouted out as they passed him. 'I'll have tea with you tomorrow in Serre.' As they made their way forward Phil found himself leading the company with the company commander Captain De Ville Smith. The captain had already gained a slightly unfortunate reputation. A private who, unlike Phil, had been with the battalion from the start, says: 'He turned out to be a right rum customer and we weren't long in giving him a nickname. With being called De Ville Smith we gave him the name "Devil Smith". He was a chap who was very strict, but what hurt us more, he used to come out with a bit of swearing. With us knowing that he had been a parson, we thought that was all wrong.'

Phil decided it was more than chance that they were leading the company together. 'He had little idea or no idea of me and I feel he probably did it to make his own estimate of what I was.' Whatever the captain's estimate of Phil, Phil's estimate of him was short and depressing: 'I think he felt the hand of death near.' Phil wondered later if he was being wise after the event but in fact he was not the only man to feel this. The vicar of Smith's old church had received a letter from the captain just two weeks before the battle and 'apprehended a certain melancholy strain'. The letter started bright and cheery, but in the last few lines Captain Smith expressed the hope that the vicar 'would not forget him at the Throne of Grace'.

They were marching on a tot of rum but they were soon too tired for singing. They kept going for most of the night, through the artillery positions, up through the communication trenches and into their designated trenches where, as one of the Pals said, 'instead of going to attack we ought to have been going to bed'. Phil was fortunate enough to be posted to Babylon Trench, the last of eight front-line trenches. The Pals from Sheffield and Accrington were in the first trenches with the Pals from Barnsley right behind them.

The first sign that things might be seriously wrong came at 7 a.m., thirty minutes before zero hour. Any chance of catching a little sleep was destroyed when they heard the German artillery replying to the final British bombardment. 'We had been given to understand that most of the German artillery would have been destroyed, but it wasn't.' Worse, at about 7.20 a.m. German machine guns opened up and Phil says 'even in our trench about 800 yards behind the front line the bullets just seemed to be skating over the parapet of the trench and one my men said to me "We haven't got to go over that, Sir?" "Yes, we have", I replied, but I had visions of half of us being toppled back into the trench as soon as we tried to get out.' If his men had any doubts about following him there were military police posted in the trenches whose job was to make sure that the doubters went over with everyone else.

At 7.25 a.m., five minutes before the attack was due to be launched, Captain Normansell climbed on to the road that divided some of the trenches and sat down in the middle of it so that he had contact with all his platoons. It was, as Phil says, a very brave thing to do – 'I was surprised that he didn't disintegrate; but seeing him sitting there untouched in what seemed a tornado of machine gun fire gave me heart, so that I thought it can't be as bad as it sounds. My watch crept round to 7.30 a.m. and Captain Normansell blew his whistle and I blew mine. I rushed up a trench ladder shouting "Come on lads, now for it." I was surprised I wasn't hit, so I ran along the top of the trench giving a hand to pull my heavily laden men out.'

They needed a hand, loaded as they were like beasts of burden with a rifle, 150 rounds of ammunition, two Mills bombs, a pick or a spade, two sandbags and other oddments like barbed wire and duckboards as well as their haversacks with two days of food – a total of about 66lbs each.

Phil describes what happened next:

> Then amidst all the din, with no very clear ideas in my head beyond that somewhere in front was something to be done, I turned, and with hunched shoulders and head bent to meet the storm, walked forward. I saw a man fall on his face. Wonderingly I thought, what has he done that for? I fell into a shell hole. At once reason came to my aid; this was silly for nothing could be done there; so I got up and went forward again.

The Germans were ready for them. For days now the men of the 169th Infantry Regiment, who were manning Serre's front-line defences, had been sheltering from the British bombardment, but now, in the morning sunshine, they watched the attack unfold. There were sitting on the edge of a plateau about 100 feet higher than the British trenches so they had a good view. An extract from the regimental diary reads: 'Over there in close rifle ranks come the attacking English. Slowly, almost leisurely, they trot along, out of the third into the second, then into the first English trench. From there they proceed to the attack, their light cooking utensils flash in the gunpowder-impregnated air.'

Brigadier General Hubert C. Rees, who was in temporary command of the Ninety-fourth Brigade, had his command post about 600 yards away from the last of the trenches on a slight elevation, which gave him a 'perfect view'. Even though it is in the formal third person, his report after the battle manages to convey the scene well:

> The brigade advanced in line after line, dressed as if on parade, and not a man shirked going through the extremely heavy barrage, or facing the machine gun and rifle fire that finally wiped them out. He saw the

lines that advanced in such admirable order melting away under the fire. Yet not a man wavered, broke ranks, or attempted to come back. He has never seen, indeed could never have imagined, such a magnificent display of gallantry, discipline and determination.

Phil does make some attempt to explain how men could walk into machine gun fire and almost certain death.

Somehow it seemed that in leaving the cover of a trench a detached consciousness had taken possession of me. There was fear, yet strangely also there was no fear. The thinking principle seemed to be acting independently of the body and not completely in contact with it. I advanced like an automaton, the mind almost blank, but with the will controlling the body. When I tumbled into Monk Trench, completing our first bound, I seemed again to repossess myself.

As they piled into the trench about halfway from where the forward Pals were being annihilated, one of his men startled him as he crawled about on the parapet by saying 'You are wounded, sir.' Phil looked down at his leg and saw a patch of blood the size of a shilling. 'A thrill went through me. "Is it a Blighty?" But I couldn't feel anything. I thought shock might account for that.'

He went into a dugout to check and found he had a neighbour, a man wounded in three places who was lying there incapable, with no one to help. Phil bandaged him as best he could and then unwrapped his puttee to look at his own 'wound'. All he found was a small spot oozing blood, perhaps from a shell fragment – 'there was no glory and not much gore' – which was certainly not a Blighty.

They were ordered to move along the trench they were in. 'When we were in the middle of a fire bay full of dead Sheffielders with limbs blown off, and faces turned black – frighteningly black – a long stoppage occurred. Then we moved into the next fire bay, also full of dead Sheffielders. Both bays had got direct hits by heavy shells. One body was lying on the parapet with its head blown off.' Phil seems so mild and matter of fact through all this, but this was too much even for him: 'The stoppage was so long it was unbearable and I ordered a return to the trench where it wasn't so catastrophic.'

They stayed there for a while until they were ordered forward again to support the very few men who had broken into the German lines. Tommy Oughton, another of the Barnsley Pals, says: 'We hadn't a chance. There you were, you could see bodies dropping here, there and wondering is it you next? I saw plenty of men I knew drop. No hope at all. Of course we didn't get far before we were knocked back. What made us stop was we got the order to retire. I don't know who gave the order.'

Phil says: 'Two bays further on I had to step over the dying body of my Company Commander Capt De Ville Smith, who was gasping his last.' Captain Smith's premonition had proved to be all too accurate. He had been standing in the trench with Captain Normansell when a messenger arrived at virtually the same time as a shell burst; Captain Smith died within half an hour, the runner got a nasty splinter wound in his chest and Normansell – who was standing between the two men – was untouched.

Amidst all this death and confusion a young lieutenant was sent forward to reconnoitre the front line which was their next objective: 'he came back shell-shocked and weeping and was of no more use while he remained with the Battalion.' With no more information to go on than this, Colonel 'Bullfrog' Wilford reported to Rees: 'As far as I can make out, General, I have two companies left. If you would like me to charge at their head I shall be delighted to do so.' Phil was part of one of those two companies but, happily for him and the other remnants of the Barnsley Pals, Rees had more sense than the Bullfrog and wisely declined the offer. Instead they waited until night fell when both sides could relax slightly and count the day's cost. Captain Normansell and Phil found a small shelter in the trench, removed a dead body from within it and turned the place into their company HQ. 'We sat down to rest, to doze, to forget. Hazily I wondered when working parties would come along to gather the human debris of our ill-fated attack.' Phil actually managed to sleep before being woken up after two hours:

> Never before or since for that matter have I ever experienced anything like that awakening. I sat up and swayed. I knew I was awake but I felt as if my consciousness and my body were separate and distinct. A voice said 'Here drink this, Sir' and a mug of tea was put to my lips. I drank and my consciousness, which seemed to be floating over my right shoulder, rushed into my body, and I became fully roused with active memory of the previous day's experience.

Haig had expected a 7-mile breakthrough on the first day but Phil and his battalion had got precisely nowhere and his unhappy task on the second day was to clear the area of the dead – while being shelled for his pains. Their first body was a sergeant with the West Yorkshire Battalion – both his legs had been blown off at the hip. 'I told the men to pick him up but was surprised to find that though the Battalion consisted of hard-bitten miners they boggled at it. I had to give them a lead, so like the coward I was I stooped to pick up the unbloody end, whilst two of them lifted the legless end.' Their hesitation compares with men who the next day heard someone still alive in No Man's Land calling for help. Two stretcher bearers plus two other volunteers climbed on to the trench parapet ready to make a dash for the man in distress. Immediately a machine gun opened up, two of them were hit and the other two scrambled back into the trench. 'Man is an interesting study in war,' wrote Phil. 'He can be selfish enough to take another man's rum ration, and unselfish enough to risk his life for a man he doesn't even know.'

On the third day Phil was sent to help Captain Pete Currin, a veteran of the Boer War, in the first-line trenches facing the Germans. Shortly after he arrived there was a torrential downpour which turned the trenches into a quagmire. But it did more than that. Captain Currin had spent much of the past forty-eight hours in an ultimately successful search for the body of his good friend and second-in-command Captain Firth. Having found his body he had it placed at the top of a communication trench ready to be taken back for burial. But a combination of the rain and the arriving troops collapsed the trench wall on top of the body. 'Captain Currin had to stand there and see the men treading more sludge into his friend's body. It was covered with four foot of mud so it had to be left.'

At the end of three days Phil was relieved. He had been shot at and shelled by the Germans almost continuously; snipers from his own side had tried to pick them off from the rear; at one point he had almost been shot by a fellow officer when he forgot his password at a key moment; above all he had to cling on to an existence amidst scenes that never in his blackest moments could he have begun to imagine. And the cost? 'When relieved the Ninety-fourth Brigade marched out 700-strong – casualties 700 killed and 1,200 wounded.'

But this is not the picture the army relayed to the public back home waiting anxiously for British success. At 4.55 p.m. on 1 July Haig sent a message to the Chief of Imperial General Staff which combined truth, hope, lies and omissions to turn the disaster of the first day of the Somme into a picture of considerable success.

> Battle is proceeding. Substantial advance has been made on our right, the villages of Montauban and Mametz have been captured [true]. We have occupied the village of Serre on our left [false – Rees reported that 'hardly a man of ours got to the German front line']. The encircling attack round Gommecourt is progressing [it was not until the end of February 1917 that the village fell]. The Germans are putting up a stubborn fight [so stubborn that two-thirds of their line had not moved].

No wonder that back in Barnsley the weekly *Chronicle* reported, seven days after this disaster: 'The preliminary British bombardment paved the way to the great success afterwards achieved . . . with the triumphant British advance the great conflict seems entering upon its penultimate and most momentous phase.' It was not until mid-July that column after column of casualties started to appear in the Barnsley paper. Amidst the reports of bravery and sacrifice the hard truth about the failure of the attack never surfaced.

To go to Serre now, visiting the graves of some of Phil's dead comrades on the way, it is hard to feel anything but despair. Here amidst the peace and the green grass of Euston Road Cemetery – a peace which marks almost all the British war cemeteries – lies George De Ville Smith, both a reverend and a captain, a yellow rose still blooming in front of his grave in the September sunshine. Nearby is Stephen Sharp, Phil's Conisbrough friend whose body was finally recovered. Here too, but to one side, is a marker for Captain Firth, dug out from underneath the Barnsley Pals' boots, with a headstone that reads 'Known to be buried in this cemetery'. (Firth's grave was known at some point, but the cemetery was so close to the battlefield that by the end of the war, when the time came to mark out the cemetery more formally, his grave had been obliterated.)

And finally, once the cemeteries have begun to merge into one – Serre Road Number One, Two or Three where 9,646 men including thirteen Germans are buried – you reach the trenches where the men from Sheffield and Accrington and Barnsley were to rise and walk slowly up the slope towards Serre and slice through the German lines. It is at this point that the whole thing becomes unbelievable. Looking towards Serre where the Germans were waiting, it is all too clear that it was an attack that relied for its success on every smallest detail going completely and utterly right – there was not room for an inch of error either in the planning or the execution. And when things went not slightly wrong, but badly wrong, the result was disaster. A memorial plaque to the Sheffielders amidst the trenches calls the battle a massacre and that is what it was.

It was not until 7 July that Phil got an opportunity to write to his mother again from just behind the lines at Louvaincourt – it is a letter that is as understated as Haig's case is overstated: 'I have been extremely busy this last week and it has been impossible to write letters. We went into action last Saturday July 1 and had a gruelling time having 50 per cent casualties. I was slightly wounded early on, but not enough to stop me going on . . . I have come to the conclusion that souvenirs of this war are best left in France. I want to forget it as soon as peace is declared.'

Within ten days he was back in the trenches again and again his letter to his Aunt Bec is more revealing than his letters to his mother.

Everybody's nerves have been shaken by what we have gone through, and a good rest is really necessary. Under existing circumstances rests are short . . .

Concerning Stephen Sharp, he went over with the first wave of the Barnsleys and from what I could gather from some of the men who went to bring in the wounded and who brought in Stephen's equipment he appears to have been killed by a shot striking and exploding a bomb that he was carrying in his pocket. All of them said it was impossible to bring in his body so it was left in No Man's Land.

HELL, that's what it was, horrible explosions, shattering everything and producing a sort of numbness to the senses. LOVE WAR? Not I after these experiences. Long horrible wars like this one are one of the strongest arguments for COs.

I had a letter returned to me the other day that I had sent to Bert. I am pleased he is in England again; it was quite a relief when I heard his sentence.

And what of Harold, who Phil had been happy to hear had been kept out of the first attack on 1 July? His turn would come. Another 25,000 men had been lost in two weeks securing the front line for a second push which came in a night attack on 14 July. Harold was wounded in this push after an initially successful British attack on High Wood was first halted and then repulsed by a German counter-attack. He and his men had stumbled around the wood for most of the night, at one stage coming right up against a German trench by mistake. In the end he was shot in the arm and had to dodge his way through the gas shells to get back for help. His war was effectively over, but he was still alive.

As for Serre, it was not taken on 1 July as the generals had promised it would be; it was not taken in the next big attack in October – the last of the year. It was not until March 1917 that the Germans themselves surprised the Allies by giving up Serre and other points along the Somme battlefront and retired to the much more easily defended Hindenburg line that they had spent six months constructing. Only then was Phil was able to walk through Serre, a walk which he says was a 'weird experience'. Serre, a small village in the first place, no longer existed: it had been 'wiped out, not one stone left on another'. The cost of the battle of the Somme was approximately 419,654 British and 194,451 French casualties and possibly as many as 600,000 Germans killed or wounded. For the British, as the military historian Sir John Keegan says, it was the 'greatest military tragedy of the twentieth century, indeed of their national military history'.

15

The Conspiracy

So in the summer of 1916 all three brothers were still alive. Harold had the 'Blighty' that was his passport to safety – a bullet in his arm bad enough to land him in hospital in England for treatment to the nerves that had been cut, but not bad enough to maim him for life. Phil was somehow surviving in France; in November 1916, trying to work out why he had been given the soft command of the Brigade ammunition dump when the next attack was made, he decided it had to be because, out of all those who had gone into action on 1 July, he was the only subaltern left in the Brigade.

Why was Bert's death sentence commuted to ten years in prison? The most dramatic theory goes something like this: what saved Bert and the thirty-four others sentenced to death in France was first the various notes, not just from Bert but from others, which alerted their supporters to their exact location in France; second, the death of Lord Kitchener on 5 June, drowned on his way to Russia when a German mine sunk the cruiser *Hampshire*. Kitchener's death meant that Haig had lost his key ally whose support he needed if he was going to have the conchies shot.

The truth is rather less dramatic but it is nevertheless remarkable, involving as it does the considerable sexual appeal of one woman; her MP husband; a philosopher; a professor of Greek and an agreement with the Prime Minister which everyone involved kept secret despite the fear and the pain this caused.

On the evening of 11 May 1916 an extraordinary little delegation managed to gain an audience with the Prime Minister. The fact that Asquith kept his appointment is remarkable in itself. The French were being pressed to the limit and beyond at Verdun; Haig was busy assembling his armies for the Somme; but of more immediate concern the Easter Rebellion in Ireland had only just been extinguished. The problem was not just the rebellion itself; the trouble had been compounded by the executions and brutal suppression that followed it – watering in blood the seeds of Irish independence. Immediately after seeing the delegation, Asquith left for Dublin in the hope – forlorn as always – that he would be the one who could sort out the Irish problem.

The meeting with Asquith had been called to discuss two key issues: the new Military Service Bill, extending conscription to married men, which was going through Parliament, as well as the belated plans for alternative service for conscientious objectors. But word had got back to London that some COs had already been shipped to France and, given the way that the military had acted in Ireland, the possibility that they might be executed now overwhelmed anything else.

The delegation was supposed to be five-strong but the meeting had been pushed further and further back through the day by the debate in Parliament on the Irish crisis. The Bishop of Oxford had had to cry off at the last moment in order to catch the 6.25 p.m. train back home. While there were four men including the Prime Minister present, there was only one woman in the room: Catherine Marshall, the woman who in many ways had held together the No Conscription Fellowship and who had co-ordinated this key meeting.

But in addition there was another woman whose presence must have been very much felt, even if she wasn't actually there: Lady Ottoline Morrell. Six feet tall with an unconventional beauty, she was both a key society hostess – sometimes known by her bitchy critics as Lady Utterly Immoral – and an outspoken supporter of the conscientious objectors. Her husband, the Liberal MP Philip Morrell, was one of the men in the room; the second was Bertrand Russell, her lover; the third was the Prime Minister. Asquith had close relationships with several women and had tried more than once in the past to transform himself from Ottoline's father figure to her lover. Although he did not appear to have met with success he remained on good terms with her and was still happy to help her husband obtain a seat in Parliament. The Labour MP Philip Snowden was the other man present.

Russell had already bumped into Asquith on a couple of occasions at Garsington, the Morrells' country estate in Oxfordshire. 'Once,' wrote Russell, 'when I had been bathing stark naked in the pond I found him on the bank when I came out. The quality of dignity which should have characterised a meeting between the prime minister and a pacifist was somewhat lacking on this occasion.'

But the Downing Street meeting was much more serious. If there were ever any official records of the meeting they have yet to surface, although Russell wrote the next day to his lover: 'The old man knew so much about the question that one could not doubt the genuineness of his interest. He was very sympathetic.'

Catherine Marshall, however, kept meticulous records and the day after the meeting she had it confirmed in writing by the Prime Minister's new Secretary David Davies that 'directions have been given to Sir Douglas Haig that no conscientious objector in France is to be shot for refusal to obey orders'. When she then wrote in her precise but polite way asking for clarification as to whether courts martial had been instructed that they could not impose the death penalty, Davies replied assuring her that if any court martial imposed the death sentence it would not be confirmed. Asquith had been battered by the war into accepting many things, but the presence of Russell and Morrell must have bolstered his own Liberal instinct to stand firm on this one.

If they needed help they had it in the form of Asquith's fellow classicist Gilbert Murray, Oxford University's Regius Professor of Greek. Murray recalled a few years later that he was alerted by Rendel Wyatt's parents that Wyatt had been transported to France. He then managed through his brother-in-law, the Liberal Chief Whip, to meet Asquith in his office for five minutes and tell him what was going on.

Asquith, according to Murray's recollection, uttered one word, 'Abominable', and assured Murray that no executions would be allowed to happen.

Bertrand Russell, in his autobiography, is absolutely clear on the role that Asquith played: 'It had generally been supposed, even by the government, that conscientious objectors were not legally liable to the death penalty. This turned out to be a mistake and but for Asquith a number of them would have been shot.'

What Asquith asked for in return for his efforts was secrecy and it is a measure of how society worked in the early years of the twentieth century that he got it. A deal had been struck with the Prime Minister which was to save men's lives but they had also agreed not to tell anyone. Davies was absolutely open about this in a letter to Gilbert Murray: 'The government do not wish their decision to be made public for the present as they fear an embarrassing increase in the number of claimants to conscientious objection.' In fact the timing was crucial: under the new Act conscientious objectors had until 24 June to apply for exemption and both the army and the government wanted to do as much as possible to discourage anyone from applying. It was not until the end of the month that Asquith was free to reassure the Commons that 'no soldier will be sent to France who we have good reason to believe is a conscientious objector'.

What this meant was that for six weeks while the fate of the COs in France was being decided, their key supporters had to keep the good news to themselves while nervously wondering if Asquith, whose days were clearly numbered, could quite deliver on his promise. The men in France, waiting in fear first for a court martial and then for their sentence, were not allowed to be told, nor were their relatives. When their names were called on the parade ground above Boulogne and they had to step forward alone to hear the verdict they had no idea of what their sentence would be. It is hard to imagine that a secret deal like this would have lasted twenty-four hours, let alone six weeks, in today's world of instant news. Murray realised at one point he had made a mistake in telling or at least hinting to Rendel Wyatt's parents that the news was good. He sent them a telegram warning them of how vital it was to keep it secret. Lady Murray immediately received back from Mrs Wyatt a very apologetic letter saying they had taken immediate steps 'to procure silence where we had spoken of it. I cannot express my sorrow that we should have been the means of giving you and Professor Murray anxiety. There is no one in the world at the moment to whom we stand more indebted.'

Seven days after seeing Asquith, Catherine Marshall wrote to the editor of the *Guardian* to thank him for his newspaper's recent coverage. But again she had to remain coy about the COs in France: 'I believe there is no immediate need for anxiety that such men will be shot, but there can be no permanent security until they have been brought back from France.'

But if Asquith was the saviour of the hour, who wanted them executed? Haig and Kitchener certainly make easy villains, but while Haig demanded more men and he saw conscription as the way to get them, there is no evidence at all that he pushed for the COs to be sent to France to be executed. Although the sentences were commuted using his name, again there is no evidence that he took an active part in deciding their fate.

Kitchener came to accept that there was a limit to the number of men his own personality could conjure up and that conscription was inevitable. But the day before he departed on his ill-fated trip to Russia he had seen a delegation of churchmen and asked one of them, Revd F.B. Meyer, to go to France to see if the COs there were being fairly treated and to ask them if they would accept alternative service. It was hardly the action of a man wanting to see them shot.

The push to have these men sent to France and sentenced to death appears to have come from a step down the command chain, from Sir Nevil Macready and the man he asked to look after conscientious objectors, Major-General Wyndham Childs – 'My beloved chief' and 'Fido'.

The evidence against these two men is circumstantial and building a case against them is not helped by the fact that, deliberately or not, only a few papers on the subject have been preserved.

If Catherine Marshall were alive today she would probably be surprised to hear of Childs' role in this. Her correspondence with him shows that she regarded him as a man who she might not agree with but who nevertheless did try to act fairly. Thus in August she wrote saying how 'very much obliged' she was for the opportunity for a long talk: 'I think it helped me understand your point of view rather better than before, though I am afraid I cannot flatter myself that it resulted in any greater respect on your part for the point of view of the CO.' Six weeks later she wrote again: 'I recognise that you are taking a great deal of trouble to deal fairly with that part of the conscientious objector problem which comes within your jurisdiction.'

In his memoirs (which he dedicated to 'My Beloved Chief') Childs wrote: 'I often wondered whether the NCF really trusted me. But I am inclined to think they did.' He is right, they did trust him; but neither Marshall nor other members of the NCF might have felt the same way if they could have read his views about them. He complains that 50 per cent of his time was expended 'in securing justice in accordance with the law for people whose sole object seemed to be to desert their country in time of peril'.

In a memo to Macready which he sent in mid-May 1916, Childs describes the NCF as a 'pernicious organisation' and states 'as far as I am concerned I have no intention whatever of making any investigation as to the treatment of members of this organisation.' He was – naturally enough – frustrated that in the middle of a war his department was having to spend so much time dealing with letters of complaint concerning conscientious objectors.

It is a revealing memo since at the time it was secret, enabling Childs to speak his mind openly. Many of the letters, he says, make complaints about treatment while in detention barracks, such as being fed on bread and water, which was allowed by the rules. 'All letters of this description

WE WILL NOT FIGHT

will be ignored.' Other letters make general complaints of ill treatment in detention barracks – these too 'will be ignored'. He claims that any more detailed complaints that he decided to investigate had so far proved 'either entirely unfounded or grossly exaggerated'. Childs also says that the general public do not understand the prison treatment authorised by military law: COs, for instance, who complain about being moved to a 'dark' cell use the adjective because it is more 'poetical', but in fact they are simply moved to cells that have been 'duly inspected and authorised'. He argues at the end of this memo for a 'discreetly worded communiqué' to the press explaining the real facts.

Childs comes across as a classic case of a soldier who believes that everything can be sorted out satisfactorily as long as the politicians do not interfere. Looking back, he says his department had to deal with about 5,000 COs and 'my own belief is that there would not have been half so many had it not been for the encouragement they received from members of Parliament.' He was operating within an army command that had little trust and considerable contempt for politicians – or 'the frocks' as one senior officer called them. Apart from Kitchener, who was in the Cabinet and thus a sort of politician himself, within the army high command there was a comfort zone where scorn for the politicians could be openly expressed. In March Robertson wrote to Haig complaining that 'the conscription Bill is proving a farce, Macready and I are attending to it'. In April Sir Henry Wilson (who later took over from Robertson) suggested in a letter to Lord Milner: 'If ever a man deserved to be tried and shot that man is the Prime Minister.'

In his memoirs Childs recalls going to see Asquith to argue that exemptions to military service should only be on religious grounds. Asquith asked him why moral or ethical scruples should not be considered. 'The only answer I could give was that I did not consider any moral or ethical grounds should be recognised, though I realised that it was impossible not to take religious objection into consideration. His answer was over my head. It left me wondering – and wondering I am to this day.' He adds, 'For my part I always thought that the No

Conscription Fellowship or at any rate its organisers [which would of course include Marshall], should have been dealt with under the Incitement to Mutiny Act.'

In May as the first rumours that the men from Felixstowe had been sent to France began to circulate and the campaign to save them gathered pace, it appears that both Macready and Childs were prepared to fudge the truth about what was going on in France. Kitchener circulated to the Cabinet a note from Macready arguing that some sort of organisation needed to be set up where the CO could be sent to serve under conditions 'rather worse than those of his comrades at the front'. At the bottom of the note was a very short appendix consisting of two cables. In the first one, sent to the Adjutant General in France by Macready, he demands: 'Inform me shortly by cable where non-combatant companies are employed and if there is any trouble with them.'

The reply came back the next day detailing exactly where each unit was and finishing: 'Seventeen men of No 2 Eastern Company are at Boulogne. There is no trouble with them.' The seventeen men were, of course, the men from Felixstowe and the report that the Cabinet received that there was no trouble with them is a lie. On the day that the Adjutant General reported 'no trouble' Cornelius Barritt was on his second day of crucifixion punishment at Harfleur prison for refusing to go on parade, and he noted in his diary: 'This day we were confined to tents and tied up as usual in the evening.' Three days earlier the seventeen had reduced the commandant in Le Havre to a laughing stock by refusing to march when the order was given. This was certainly trouble in a form that the army had no idea how to deal with. Yet the Cabinet and Kitchener were being reassured that all was well when both Macready and Childs must have known that it was anything but.

When the absolutists continued to be held in prison in England, Childs represented himself to the NCF as one of 'those who were endeavouring to get the "Absolutists" out'. But in private he took a very different stand. He wrote to the King's Assistant Private Secretary in

September 1917 warning of dangerous propaganda on behalf of the absolutists: 'The day that *absolute* exemption is granted to anybody whether his objection be based on religious or on other grounds we are beaten.' A few months earlier a Downing Street official had circulated a memo which proposed to the Prime Minister that the absolutists should be freed and Childs replied: 'I am sorry to say that I totally disagree with your proposals. The release of the first absolutist from military service would be the beginning of the end.'

The only evidence of what he actually felt about executing conscientious objectors comes towards the end of the war when the army was getting so desperate for men that it was proposed to extend conscription to cover Ireland. Childs was concerned that the Sinn Feiners would simply follow the example of the absolutists in Britain. His solution was a court martial where, if a death sentence was imposed, it would be carried out 'if it appears that their objection is based on political and not religious grounds. If this proposal is adopted it is no good disguising the fact that it will in certain cases mean shooting, and it should be recognised that Sinn Feiners will be shot as well as the anarchical atheists in this country who on termination of their sentence of imprisonment again disobey the lawful commands of their superior officers.' He never got to put this policy into action. America entered the war in 1917 and eventually American troops began to flood into Europe – at one point their Commander in Chief, General Pershing, had written to the Allied commanders: 'Everything that we have is at your disposal – we are here to be killed.' There was no need for an attempt to conscript the Irish.

At the time of writing, ninety years later, it is impossible to say with absolute certainty who sent the thirty-five so close to their death. But it was not by accident that they were ordered to Boulogne, given orders that they were never going to obey and then court-martialled and sentenced to death. Macready and particularly Childs were the two men directly responsible for them; they did not take kindly to the COs nor to their ever-vocal supporters; their attitudes were mirrored by their superiors who were constantly pushing for more men; and at least at one stage Childs saw the death penalty as the best way of enforcing conscription. The conclusion must be that, if Asquith had not intervened and Macready and Childs had been left to their own devices, then some at least of the conscientious objectors shipped to France would almost certainly have been executed.

16

Sacrifice

A month after the thirty-five returned to England, a member of the Non Combatant Corps, who was also a young preacher 'enthusiastic to win souls for the master', wrote to a young lady he had met on a train to try to convince her of the rightness of his cause. She wrote back politely, thanking him for his letter but adding that if 'Heaven was inhabited by conscientious objectors she had no wish to go there'.

The thirty-five soon learned that while they were safe they certainly were not popular. At Southampton, when the biggest group arrived from France, onlookers at the docks suggested to their escort that instead of looking after the conchies they should stick their bayonets through them. When they reached Winchester it got worse because somehow the word had got out that there were conchies on the train. Bert remembers: 'The station was crowded with hundreds of people who were seeing off a train-load of soldiers bound for the land we had just left; on one line the warriors, on the other the conchies returning victorious from their struggle. The air was electric; emotions at fever heat. People gathered around us to hiss and hurl insults.' Bert found comfort singing hymns to himself as the crowd bayed for blood until eventually the conchies were escorted along a back route to the prison. There they were grateful to put on broad-striped prison clothes and discard their khaki – while it was decided what should be done with them next.

Almost immediately after they had been sentenced in Boulogne, Murfin remembers that the soldiers who were in prison for various

SACRIFICE

misdemeanours taught them the prison Morse Code – two taps for a dot and one for a dash – it was 'an interest and besides it was fun'. And now it was essential, for in Winchester a strict rule of silence was enforced. Visits too were strictly limited but at least, Bert thought, he had two visits he could look forward to. Unfortunately both were to prove disappointing. His first was from the prison's Church of England chaplain who made a point of visiting every newly arrived prisoner. The visit proved a disaster. Instead of understanding, the vicar came bearing pure malevolence; a man, in Bert's words, 'of very sour countenance'. He told one CO, 'Christ would have spat in your face' and as for Bert he was 'a disgrace to humanity'. When Harry Stanton told him he thought it was unChristian to fight he replied that such thoughts were 'piffle'. Howard Marten remembers him as 'undecided as to whether I ought to have been shot or whether that was too good for me and that it was fitter I should linger in a prison'. Harry Willson, a Socialist, told him he should have been a prize fighter not a parson and got three days' bread and water for his insolence.

Bert obviously hoped for much more from the one visit he was allowed from his family, but even this was not a happy meeting. The prison authorities were soon to discover that the absolutists had left none of their principles in France. When Bert learned from his fellow conchie in the next-door cell – by Morse Code – that the sacks they were sewing were going to carry coal for the navy, they both refused to sew any more. Mailbags were one thing, coal bags another. The chief warder naturally took a dim view of this: 'It's a pity they didn't put you below the ground out yonder' he told Bert before sentencing him to three days' bread and water in a solitary confinement cell in the basement.

When he returned to his cell on the top landing after his three days the sacks were waiting for him to sew; inevitably he refused to do so and just as inevitably he was sent back to the punishment cell. It was at this point that his father, mother and fiancée Annie Wainwright turned up for the one visit each prisoner was allowed at the start of their sentence. Annie's support for Bert remained just as absolute as Bert's opposition to the war despite the fact that her brother Gilbert was now fighting in France with the Royal Artillery. Phil bumped into him at the front in September, face all black as he overhauled a field gun. Phil wrote home: 'He seems to be growing, he gave me the impression of being as tall as I am.'

They arrived in Winchester only to be told that they could not see Bert because he was on a punishment regime. But Bert's father, having travelled 200 miles or so from Conisbrough, was not going to let it go at that. Being a Justice of the Peace himself he found the nearest magistrate and persuaded him to write out a document ordering that the visit must go ahead. So they duly met in the visitors' room for a visit that was anything but intimate. On one side of the room was Bert who faced a corridor of two wire screens, in the middle of which sat a warder. On the other side sat his family. So the conversation was carried on past two screens and one warder. Bert writes:

Father began to question the wisdom of refusing to make coal sacks. He said it was a good thing we had a navy. I said that the navy was one of the factors that helped to start the war.

I remember Father asking me what work I was prepared to do, if any. I said I would sew mailbags. He asked if that was not also war work as they would be used to carry letters for the soldiers. I said I saw no harm in soldiers having letters from home.

It must have been heartbreaking for both father and son – Bert admits only that it was 'sad'. Here was a father who had supported his son throughout his ordeal now effectively saying 'Come on be reasonable', and here was the son, the biggest career success of the family, the London-educated teacher, who had come back from the brink of death and was now sitting in prison arguing over what kind of bags he was prepared to sew.

'We quickly realised that we had only twenty minutes and that it would be a waste of our precious time to argue about pacifism. Mother told me later that as they left the prison she and Annie wanted a quiet place to weep together.' In future they decided it would be better to swap a letter for a monthly visit, upping the number of letters allowed in and out to two a month. Bert was proud of his tight family bonds and the argument over the coal sacks was the nearest they ever came to breaking.

Bert's experience was not unusual. Harry Stanton had a visit from his mother in the same visiting room, but this time the warder sitting in the corridor could not contain himself. He 'broke into our conversation to express his views "as a Christian man" on the righteousness of the war; my mother firmly reminded him that she had come a long way to pay this visit and that he had no right to take up so much of the time which was all too short . . . I determined never to repeat such an unsatisfactory experience.'

If Bert was suffering in Winchester, brother Phil was enduring much in France. He was having ever-increasing doubts about the war and letters to his family were the only way he could express them. After a short relief he had been moved up with his now desperately under-strength battalion to hold the front line at Neuve Chapelle. From there he wrote to his aunt:

> We have been in the trenches now eleven days and have had a gruelling time. I have had quite a number of providential escapes and some nerve-shattering experiences that are absolutely too horrible for words.
>
> I feel that my eyes have been opened to the reality of war; GOD isn't in this war, it is of the DEVIL, devilism.
>
> I am delighted to know that Harold is safely wounded and in England and I pray that he may never get out to France again. I am also jolly glad Bert is in England again. I shouldn't worry too much about him; he will doubtless be pleased to suffer for his opinions and I am hoping that when the war is over these sentences will be remitted.

For now there was no question of Bert's sentence being remitted, but what had happened to him and the other thirty-four COs taken to France had shown both the government and indeed the army that the system simply was not working. It could not have an endless flow of conscientious objectors being sent by tribunals to join the Non Combatant Corps, who then refused to have anything to do with the military and ended up first being court-martialled for disobedience and then imprisoned.

So the Central Tribunal, the ultimate appeal court, which had spent most of its existence turning down the appeals that had reached it from COs' tribunals, was now asked to look at their cases in a new light. If satisfied that their claims were genuine – and in the great majority of cases it decided they were – then from July 1916 onwards they were to be offered work of 'national importance' under the leadership of a new committee (named after its chairman, William Brace) set up by the Home Office. However, they would still be listed as members of the army reserve.

It was a scheme which even its critics admit was 'launched with the usual flavour of good intention' but it suffered from the politicians' and the public's demand – expressed vociferously in the press – that there should be equality of sacrifice: the COs should suffer as much as the men at the front.

But how could this ever happen? Phil wrote home to his aunt at the time Bert's case was being reassessed:

I have been very grieved this last week, a fellow named Wise joined us about a fortnight ago and relieved me of my duties so that I could go on a course. When I rejoined the Battalion I heard that he had been killed by a rifle grenade. He had only been a fortnight in France. I pray God that the war will soon be over. It grates on my nerves horribly the thought of killing and the cold blooded way in which slaying the Boches is talked of. They might be vermin so horribly callous is it all.

There was no scheme that could equal this horror; instead what became known as the Home Office Scheme offered more in the way of punishment than work that could in any way be considered of national importance – this was to be no soft option. Nevertheless to someone like Gilbert Murray who had campaigned all along for the rights of COs it was enough; he urged them to take part in the Scheme: 'They have made their protest. They have vindicated their courage. They have established the rights of conscience.' In response the editor of the No Conscription Fellowship's *Tribunal* wrote: 'If our action was merely a refusal to help our fellows because we were asked to do so by a Government with which we disagree, it would be hard to defend. But it is nothing of the sort; it is an active protest against what we consider the greatest evil in the world, and our method of protesting is to refuse to acquiesce by a single act or deed in a system which is indescribably evil, both in origin and purpose.'

When it was the turn of the men from France to come before the Central Tribunal, only three refused to have anything to do with the Home Office Scheme. When the tribunal members asked Bert if he would do work of national importance he told them he 'wanted to help the community but not the war' – in other words, he would give it a try. The COs were sent to Dyce, a desolate quarry near Aberdeen where they were to sleep in tents during the night and break stones during the day.

Dyce, established at a time when neither the country nor the politicians knew quite what to do with conscientious objectors, turned out to be a complete failure. It lasted only three months before being closed down. Ramsay MacDonald, later Prime Minister but in 1916 an MP, walked 3 miles from the nearest railway station to visit the men working in the quarry. He told an Aberdeen newspaper the place was 'no better than a pigsty'. He told the House of Commons it was a 'melancholy spectacle. There were very few men there earning even the small pay they were getting. They were just getting in each other's way and they were to put it mildly, very round pegs in very square holes.' He then went on to suggest the sort of work they *should* be doing: 'It must have some relation to the training and capacity of the men who are doing the service and it must have some relation to national needs.'

But the subject was too emotive for this sort of sensible suggestion. Eventually Labour MP Charles Stanton decided he had had enough after listening to all the complaints of the men of Dyce: 'What about our sons and brothers and others who are at the front?' he asked. 'Do they cry out about a little mud in their camps? What about the boys whom I saw out at the front, my own son among them, up to their eyebrows in mud – boys who are risking everything?' (MPs' sons and on occasions MPs themselves fought in the war; the Prime Minister's eldest son Raymond was killed in a second 'push' on the Somme in September 1916 and the elder son of Walter Long, the minister responsible for dealing with conscientious objectors, was killed four months later.)

Although many of the men at Dyce complained, Bert was his usual positive self: organising concerts, listening to debates and taking part in the 'highlight of the week' – a 6-mile tramp to Aberdeen for worship at the Friends Meeting House there. Harry Stanton was less sure: it was not the mud that worried him as much as his fellow COs. He was soon writing to Catherine Marshall:

> I have had an uncomfortable feeling that the camp is not all that can be desired. There are a number of Revolutionary Socialists and Anarchists here and I believe, though of this I am not sure, they have considerable influence on the committee [a management committee elected by the COs]. Also one concrete fact, there is a certain amount of bad language to be heard. One has grave doubts as to whether we should not have to recommence the struggle and give a definite lead in a different direction.

It was not bad language which ended Dyce but the rain that arrived in the autumn. On the bleak hillside where the 250 men were camped the old army tents they had been given were completely inadequate. Even

Bert said the rain transformed the camp into a quagmire and the 'all-pervading dampness of ground, tents, clothes and bedding could make life a burden'. In the hospital tent he saw Walter Roberts, aged twenty, who had been one of the first, if not the first conscientious objector to appear before a tribunal, fighting a losing battle against pneumonia. He was dead within five days. In the NCF's newspaper Fenner Brockway proclaimed: 'To all of us, his life and death must be an inspiration,' but although his death hastened the closure of Dyce it achieved little else.

It was clear that even the tents signified the authorities' determination to make them suffer for their opinions. It was only after Roberts had died that they were allowed to move out of their tents and into various barns where, Bert says, there were 'dry floors under us, and good roofs over us and we felt we were living in absolute luxury'. But the luxury did not last long. In prison the argument had been over what the bags they were sewing were to be used for; now it was not bags but stones they argued over. They had been assured that the stones they were quarrying were for civil roads, but these were not men to take anyone at their word. One Saturday two of them went to the trouble of tracking a trainload of stones on their bicycles and discovered they were now being used to build a road up to a new military aerodrome. Bert took this news to one of the many camp meetings, arguing that they should stop work, but – surprisingly – only one man supported him. For Bert, troubled in any case by the whole idea of alternative service, what he had heard was quite enough; he simply left the camp and returned home. The local Conisbrough newspaper, reporting every coming and going within the town, headlined its paragraph on his arrival 'Unexpected Visitor' and said he had been granted 'leave of absence' for his 'reported good conduct'. His 'leave' ended after six days of freedom when he was arrested by 'the most gentlemanly police officer I have ever met' and escorted to Armley jail in Leeds.

Three weeks later the camp closed down. Its closure was marked by a debate about the farewell concert put on by the men which only emphasised – to a laughable degree – just how determinedly individual each one of these conscientious objectors really was. Two or three of the COs said they wanted to bring beer to the concert; there was a vote and they were opposed by a huge majority, many of them holding strict religious beliefs. Whereupon the 'libertarians', led by Herbert Runacres, who had been studying for Holy Orders before conscription was introduced, said they wanted no beer for themselves but they must support the right of the minority who wished for it. Although Runacres was a strict teetotaller he announced he was going to drink a glass of beer himself on the night as 'a protest against bigotry'. Thus the camp closed as it had opened – with argument and anger and no one quite sure what its purpose was supposed to be.

'I had naively assumed that this Home Office Scheme was designed to meet the scruples of men such as me,' says Bert. 'But now I was sure that the aim was to wangle us somehow into the war machine, and therefore the only satisfactory attitude was the absolutist stand. If the authorities had offered me say agricultural or hospital work I should have felt it my duty to do such service; but there never was such an offer. There was no alternative but to go back to prison.'

But others *were* offered an alternative. The artists and writers of the Bloomsbury group, for example, would do everything possible to avoid a war which they considered both immoral and irrational. But that was as far as they went; not for them 'crucifixion' nor court martial, nor arguments over mail sacks or coal bags or whether stones were for ordinary roads or military roads.

The writer Lytton Strachey set the style; when the war started he had decided the best he could do was to knit mufflers for the soldiers and learn German just in case. When he faced the inevitable tribunal in Hampstead to plead his case for conscientious objection he wrote to his brother: 'I am quite ready if necessary to tell any number of lies.' But lies were hardly necessary; if the tribunal was not put off by what one writer calls the 'bearded stick insect' who appeared before them, then the sight of one of Lytton's sisters carrying a light-blue air cushion for him to sit on because he was suffering from piles must surely have convinced them that he was not going to make a soldier. Nevertheless the military representative was foolish enough to ask him: 'What would you do, Mr Strachey, if you saw an Uhlan attempting to rape your sister?' To which Strachey replied: 'I would try to interpose my own body.' The tribunal granted him exemption only from combatant service but unsurprisingly the medical examiner declared he was unfit for any form of service.

For the artist Duncan Grant and his lover David 'Bunny' Garnett life was rather more complicated. They decided they would have more chance of winning a case before a tribunal if they moved from London to Suffolk. There Grant's father, Major Bartle Grant, who always referred to Garnett not as Bunny but as 'Garbage', reluctantly helped set them up as fruit farmers. The hope was that this would help them in their plea for alternative service. Although they knew next to nothing about fruit and farming, they did however set out for the countryside armed with three volumes of bound-up leaflets from the Board of Agriculture. The natives did not take to them, partly perhaps because of their views and partly because they thought they were being made fun of (particularly after the pair dyed the tails of six pedigree Leghorn chickens blue so they could recognise them amongst the other birds).

At the same time as Bert was in his cell in Richmond Castle, Grant and Garnett's case was being heard in Suffolk. They could summon considerably more help to their cause than Bert could. Grant was the lover of Vanessa Bell (sister of Virginia Woolf) and thus they had her brother Adrian Stephen arguing their case as well as the economist Maynard Keynes, another of Grant's lovers. Keynes could impress the appeal hearing by asking that the case be heard as swiftly as possible since he had to get back to his work at the Treasury. They were turned down on appeal but rather than being dispatched to the army's Non Combatant Corps, their case went to the Central Tribunal. There they argued, 'based on the sales of our blackcurrants, which had been unexpectedly profitable and had made up our losses on ducks and fowls', that their work was of national importance and it would best be continued in Suffolk. The tribunal agreed that they should be allowed to take advantage of another scheme that was offered to COs but not widely known about at this stage. This was the Pelham Committee – set up to advise tribunals, which often ignored its advice, about the sort of work that could be considered of national importance. In total about 4,000 COs eventually took work under this scheme, including 1,400 members of the Christadelphian religious sect.

It was agreed that Grant and Garnett should be allowed to continue farming work, albeit not as their own bosses on the Suffolk fruit farm, and they were given two weeks to find appropriate work. (Explaining all this to a friend serving with the Royal Army Medical Corps in France Garnett was surprised to receive a letter back which ended: 'Have Rupert [Brooke] and Nurse Cavell died in vain? I spew you out of my mouth.')

Vanessa Bell was dispatched to Sussex to find a new base for them. There she found Charleston, a pretty farmhouse with a small lake in front of it, as well as jobs with a local farmer. There was an attempt to make Grant's life even easier by making him the Charleston 'gardener' and asking that this should be considered his 'work of national importance', but it was considered a step too far. Garnett in his auto-biography talks of their 'sufferings' over the winter . . . but with Grant's farm work eventually being reduced to mornings only because of a severe attack of rheumatism and Vanessa's husband, Clive Bell, appearing at intervals bearing 'Manilla cheroots and bottles of wine' life must have been more than bearable. Indeed, the extraordinary way in which Grant and Vanessa Bell transformed the house in between the farm work is still beautifully preserved at Charleston today.

As for Vanessa's husband, Clive, he too was doing work of national importance although he chose not to do it with his wife but at Garsington, the country house of MP Philip Morrell and his wife Lady Ottoline Morrell, who, as noted earlier, in their different ways had both played a key part in persuading Asquith that the conscientious objectors transported to France should not be shot. Here Bell and other conscientious objectors were housed in the bailiff's house opposite the manor, and Bell did a little light hoeing with the village women. Their actions saved them from the army but the Morrells got little or no thanks for it; Ottoline Morrell's biographer, Miranda Seymour, writes: 'From the COs' point of view it was an unsatisfactory way of life. They were not cut out to be paid labourers. Most of them, regardless of their inexperience, felt that they were being exploited as cheap labour under the guise of idealism.'

From time to time the inevitable whiff of class blows unmistakably through the story of these first conscientious objectors. At Duncan Grant's tribunal there was a wonderful moment where the military representative tried to trap him into agreeing to do some war work by asking: 'You would not push your objection to war-work so far as to refuse to make a pair of boots, I suppose?'

'Under no circumstances whatever would I consent to make a pair of *boots*,' replied Grant, furious at the suggestion he might be taken as a mere tradesman. No, Grant was no tradesman, and the fact that Virginia Woolf had put in a plea to the chairman of the Central Tribunal via Lady Robert Cecil, and that MP Philip Morrell had been there to give evidence for them must have been a help to Grant and Garnett's case.

Thus while Bert Brocklesby and the others from France were breaking stones at Dyce, for about three shillings and sixpence a week, Duncan Grant and Bunny Garnett were farming at twelve shillings and sixpence a week and enjoying the Sussex countryside.

At the beginning of December Bert was transferred to Wandsworth prison, from where about thirty prisoners, chained in groups, were sent off in buses to Victoria Station on their way to Maidstone prison. The bus took him through the Pimlico streets where a few years earlier, studying at the Westminster Training College, he had been accepted as an honoured preacher. 'I wondered what those people would think if they could see me as a chained criminal.'

17

The Forgotten Men

As the war that was supposed to be over by Christmas 1914 dragged on into 1917 there still seemed no end to it. With both sides still believing that they would be victorious – whatever the price – two attempts at the beginning and end of 1916 by the American President Woodrow Wilson to negotiate peace had ended in complete failure. Yet, despite this rejection, war weariness had begun to spread. In June 1916, when Lloyd George replaced Kitchener as Secretary of State for War, Margot Asquith wrote in her diary: 'We are out: it can only be a question of time now when we shall have to leave Downing Street.' Within six months she was proved right. Asquith had been forced out of office by a combination of Lloyd George's ambition and a feeling in the country – fuelled daily by the Northcliffe Press – that for the war to be won the country needed a new leader.

In April a disastrous attack by the French at Chemin des Dames came to a swift end with around 130,000 casualties, the dismissal of the commander in chief, and a series of mutinies so widespread that it was left to the British to continue the war along the Western Front for much of the rest of the year. British successes at Arras in March, where the Canadians captured Vimy Ridge, and Messines in June were followed by the nightmare of Passchendaele where British casualties numbered about 300,000 men. In March acute shortages of fuel and food in Russia brought the overthrow of the Tsar and saw Russian soldiers, in Lenin's phrase, 'voting for peace with their feet'.

Throughout 1916 and 1917 Phil remained at the front. The usual pattern was a few days in reserve, then back up into the trenches again, out on raiding parties. In November he wrote home about a raiding party that brought home four prisoners, 'two wounded and two unwounded. The two unwounded were nothing more than lads, looked to be about sixteen or seventeen. One had only left Berlin three weeks before. The poor kid looked quite pleased that he had been taken. It grieved me very much to think that we were there to slay youngsters like him.'

In December 1916 he went on a six-day course to learn about the Lewis gun and from there he wrote to his mother: 'This is the first Christmas I have spent away from home. We are having a slack day on the course and so I am playing footer this afternoon. I have often thought how wonderfully good Providence has been to me.'

The following February he was writing home to his mother for some more anti-lice cream because 'I have got some more visitors. I get shocks every time I see one. I subjected one to pressure between the table and the knife the other night and its drops of blood spurted and hit me in the eye. Ugh! You don't know what the horrors of war are. It makes me want to burn my clothes.'

In early May Phil led his company up to the front yet again; there was the smell of death in the air as they passed dead mules still in their wagon tracks and dead men lying where they fell – 'I was impressed when passing round one shell hole to see two bodies, one had stiffened on his knees as if he had sobbed out his life praying to his maker.' In the midst of all this his commanding officer, Colonel Wilford, rode up and started chatting: 'They tell me Brocklesby you don't want to kill a Boche.'

'Oh I shall be there when the occasion arises,' replied Phil carefully as he kept on towards the front. The colonel did not press the point further. Phil was sure that a new captain who had joined the battalion from Conisbrough eight months earlier had brought news of Bert's stand and that it now reflected on him. Yet in one way the colonel was right. Phil was marching to what easily could be his death; he would do his duty, he would look after his men, he would kill if he had to but if he could avoid killing anyone he would. (Only once did he admit he might have killed a German, when pulling the firing handle of a gun aimed at the Germans in the village of Bucquoy, but since Bucquoy was some 3 miles away he never found out.)

Just a couple of weeks after this exchange with his colonel he wrote to his mother: 'I sometimes envy Bert, his is purgatory but this is hell. I am gradually losing faith in mankind and if this goes on much longer, when it is over I shall go and isolate myself from the rest of the world. I have long thought that most of the people I rub shoulders with consider me mad and I am beginning to agree with them.'

His next letter was to his aunt: 'I have just been through the roughest month I have had out here and I have had the three narrowest escapes of my life.' He followed this with a letter to Harold which gave a glimpse of the effect all this was having:

I feel that I shall come through safely, but the horror of it all has settled on my nerves. The last time I was in the trenches I buried a Sergeant of the South Staffs who had been killed four weeks before. The poor fellow was black through decomposition although he was in good condition compared with some other poor fellows. When I see sights like that I think of the people at home who under comfortable conditions talk glibly of the glory of dying on the field of battle.

It was at this point that his father must have become seriously concerned by his letters and suggested he go to see the doctor. But Phil would have none of it: 'I am eating well and sleeping and I wouldn't have the face to go and see the doctor except to ask him how he is. I am not suffering from SHELL SHOCK. My particular complaint is a sort of combined spiritual and physical nausea of all that warfare means and is.'

His letters reflect the haphazard nature of life on the Western Front. One moment there is tea with Valerie, a 'charming little French maiden of seventeen' who would not come to the cinema with him without her parents or brothers as chaperone; the next he was buried up to his neck in earth when a German shell landed far too close to him in a front-line trench. It was not until December 1917 that Phil was allowed home for the first time on ten days' leave and even then he could not stay for Christmas. On his way back to France he made a surprise visit to Maidstone prison. Bert remembers it vividly: 'One day, all unexpectedly, I was called from work to receive a visit. Since that sad affair in Winchester I had never asked to be visited. Behold! My two officer brothers.' Although Harold was still recovering Phil had brought him along too as extra support. Phil had no visiting order, relying instead on the power of his uniform to get him inside the jail.

'The Governor allowed the visit,' wrote Bert. 'Perhaps he thought that my two brothers might persuade me to give up my resistance, but I am sure they never entertained any such idea.' Their meeting – they were allowed thirty minutes – was 'full of joy, one might even say mirth. One item sticks in my memory. Phil told me: "The Governor asked me if I would like to take you with me to France. I asked him if he would like to go too."'

Bert's life was never again in danger. He never suffered from the mud, the shelling, the lice or the high-ranking army officers in the way that Phil had to, but it was nevertheless an unhappy life in Maidstone prison, made particularly unbearable by the rule of silence. His existence was alleviated by a visiting Methodist minister who was a different sort of man from Winchester's prison chaplain; and by the fact that a number of Bert's friends from France joined him in prison rather than continuing with the Home Office Scheme. When Harry Stanton arrived one of the first people he saw was the irrepressible Bert who was not allowed to say a word of greeting but 'began to execute a silent war dance to express his delight at seeing us'.

The Reverend Robert Wardell was Bert's first and, for a long time, only visitor and Bert says that for him 'I shall ever feel deep gratitude.'

'Well, young man, what are you here for?' he asked Bert when he entered his cell.

'I am here because my conscience will not allow me to take part in war.'

'It is very difficult to understand how conscience drives men in exactly opposite directions,' said Wardell. 'Both my boys joined the army as a matter of conscience and one has paid with his life.'

Bert writes: 'Poor bereaved Mr Wardell. Before he left Maidstone he had to tell me that his remaining son had followed his brother. Yet never did he by word, look or gesture, express any condemnation of my attitude.'

Wardell's obituary talks of a preacher who had an ardent desire to help men, who demonstrated utter simplicity, practical knowledge of life's difficulties, wise judgement and sympathy, and who 'won the affection of all who knew him'. He must have been a remarkable man, able as he was to live with his sons' deaths and conscientious objectors at one and the same time.

It was not the food, nor the corrugated iron cells, nor the cold that really got to the men but the rule of silence. After eight months of silence one CO wrote: 'The cruelty of absolute silence tells on me a great deal. To deprive the human mind of expression both in speech and writing is like stowing precious stuffs away in the damp – there is danger of mould and decay.' There was no meeting together apart from when they were working in the tailor's shop, the printers (where they worked under the expert tutelage of a man doing eight years for forging £100,000-worth of notes) or the laundry. After three months of good conduct they were allowed 'talking exercise' every Sunday afternoon and only after five whole years was this privilege extended to every day. Until then even their daily exercise, filing around the parade ground every morning, had to be conducted in silence. Any breaking of the rules meant solitary confinement on bread and water. (Bert was once caught with an illegally produced 'news bulletin' – it was just one sheet of paper rolled up into a ball and stuffed in the waistband of his trousers. He got three days' solitary and was demoted from the printing shop to the laundry.) For the first two years in jail a prisoner could write a letter and receive a visit once in four months. After that things began to improve marginally.

It was not as though the 'Frenchmen' were treated any differently from other prisoners. Unusually, the group had been put in the 'Third Division', a very tough regime. Prison rules could be set at any of three standards – with third being the hardest and first being the softest – and usually a man jailed for 'offences of opinion or conviction' was held in the relative luxury of the 'First Division'. In 1918, when Bertrand Russell was sent to prison for six months under the Defence of the Realm Act, he was put in the 'First Division' where life was rather different. He paid two shillings and sixpence a week for a bigger cell, and sixpence a day for a fellow prisoner to clean it. He was allowed one visit a week from three visitors; most of his food was sent in and he had unlimited access to writing materials, books and newspapers. Thus he could send out messages to his lover, Lady Constance Malleson, and receive messages from her hidden in the personal column of *The Times*. Any written work he sent out, however, had to be censored first and the book he wrote in his cell, *An Introduction to Mathematical Philosophy*, was sent to the prison chaplain to censor.

Under pressure from outside, the prison authorities eventually allowed those in the 'Third Division' three 'educational' books in addition to the prison library, and as a birthday present for Bert, Annie sent in three oratarios – the *Messiah*, *Creation* and *Elijah* – bound into one volume. It didn't work, the warder still counted them as three, but anyone peeking into Bert's cell would see the bed boards balanced between his table and his rolled-up mattress to make a 'dumb piano'. Bert played away with the score in front of him so regularly that when he returned to the outside world he found he could still play without any sense of being out of practice.

The only thing that made an unbearable system workable was the widespread use of Morse Code. With the help of the right heating pipe chess could be played with a prisoner several cells away, although two of the 'Frenchmen' were caught and punished for transmitting Gray's

'Elegy' in Morse. Even more important was the fact that among the warders the 'slackers' wanted an easy life and the 'blackguards' would look the other way if the bribe was right. Prison was not quite as silent as it was supposed to be.

Nevertheless it was still a harsh regime and there was now, in the form of the Home Office Scheme, some sort of alternative, which came with much greater freedoms. Harold Blake, once a chemist but now confined in Wandsworth prison, found it very tempting: 'Why should I remain in the cheerless prison when by merely signing an unimportant paper I could end my lonely isolation in comfortless confinement? . . . No one save he who has been confined for months in the prison cell, can have the faintest realisation of the fierceness of such a temptation to lower the standard.' In his diary he put the absolutist position very clearly: 'To accept ANY condition of exemption from military service is to me equivalent to entering into a bargain with the government that, provided I am not required to do the killing, they can carry on with the war and kill as long and as hard as they like.' (Although tempted on occasion, Blake stayed in prison until the end of the war.)

For some, torn between prison or the limited freedom offered by the Home Office Scheme, the pressure proved too much. Alfred Martlew, a Quaker and, before the war, a clerk in Rowntree's Chocolate factory, had been one of Bert's fellow prisoners at Richmond Castle and had duly been sentenced to death with him in France. In July 1917 his body was found in the River Ouse. Under the headline 'Sentenced to Death', the *Yorkshire Gazette* reported that Martlew, like the other thirty-four, had been at Winchester prison and had subsequently agreed to go under the Home Office Scheme to Dyce. A friend who saw him shortly before his death said that he was 'very depressed' because on three occasions the Home Office had broken their pledge to him regarding the work he was to undertake. He had been 'missing' for some weeks but he had decided he would come home to York to give himself up and serve the rest of his sentence in prison.

His fiancée saw him on the moor about a week before his body was found. He told her too that he was going to give himself up. 'He gave me his money, his watch and several other articles, but he did not give me any papers.' Shortly after this final meeting he killed himself.

With Dyce closed, the government's next step as part of the Home Office Scheme was to turn several prisons into something more akin to primitive boarding schools. The war had cut the prison population in half (although bigamy was one of the few crimes that statistically increased) and disused prisons at Wakefield and Warwick were reopened and christened Work Centres. When, a little later, Dartmoor Prison became the Princetown Work Centre as CO numbers increased, the ninety convicts remaining there were transferred to other prisons. The locks came off the doors to the cells which now became 'rooms'; the warders became 'instructors' and the governor became the 'agent'. At Wakefield the prison doctor was promoted to agent and insisted on walking around the centre, accompanied by his small brown dog, carrying an old-fashioned stethoscope under his arm. The COs could elect a committee to help run the Work Centres. There were some among the Prison Commission who believed that this would be the way forward for prison management once the war was ended. If so they would have been gravely disappointed.

It was not prison, but it was not freedom either, for it takes more than removing the locks from a cell to turn a prison into something else. Stanton remembers in the early days at Wakefield, 'A prison atmosphere hung about the place . . . men conversed in low tones as if exercising a privilege which might be forfeited if too frequently used.'

At Wakefield COs had to work from 8 a.m. until 5 p.m. for little money. They were allowed out on weekdays until 9.30 p.m., and for most of the weekend. They had their own keys which they had to hang up on hooks if they were out. Percy Leonard, who used to work in the family tailor's shop before he ended up in Wakefield, says: 'The warders didn't have anything to do with the cells. Men would go home for days. Sometimes people would be substituted for them, sometimes people who the army was actually looking for.' He used to go out most evenings to a Quaker family in Wakefield although one evening towards the end of the war 'there was a riot outside their house. They threatened to burn the place down. There were a number of conscientious objectors there and they packed us down to the cellar.'

As for work, 'the basic job was mailbags. It was ridiculous to call it work of national importance. In fact it was work of no importance at all.' Warwick Work Centre was run by a Quaker who tried to make the Home Office Scheme a real alternative. But a mix of useless work, a minority of COs who were hell-bent on finding trouble wherever they could – they threatened a strike on occasion, much to the consternation of the NCF which realised this was unlikely to go down well with public opinion – and the continued public desire to see 'equality of sacrifice' meant that neither he nor the other agents had much chance of success. The Warwick agent eventually resigned after being pressured to make the regime tougher.

If a CO broke enough rules he was returned to 'real' prison. Jack Foister was bowling a fast overarm across the Wakefield courtyard using one of the prison's home-grown turnips when the agent unfortunately came by. He claimed that Foister was not just misusing a turnip, he was behaving in 'a contumacious manner likely to bring scorn upon the institution'. This together with another two previous rule-breaking incidents was enough to send him off to Maidstone prison to join many of the other 'Frenchmen'.

There he soon met Stanton again who, along with seven others, had decided that without any work of real national importance at Wakefield Work Centre they could no longer justify the relative freedom they had there. They remained studiously polite throughout. They wrote telling the authorities that they would not work any more, that they had made a mistake in joining the Scheme and they would be 'available for arrest when required' and then went off for a trek across the Yorkshire Moors. When they came back they were duly arrested.

Other smaller schemes did not fare any better and the Princetown

Work Centre at Dartmoor antagonised outsiders more than any other. While the locals thought the COs should be grateful to be so far away from the battle, the COs saw it very differently. The conditions were poor and the work was meaningless. In addition, as the CO who became secretary of the camp recalled later, there were men there who were 'destructive for the sake of being destructive. They didn't want the scheme to work and they weren't prepared to work it.'

The result was seething resentment on both sides. Joseph Hoare, an unusual CO in that he had been in the school corps at Repton before going up to Oxford, accepted alternative service and was sent to Dartmoor. 'I remember two or three of the COs from Princetown going up to the church for communion and getting stoned away. Sounds incredible doesn't it. The parson was standing on a tombstone. I won't say he was cheering them on but he was encouraging them. It makes the point that animosity comes from people who don't know you.' After a visit to the Work Centre, the Bishop of Exeter, who had lost three sons in the war, came away furious. He saw revolution brewing on the wild moors of Devon and wrote to *The Times* to complain that 'sacks of letters come and go carrying instructions for those plans of bloodshed which may at some time in the future bring . . . ruin to England'. He suggested that the 'religious conchy' should be released, but the political objector should be allocated to that portion of England 'which is frequently visited by enemy aeroplanes . . . the whirr of the midnight raider might help them to a truer view of the political situation'.

If there were not strikes there certainly was 'slacking'. The *Daily Mail* called the culprits the 'Dartmoor Do Nothings' and 'The Coddled Conchys' and captioned one photograph: 'Warmly clad and with cash in their pockets the conchys sally forth to spend their money in the Princetown shops.' At a public meeting in Plymouth the Mayor rebuked his fellow citizens for their intolerance but it did no good, the meeting still voted unanimously in favour of keeping the 'bastard political agitators' within the boundaries of the prison grounds.

There were some who tried to get something out of it all. Eric Dott wrote home: 'Lately there have been a great number of classes started: English, French, Shorthand, Logic and many others.' A newspaper was started, the Dartmoor *News Sheet*, although it could hardly compete with the paper produced at Dorchester jail – *Instigilo* – which was written entirely in Esperanto. At lunchtime on the moor, according to Dott, they would break off from their shovelling and 'have meetings with learned discussions on philosophy and socialism and religion and all that kind of thing'. Donald Grant joined a political discussion group: 'Once a week we would meet in the cells of Banks the anarchist, and there would be coffee in a mug and a candle in a bottle.'

At Wakefield one prisoner kept an autograph book – slightly smaller than the ones that little boys used to wave at cricketers – which should have won a prize for intellectual quotations. Here is Ibsen: 'The most dangerous enemies of truth and freedom in our midst are the compact majority'; here is Disraeli: 'We put too much faith in systems and too little in men' and here too is Nietzsche: 'Whatever the state saith is a lie, whatever it has is theft; all is counterfeit, the gnawing, sanguinary insatiate monster.' Kant, Liebnecht, Spinoza, Byron, Thomas Carlyle, Robert Burns . . . they are all there, quoted by fellow COs as they sign their name. Others left their own aphorisms: 'Every professing Christian who is not a pacifist is a hypocrite.' Duncan McInnes from Glasgow tried poetry:

> Hark! The battle cry in ringing
> The patriots are loudly singing
> Join the army did they yell
> But all I answered was go to hell.

In Dartmoor the programme of lectures and debates for the autumn of 1917 included 'Life History of some common trees', 'Fairy tales and their origins', 'The dangers of pacifism' – which would have been an interesting debate – and 'The message of Robert Burns'.

But for Joseph Hoare the 'absolutely farcical nature of the scheme', the 'tendency [of some COs] to make things uncomfortable for the government which really wasn't at all my particular line', and the death of a fellow CO forced to work in the quarry when he should have been in hospital all made him decide he had had enough. As he sauntered out of Dartmoor to the railway station, the chief instructor (previously the head warder) saw him and shouted 'You can't do that', to which Hoare replied 'Well, I am.' He continued on his way, even though he knew he would end up in prison, where the regime would be tougher – but his conscience would be much clearer.

If the public and the COs had doubts about the Scheme so too did the No Conscription Fellowship. In short they would have liked to have seen many more absolutists challenging the system directly, but instead, as the months went by, the majority were choosing to work within the system. Howard Marten, another 'Frenchman' prepared to work the Home Office Scheme, says this made him and others like him so unpopular that some at the NCF, led by Catherine Marshall, 'thought it would have been very much better if we had been shot'.

In contrast Corder Catchpool was one of the men who, like Bert, would make no compromise. Catchpool, as we have seen, resigned from the Friends Ambulance Unit in May 1916 when conscription was introduced. A tribunal dismissed his plea for absolute exemption and in January 1917 he was court-martialled for refusing to wear khaki and sentenced to 112 days in Wormwood Scrubs. He was now ensnared in the debilitating system known as 'cat and mouse'. The way the system had evolved was this: arrive at army camp, disobey an order however trivial; face a court martial for disobeying that order; receive a sentence, usually 112 days, sometimes a year, occasionally two (but never the ten years that the men in France received); serve your sentence; return from prison to the relative comfort of the guardroom cells; disobey another order; have another court martial and receive another sentence.

During the guardroom spell COs could receive visits and send out letters. This was a considerable relief – and thus provided temptation to fall into line before starting all over again.

Philip Radley, Corder Catchpool's brother-in-law and a fellow CO, remembers one such spell during which his mother came to visit him every day at a camp on Salisbury Plain. Both he and his mother struck up a relationship with the guards. 'This young sergeant was embroidering a cloth for his wife and he roped my mother in to help and she did some of the work for him. Eventually the sergeant said "You know Mrs Radley we can't keep him out much longer, we shall have to give him an order." "Well," she said, "I shan't get this cloth finished." But we got our order in due course.' Back to prison he went.

When Catchpool had served his first sentence he was court-martialled again and sentenced to two years, reduced to one year 'in recognition of services in ambulance work' and eventually reduced to six months. Before the war ended he had to go through the whole process twice more.

The tragedy was that the system just could not deal with a man like him. At his last court martial in March 1918, when the German army was making one final and, for a short time, very successful push on the Western Front, he admitted: 'There is hardly a moment when my thoughts are not with the men in France, eager to help the wounded by immediate human touch with their sufferings. At times the impulse to return to this work becomes almost irresistible. May God steady me and keep me faithful to the call I have heard above the roar of the guns.' When the court had decided on its inevitable verdict – guilty – and its sentence – two years this time – Catchpool was summonsed to hear it read out. Only then did he wear the Mons Ribbon given to him by the War Office in recognition for his work in 1914. The officers at the court martial were, understandably, astonished.

Of the 16,300 conscientious objectors almost 6,000 men were arrested, court-martialled and sent to prison (521 were court-martialled three times and twenty were court-martialled five times). The 1,300 absolutists, including Catchpool and Bert Brocklesby, remained in prison until five months after the end of the war; but another 9,100, like Duncan Grant and Bunny Garnett, accepted some form of alternative service whether it was farming at Garsington or, on a rather different level, quarrying at Dartmoor.

Howard Marten was let out of Dartmoor in 1917 to work with the Friends War Victims Relief Committee. As Marten says: 'they might have let me do that at first rather than at last'.

Some years after the war Fenner Brockway admitted: 'Clifford Allen and I took the extreme view. We felt it would be a compromise to accept alternative service; that in a sense it would be accepting conscription, accepting the authority of the government for war purposes to order us about.' Both leaders of the No Conscription Fellowship practised exactly what they preached. Allen ended up in prison in August 1916 and Brockway in November the same year. They did not stop there. Allen, an introspective man at the best of times, decided during his third term of imprisonment to refuse all prison work even though he knew this meant solitary confinement and the 'torture of enforced and perpetual silence'. Brockway refused to obey the silence rule and suffered eight months of solitary confinement.

Brockway was kept sane in part by sympathetic Sinn Fein prisoners, including Eamon de Valera who had been imprisoned after the Easter Rising. They were being held under much looser conditions than Brockway and they managed to get a note to him saying they could do anything he wanted 'except get you out'. What he wanted was a daily copy of the Manchester *Guardian* (the Sinn Feiners were allowed all papers apart from Irish papers), and they managed to leave it for him behind a loose brick in the wall of the lavatory that he used. As Brockway says, the warders must have known the newspaper was coming in and felt some sympathy towards him.

Allen, who had something of the martyr in him, could well have died in prison, but for the efforts of Mrs Henry Hobhouse. She was concerned not so much with Allen's release but with the release of her son Stephen, a product of Eton and Balliol who had been doing social work in the East End of London before he was imprisoned as a conscientious objector. Her opponents labelled her 'a pernicious woman' but that was the measure of her success. Her husband was a former West Country Liberal MP, and she enlisted a glittering array of supporters, including Lord Milner, Lord Curzon and General Jan Smuts. Bertrand Russell, who was the ghost writer of her short campaigning book on the subject, was kept well in the background. Her contacts and her sheer persistence forced the government to announce in December 1917 that it would release those absolutists who were in poor health. Her son was released within days and Allen soon followed him. Under this fudge some 333 absolutists were released before the war ended. When Allen emerged from prison he weighed less than eight stone, and he was suffering from the onset of tuberculosis: the doctor at Winchester prison said he was only a few days from death.

Stephen Hobhouse was released from Exeter prison on 8 December, and his wife, who had been tipped off by the prison authorities, was waiting in lodgings for him in the city. Four days later another absolutist, Arthur Butler, a former scholarship boy at Stockport grammar school with none of the same connections as Hobhouse, died of consumption in Preston jail. As his condition worsened his mother had eventually been allowed in to see him, but when he begged that she should be allowed to stay beyond the regular visiting hours the governor refused. Butler died the day after her visit.

Figures compiled after the war show that ten COs died in prison and a total of seventy-three died as a direct result of the treatment they suffered either in prison or while being held by the military. These deaths included men who, their health weakened by their stay in prison, caught tuberculosis or a lethal 'flu virus that swept through Europe in 1919. In addition there were another thirty-one who 'lost their reason' because of the conditions.

For Bert Brocklesby and the other 'Frenchmen' who remained in Maidstone prison, ten years was ten years and life hardly changed at all. Bert would sometimes have 'dainties' delivered down to him dangling on a mailbag string from the window of the prisoner in the cell above him, who had long-term privileges. He eventually got into the tailor's shop where he was promoted from darning socks to patching shirts. But he still had to live in silence. He had some books, he was allowed to play the organ at the Methodist service every three weeks and that essentially was his life. The only thing that could be said for it was that it was a safe life – safe from the front and safe too from the treatment that a minority of others received.

Within the lower ranks of the army there was an inevitable feeling that the COs should not be allowed to 'get away with it'. Retribution was sometimes referred to as 'horseplay' among soldiers, but on occasions it was much more than that. For men stripped and left out in a tent on the cliffs above Dover for several nights, thrown into a stream in the New Forest, put on the railway track at Kings Cross or flogged in Manchester, the treatment consisted of rather more than a playful prank. The COs prided themselves in being able to make soldiers understand them – given time – and they certainly did achieve this on some occasions. But when one private with the Tenth Battalion Rifle Brigade was asked after the war about the attitude of soldiers to the COs, he replied 'They was vile to them. If they got a chance they would knock them silly.'

Sergeant Charles Lippett, a regimental policeman who was interviewed after the war, said, 'The thing I must emphasise is the treatment we were forced to mete out to these poor blighters because they thought as they did.' He tells of one incident where a CO refused to wear khaki and the guards were instructed to take measures to 'remedy this state of affairs'. On a very cold night they took him to the baths, stripped him and forced a uniform on him and then left him in an open compound knowing he needed the khaki to keep warm. 'During the night he stripped himself of this khaki and shredded the whole of the suit up and hung it around the barbed wire, and that man walked about all night without a shred of clothing on him. That was the type of treatment we had to mete out, and I am bitterly ashamed that I was forced to take part.'

At Atwick Camp near Hull, John Gray, nineteen, was subjected to a 'breaking down' campaign of beatings by physical training staff which included being dragged around a field and then repeatedly thrown in a pond and dragged out by a rope attached around his waist. Interestingly at least eight soldiers refused to obey orders to impose the treatment, but in the end the campaign, which included being threatened with a Mills bomb, was successful. Gray gave in and became a soldier – albeit a guilty soldier – writing to Catherine Marshall, 'I reprove myself for being so weak and having to bow down to militarism.'

At the army camp in Cleethorpes where the commanding officer had ignored War Office orders and sent five COs to France, James Brightmore was sentenced to twenty-eight days' solitary confinement. Since no cell was vacant, a muddy pit ten feet deep and three feet wide was dug for him where he had to serve his sentence. He was told 'the five lads have been shot' and promised that he too 'would be shot like a dog when I got to France'. After eleven days of this a sympathetic soldier smuggled out a letter detailing his treatment which reached the Manchester *Guardian* – Brightmore was taken out and the hole filled up as soon as the letter was printed.

Major General Wyndham Childs relieved the commanding officers at both Hull and Cleethorpes of their posts – although they were both re-employed by the army towards the end of the war. Childs recognised that any institutionalised ill-treatment was counter-productive, for there was now a system in place whereby the most determined of the COs were given a choice of prison (with an escape route for anyone who looked like dying) or meaningless work of national importance. The key leaders of the NCF were imprisoned, as were many of its members. The pressures Parliament faced had been skilfully relieved by the release of Stephen Hobhouse, Clifford Allen and others. The problem of conscientious objectors did not go away but it was relatively easily contained for the rest of the war.

18

The Cost of Conscience

In January 1918 Phil wrote home to his aunt: 'We came out of the trenches on Xmas day and we were in again for New Year's Eve. There were the usual New Year's greetings from both sides but we had no casualties. There is a feeling of fed-upness slowly growing, evidenced by the lack of enthusiasm in the men, it has become a sort of dull routine.'

Fortunately, though, he was about to escape this dull but still very dangerous routine. The War Office ordered that some of the junior officers who had been in France for a long time should be replaced by those who had never left the safety of England. Phil was the third in his brigade to go. Ironically his last task before leaving France was to sit as the junior officer on a court martial of a soldier charged with desertion. The man, who had no one to represent him, appeared guilty enough. But he did not know how fortunate he was to have Phil as one of the officers trying him, for Phil admitted later: 'I was unjust in my approach to that trial for, without hearing the evidence, I had already decided to do my best for the man.' He was found guilty, but when it came to sentencing, Phil, as the junior officer, had to speak first and opted for five years' penal servitude. Since the death penalty required a unanimous vote the other officers could only follow suit and the deserter was spared.

The end of the war found Phil in the peace and comfort of the First Huntingdon Cyclist Battalion patrolling the north-east coast of England. In a way it was his prize for surviving. The Germans, having held their new line in 1917, were now ready for one last gamble. They had imposed a humiliating peace on the Bolsheviks, enabling them to switch men and munitions from east to west, and they knew their only hope of victory in the west was to attack before the newly arrived American troops could get fully involved. Phil left France just five weeks before the Germans launched their all-or-nothing offensive which at one point brought them to within 40 miles of Paris before finally being brought to a halt.

Reinforced by American troops carried on a 'bridge of ships' at up to 300,000 men a month, the Allies started to push the Germans back across France and Belgium. Germany, beset by the disintegration of its allies, hunger at home, disillusionment amongst the army, mutiny in the navy and revolution in the cities had to ask for peace, but its army still, somehow, remained a fighting unit. In the last few weeks of arguing over the terms of an armistice more than half a million soldiers were killed or wounded, including the war poet Wilfred Owen and Annie Wainwright's brother Gilbert.

But the north-east of England was a far cry from all this. At one point Phil was sent to dancing classes at the big hotel on the Whitby seafront because his colonel wanted to turn his officers into social successes. At a New Year's Day officers' beano the year before in France Phil had performed a clog dance much to the amusement of his fellow officers, but ballroom dancing was probably new to him. However, he was transferred on to a revolver course before he could perfect his dancing steps. Once the armistice was signed in November 1918 the army could find even less for him to do. He was allowed home on Christmas leave, but it was not until three months after the armistice that he was finally demobilised. Phil's war was over.

Over, but not over, for during the years after the war he suffered from nightmares which nearly always consisted of finding himself up in the front line without his gas mask. Thirteen years after the war ended he returned to the battlefields with his brother Harold and two friends, and talks of 'wandering over the ground of sacred–profane memories' and the 'scars' these memories left. In the end he turned to theosophy, a philosophical movement which draws much inspiration from the religions of the East, and it was this that slowly helped him. After four years, he says, 'the stress of war had gone from me'.

In Sussex, as soon as the cowman told Duncan Grant and David Garnett that the armistice had been signed, they abandoned their farm work, bicycled off to the train station and set off for London. There they found a city where the excitement that had greeted the beginning of the war was more than matched by the emotions that greeted its ending. 'The streets were thronged with crowds, singing and laughing, dazed with happiness.' After a day of partying Garnett ended up dancing with the wife of a millionaire Cabinet Minister in Trafalgar Square amongst people 'beside themselves with joy . . . love and goodness were all about me and the same pure happiness animated us all'. Siegfried Sassoon saw things rather differently; he ended the day at a dinner party in Chelsea with hosts who had been nowhere near the front but whose sympathies were with the flag-waving mob outside, 'a loathsome ending to the loathsome tragedy of the last four years'.

In Maidstone prison Bert Brocklesby and his fellow prisoners received their news from the chaplain who once a week read out a summary of what was going on. So they knew that the war was drawing to a close. At the eleventh hour of the eleventh day of the eleventh month Bert was working in the tailor's shop when 'suddenly all the buzzers in Maidstone began hooting and we could hear frantic cheering. Fred [Murfin] was working at a table about two yards from me and he smiled across and uttered a fervent "Thank God!"'

In Winchester the prison chaplain loathed by all COs announced the good news to the whole prison population. 'He almost had tears in his eyes and his voice,' says one CO, 'because he was so sorry the war had come to an end before we had sacked Berlin.'

Corder Catchpool was sitting alone stitching mailbags in his cell. It was 11 a.m. – he could always tell the time to within five minutes by the number of mailbags he had sewn. A hooter broke the silence and he thought at first it was just a tramp steamer in the docks. Then the prison bell rang out:

> . . . daring, loud and long. Suddenly I went a little mad too and did unheard of things. I rang my Emergency Bell! A warder unlocked the door. The war *was* over. Click, click, went the lock again. I stood confused and started to sing the 'Te Deum', but stopped halfway. I was overwhelmed, oppressed with a sense of the awful responsibility of being spared, going on living, a sense of not knowing how to try harder to do more than in the past.

The government was more concerned about demobilising disgruntled soldiers than it was in looking after conscientious objectors. In January 1919 the clerks at some dispersal units refused to process members of the Non Combatant Corps because of the strength of feeling against the 'No Courage Corps'. In response the War Office virtually gave in, saying that NCC men over the age of thirty-seven would have to be demobilised – but they should wait until last, while those under the age limit should continue to serve. In the same month Winston Churchill, the new Secretary of State for War, started pushing for the release of imprisoned COs. By this time he had the backing of the army. It was becoming clear that they would soon be released; for instance Stanton was given an ex-bank manager, in prison for embezzlement, to train up as his replacement as the prison book-binder. But it was only in April that Churchill managed to persuade the Cabinet to allow almost all of them home.

'April 12 1919 was our day of liberation,' writes Bert, 'to the great annoyance of those who were still waiting to see their boys demobbed from the army. "Why should skunks and shirkers get free before men who have been fighting for their country?"'

Bert was in the tailor's shop, where he had been further promoted to making shoes, and was taking considerable pride in a pair he was working on when he was summoned. 'I'll come back and finish these' he told his fellow workers, but it was a promise he was never going to keep.

Stanton had to spend a frustrating day waiting for clothes that he could wear to be sent in – 'I had to resort to my old pastime of cancelling vulgar fractions.' But Fred Murfin, Norman Gaudie and Bert were taken back to their cells to collect what personal possessions they had and as they walked past the men in the hall waiting to go out to work, Bert says 'a low muffled cheer began, swelling higher and rolling along that house of pain. It was against all the rules, and I doubt if such a thing ever happened before or since. It gripped my heart and almost made me weep.'

Foister's memory is less dramatic. When he was called out from the printing shop he thought he was on his way to the punishment cells for refusing to have his hair cut. Instead a warder took him to the visiting area 'and my mother was there with a suit she had brought for me to wear and she said "You are going out now."' Fred Murfin had been due to take the tenor solo in the Easter anthem eight days later – he was the only tenor lead in the prison – but they would have to manage without him.

In Dorchester jail, where Wilfred Littleboy, a chartered accountant, was held, the problem was actually getting out. 'The prison governor was almost sentimental. I happened to be the first to go in to say farewell to him and he rambled on and said how nice it had been to have people like us in and that sort of thing and I thought "Good heavens, if he's going to say this to everybody we'll be here till tea time." But when I went out he said, "Oh don't send any more. I don't want to see anyone else." I think he got rid of it on me.'

The COs were going out into a world where much had changed: the first thing Bert noticed was that ladies had abandoned long flowing skirts and were walking about in 'scarcely more than knee-length skirts'. His mother had sent him a suit but had forgotten to include a pair of braces and it was in buying a new pair that he discovered how much prices had risen. With trains few and far between he stayed the weekend with a Methodist minister in Maidstone and then made his way up to London where he had time enough between trains to visit the British Museum. There cannot be many prisoners whose first ports of call after almost three years inside are a Methodist service, a Quaker Friends' Meeting and the British Museum.

He had cabled Annie Wainwright to tell her the time of his arrival in Doncaster and his faithful fiancée was there to meet him. 'I had made a sentimental compact with her that we should meet at the very spot where we had parted in 1916, just outside the police court. All this worked as planned and she took me to where my brothers were considerately waiting around the corner.'

For Annie Wainwright this must have been a very difficult moment. She had said goodbye to him three years earlier. She had seen him once since then when she had come with her prospective in-laws for what turned out to be an awkward and unhappy meeting at Winchester prison. Bert's drawing of her on the wall of his cell in Richmond Castle might interest today's conservationists but Annie was never to see it.

She had waited patiently for a man who refused to go to war, yet exactly a month before the war ended her brother Gilbert had been killed at the age of twenty-two when a faulty shell exploded as his gun crew fired it. On his gravestone in one of the British cemeteries which are scattered in over-abundance across Northern France are the words 'Peace Perfect Peace'. He lies buried next to the others in his gun crew, who all came so tantalisingly close to surviving the war. On the wall of the Methodist chapel in Conisbrough where Annie, Gilbert and Bert all worshipped together his name is the last of the thirty-five members of the congregation who gave their lives in the war. Whatever question marks there might have been in her mind, she remained as loyal as ever to Bert.

From Doncaster all three brothers and Annie took him by taxi the few miles to the family home in Conisbrough. In prison Bert had had a serial dream, which started with him climbing through a breach in the prison wall and then embarking on the long walk back home. Every time he repeated the dream he got ever closer to home. And now, at last, this was real. His father stood at the door to greet him: 'Welcome home Bert.' Bert says of his father's attitude:

> It was a lovely Christian welcome. This was his answer to the people who said he ought to turn me out of the house. He was a true Liberal who, though he did not share my pacifist views, thought I had a perfect right to them, and was glad, I must believe, that I had defied and beaten the Conscription Act which he had detested. Aunt Rebecca had been hoarding a pile of tinned goods which she fondly called the 'fatted calf' so now it all came out and we had a feed, sumptuous by any standards, but luxurious by the semi-famine conditions of the post war period.

Fred Murfin remembers some of the same sort of excitement. He too went from Maidstone up to London and then took the train to Louth in Lincolnshire to see his parents. 'The train seemed very slow. I was out of the train before it stopped. I ran to give up my ticket and then ran most of the way home. I looked in the front window and heard mother say to Dad "There's the train, he may be on it." It was cherished memory. We had three years to talk about.'

Looking back on all this in 1984, Fenner Brockway suggested that 'things changed from the beginning to the end of the First World War, especially the attitude of the soldiers. We were bloody heroes at the end of the war.' Given what he had been through it is easy to see why he would like to remember events like this, but the picture he draws has only a remote connection with reality. Some COs might have had it easier than others but none of them suggest that anyone but their supporters saw their action as heroic. They were fortunate if they were accepted back into the community without too much trouble, even more fortunate if they got a job.

Leonard Payne was allowed home to the market town of Lutterworth early in 1918 with his brother Ronald to help their father making baskets used for carrying supplies to the troops. He was

WE WILL NOT FIGHT

accosted one afternoon by a group who included the police super-intendent's son, pulled off his bike and thrown in the river. The family's house and workshop was pelted with stones and both brothers left their home and the town immediately. They did not return until 1920 when Len's prowess as a rugby player won him a place on the town's first team despite the fact that most of his team-mates were ex-servicemen. They won all of the cups in Leicestershire 'and that was the finish. Nobody bothered with me anymore. I was just one of the heroes.'

In 1917, almost certainly as part of the deal for allowing out some absolutists on the grounds of ill-health, Parliament had barred all conscientious objectors other than those who had enlisted in the Non Combatant Corps from voting in national or local elections for five years. It was a spiteful act that had little effect – although an objection was lodged against Len Payne – for in many cases neither registration officers nor COs knew anything about it. In reality losing their right to vote did not have as much effect on COs as prison and the scorn that followed. Some coped better than others but reading through the stories of men like Bert Brocklesby and Norman Gaudie there is the unmistakable feeling that they never quite achieved in life what they could have achieved if they had not taken their stand.

The first Sunday Fred Murfin was back he went to the chapel with his parents where he knew everybody. The mother of one of his former playmates said 'she was pleased to see me home, but she couldn't shake hands with me', but at least the minister of his church welcomed him back and he 'didn't meet with any cold shoulders'. In this he was more fortunate than Percy Leonard, who went back to his Congregationalist church where for years he had been a volunteer church worker. 'The minister used to make a practice of going to the door and shaking hands with people as they went out. When he saw me he refused to shake hands. It was the last time I went to the church and it was the last time my wife went to church.'

Mark Hayler rose to become director of a building society, but he says his record as a CO 'dogged me all my life . . . When the whole war was over I got many jobs, many good jobs and then I was interviewed by a committee and the last question was always "What did you do in the Great War?" I knew that was the end. I remember getting one very good job and the secretary came to me and said "We're very sorry about it, we really are sorry, but we couldn't possibly employ you having a record like that."'

Bert Brocklesby was lucky to have the support of his family, for some COs had not only professional but also personal problems. When in later years Harold Bing was asked to recall his days as a CO, he was quite cautious about the effect of his stand on his family but his sister Dorothy was much less so. They lived in Croydon, south London, and Dorothy says:

> My mother came from a very united family. During my childhood we were constantly taken to see her sisters and their families. And as soon as they realised that Harold wasn't going to fight for his country they just cut us dead completely. Then after the war was over it was never healed; they wouldn't have any more to do with us at all. One of my aunts lost a son, the only son and they were terribly upset. He had practically decided to become a pacifist because he was great friends with my brother.
>
> When I was a student teaching in Catford where they lived I went purposely, I made a visit to try to heal the breach, I did my very best because it was terribly hurtful to my mother. And they just looked at me and no, nothing came of it at all. And they didn't come to the funeral when she died or anything. Of course my mother was very loyal to her husband and her son and I think she suffered a great deal.

As for her brother, he wanted to be a teacher, 'but if you looked through the advertisement pages very frequently at the head of the advert was "No CO need apply." Advert after advert had that.' He asked his local council to sponsor him through training college but that was a hopeless thought: 'The education committee said they would have a rebellion on the part of teachers and parents if pacifists were put in to teach their children.' However he did eventually get a job in a private school in Cheltenham where the new headmaster had been in the Non Combatant Corps.

Among the other 'Frenchmen' Norman Gaudie might have been a good cricketer, but the chairman of the Boldon Cricket Club would having nothing to do with him: 'If that fellow comes back to the club I resign.' Instead he went and played for the miners' team where they were rather more understanding. A fellow cricketer recalled that Gaudie was 'ostracised by many of his "ain folk" with whom he worked and played but he never allowed his spirit to be dimmed'. His son Martyn says: 'He couldn't get a job until 1921. Eventually an insurance agent gave him an "insurance book" where you go round getting people to pay their penny's insurance and from there he did very well.'

If the COs were patient and persistent they nearly always found employment in the end, but it was seldom what they hoped for. Jack Foister had interviews with three different headmasters who all said the same thing. 'They were very willing to take me but they did not dare run in the face of public opinion and therefore they had to turn me down.' Eventually it was the brother of his professor at Cambridge who got him a job in a school. Alfred Evans wanted to go back to his profession as piano tuner but he says he was 'drummed out of London' after the war. However he had no trouble in the provinces where there was a shortage of piano tuners.

After his work with the War Victims' Relief Committee, Howard Marten managed to get a job with his old bank, but 'they made things as difficult as they could. I was put at a branch which was known in my earlier days as the convict settlement because any man who blotted his copybook was sent there.' He tried visiting his old friends at his previous branch, 'but the manager found me and said you are no longer on the staff. You mustn't come round. But then again it was understandable. He had lost a son in the war and I suppose he felt pretty raw about it.'

For most of the country the heroes were not Fenner Brockway's heroes, they were the men who had won the war – for if they were not heroes then what was the point of the suffering the country had been through? The weekend before Bert arrived home the town had welcomed back Sergeant Laurence Calvert who had won the Victoria Cross two months before the war ended. Bert's father, still chairman of the town's War Relief Committee, was among the official welcoming party when Calvert stepped off the train. After the brass band had played their welcome there was a tour of the district in motor cars and then a 'patriotic concert'. There Calvert was presented with an illuminated manuscript recording his deed of valour: two months before the war ended he had single-handedly destroyed a German machine-gun post that was putting in jeopardy a British attack at Havrincourt – 'he bayoneted three and shot four'. He was also given £500 in war bonds, a purse containing £20 in cash and a gold watch.

There are some soldiers who remember their war years as the most exciting moments of their life – even if they remember particular episodes with horror. Bert too, if he was alive today, might even admit to a certain nostalgia for the days when he faced down both the government and the army.

Bert, whose family home was just 100 yards away from the Calvert's home, was certainly not expecting any welcoming committee other than his family, yet he was certainly hoping for more understanding than he got. The head teacher of the school where he taught until he was imprisoned did not hesitate to offer him his job back, telling him, 'Never mind what people say; they'll soon forget about it.' But Bert was painfully aware that people did not forget. 'I was surprised to find how bitter local feeling was against me; it seemed much worse than in 1916. I had thought that having proved myself sincere they would give me credit for it. But no! We had beaten the military and they hated us for it. I could feel it as I walked in the streets, and I saw it in the faces of people who at one time pretended to be friends.'

Before the war he had seemed such a central part of life in

Conisbrough, but now within his church the local employers – the men who mattered in the town – insulted him. He continued to help with the music when he could, although one long-standing member told Bert that on seeing him back at the organ stool for the first time, 'he had never felt so uncomfortable in God's house in his life'. Bert believed his church was another victim of the war; the 'beautiful family spirit' had been replaced by 'cliques, bickering and strife'. He never went back to work in the town again.

He had other problems which fellow COs perhaps did not admit to. He and his fellow COs were not career criminals; the last thing they must have thought of when they were dreaming their teenage dreams was that they were going to end up in prison. Yet that is where they found themselves. After adapting to prison life, they now had to cope with life back on the outside.

His two and a half years in prison, mostly spent in silence, had left Bert so rusty that 'in conversation I would suddenly become tongue-tied. I was fully aware of the idea I wished to express but the words to express it would not come.' There was too what he calls the 'spiritual damage'. He writes like a present-day prison reformer: 'For years the prisoner has had no responsibilities, neither to decide to work, procure his food, nor even to open or close a door. All these are done for him. He comes out feeling unable to take responsibility or to make decisions.'

Alfred Myers, a methodist and an ironstone miner from Carlin How, a small village in Cleveland, was a good example of this. He had come out of Maidstone with Bert, who had guided him through the Codices and Scott's Antarctic diary at the British Museum and then taken the train north with him. But while Bert had a resilient personality and was strong enough to cope with most things, Alfred Myers was suffering from 'an emotional or nervous reaction and felt unable to go further alone'. So Bert arranged for him to stay with a friend for two or three days until he felt able to travel back to his home town.

Bert's first job was as a teacher with the deaf and dumb in Doncaster. It lasted exactly a week. 'I cannot think the Board of Managers thought I might corrupt the poor deaf boys (who were of no military value anyway) so it must have been the common repulsion of having a CO on the staff.'

One week's work and then nothing. Weeks went by with Bert, usually such an outgoing, cheerful man, feeling 'redundant and worthless'. Then a friend suggested he apply to Durham County Council – which had a Labour majority – and he got a job in a school used by miners' children. Even at this school, though, not everyone accepted him. One of his colleagues suggested they should all stop work until Bert was forced to leave, but there was no support amongst the other teachers.

After five months' teaching Bert decided he needed to do something more to help those still suffering from the war – and in particular those children of Britain's recent enemies who were suffering. He volunteered to go to Vienna with the Friends War Victims Relief (FWVR) to help feed the children in the city. While an American relief organisation here brought field kitchens from France to feed soup to the school children, the FWVR concentrated on the under-fives.

The *Arbeiter-Zeitung* reports in somewhat lyrical terms the reception he received in Vienna, which was far different from anything he was ever going to get in Conisbrough. It describes a crush around the English mission where there was one queue for food and another queue for the doctor:

A motor drives up. The fair giant who gets out is an English school-master. He was condemned to death because of his refusal to take up arms, but the sentence was commuted. He is tall, powerfully built and very British and he looks down on the women who press around him with their questions with amusement. His answers come slowly as he has to think very carefully over each syllable: sugar, milk and flour. He then takes off his hat and drags along the first heavy sack. A small dark-haired American follows, bent double beneath the weight he is carrying. The two of them patiently unload the great lorry and the Vienna women stand by and look on with emotion. 'God Bless England' says one when the work is finished.

Annie did not see it that way. When Bert told her he was going to Austria she told him bluntly that he was going to feed the people who had killed her brother. Bert explains what happened next: 'I said that the children of Vienna had nothing to do with it. She said that if I went she would consider herself at liberty till I returned. I said that if our engagement depended on such a condition it were better broken. But the engagement was not broken yet.'

Three months later Bert received a letter from Annie telling him that now the engagement was over. That night he went to hear Schubert's *Death and the Maiden*, 'and my heart seemed dead too'. For once Bert's emotions overcame his stubbornness – he decided to abandon Vienna to see if he could put the pieces back together again. 'I shall never forget how hope sprang up as I travelled home. But it was the last leaping flame of a dying fire. Annie had gone. It was her decision and I cannot but think it right.' When Annie's picture was on the walls of his cell in Richmond Castle, she somehow seemed so right for him. But in 1920 she was almost twenty-three, and no longer a soprano in the choir in awe of her choirmaster. Bert's determination – his complete faith in the fact that he was always right – had become a burden not a blessing. Before the year was out she had married a local bank manager in the same chapel where she used to sing in the choir that Bert led. Looking back in later years, Bert said that the decision to leave all the work he was doing in Vienna in this desperate bid for Annie was the biggest mistake he made in his life. He recognised that Vienna had shown their 'incompatibility' – the relationship would never have worked out 'without some radical change in one or both of us'.

*

So Bert was now back from Vienna without a fiancée and without a job, although his father, having asked him how much his annual savings had been before the war, gave him £120 because he did not want him to be 'out of pocket' because of his stand.

At one point in his search for jobs he noticed pin pricks on the top of his application folder and was told by the Director of Education for West Riding that these came from his file being sent to several local education committees who had all rejected him because of his background. In future, the director advised, it would be better not to mention that he had been a conscientious objector when applying for a job.

Bert did eventually find another teaching post but he was still a restless man. He had finally joined the Quakers a year after he came out of prison and in 1922 he travelled to Buzuluk in south-east Russia for fifteen months with the Friends Relief Service. War followed by revolution and drought here had brought such famine – coupled with typhoid – that people were left to die on the streets. His brother Harold came out to join him in his work. 'Each morning as we set out it was with a sort of horrified expectation that we turned each corner, not knowing where we should see the fresh corpses. One morning there was one on the footpath just opposite our house, and I saw a well-dressed lady stepping daintily round it to pass on her way.' At the worst point the Quakers were feeding 260,000 people daily with supplies that came from well-wishers across the world. Foreigners had not yet learned, wrote Bert, 'that the "dictatorship of the proletariat" was a lying catchphrase'. Yet through it all he remained remarkably resilient, travelling to Moscow on one occasion to bring back copies of music by Haydn, Mozart and Beethoven and then forming his own string quartet – including his brother on viola – to play his newly acquired volumes.

While he was back in England teaching again, his father died. John Brocklesby collapsed at the end of a ceremony in which he had been presented with a gold-mounted fountain pen in celebration of fifty years of preaching. He died eleven days later, on Christmas Day 1927.

The bond between father and son had been tested but never broken and at the end Bert sang to him and prayed with him. He wrote movingly: 'We felt as though the strong oak under which we had sheltered so long, that refuge that was always ours was removed.' Ten months later he was off again, this time fulfilling his childhood dream to become a missionary. It was during his training that he met his wife Ethel, a fellow trainee who was, among other things 'that rare creature (for me at least) a woman pacifist'.

Bert spent four years with Ethel in Pemba, an island off the East African coast. It was there that Mary, the first of their two daughters, was born. During his time overseas Bert was, as always, hard on himself – refusing to take any quinine initially and, predictably, coming down with malaria. More surprisingly he was also hard on the inhabitants, some of whom he thought were being 'paid to be Christians' and who he tried to encourage – amidst considerable resentment – to be more independent. Whether it was cutting back on the useless work they were paid to do, selling the mission's herd of cows because they produced very little milk, building a smaller house to replace the huge missionary's house they lived in, or trying to stop girls being sold off for marriage to the highest bidder, Bert was predictably different. He was eventually recalled to England where this time he settled into a rather quieter life of teaching.

While Bert had troubles, brother Phil prospered. Having started with his own small chemist's shop in Hull he moved back to Conisbrough and opened his own pharmacy and optician's which was to prove very successful. He married, although he never had children, and ended up living next door to his brother Harold. Although he gained considerable respectability in the same home town that Bert had abandoned – becoming a freemason, member of the Rotary Club and chairman of the British Legion – Phil never for a moment tried to disown his older brother.

19

The Legacy

By the time of the Second World War the thirty-five 'Frenchmen' were past the age where they needed to fight the battle of conscription all over again. Nevertheless Hitler posed new decisions for them and their responses were very varied. Bert Brocklesby was teaching in Scunthorpe and he took considerable trouble to erect a noticeboard in his front garden where he would stick up various newspaper stories and anti-war articles that he collected. His daughter Mary remembers: 'I was impressed by the policeman who came to our door to tell him to take it down.' At another stage in his life Bert might well have refused and gone to jail again, arguing that he was doing no more with his noticeboard than exercising his right to free speech. But by then he was on his own with two young children to bring up following his wife's death from cancer, and so the noticeboard came down. Mary also remembers him taking turns to be a firewarden in his school – 'We used to go along with him at night time, it was quite an adventure.' Crucially, he was not an official fire watcher, he just volunteered to help; nevertheless it was an activity that he might have considered as aiding the war effort in his earlier purist days.

To judge by Phil's despairing letters from the front it would have seemed impossible that he would want anything further to do with war; and besides he was forty-six by the time of the Second World War and too old to fight. Yet he volunteered instantly for the Home Guard, was elevated to major and with another veteran from the First World War as his second-in-command he organised the defence of Conisbrough.

The likelihood of the Germans reaching Conisbrough was minimal, but Phil was so enthusiastic he even went to the length of constructing a rifle range near the walls of the castle in the town to give his men the target practice they needed.

Jack Foister, one of the 'Frenchmen' who was imprisoned in Harwich, joined the Home Guard once the war had started and ended up as a lieutenant. However, his fellow 'Frenchman' Alfred Evans refused to participate in the firewatching duty he was ordered to do. He was taken to court, fined and, when he refused to pay, he was jailed. 'It was absolutely absurd they put me inside on Christmas Eve,' Alfred comments. The governor of Bedford jail said I should be "pushing up daisies."' It was two months before he was let out. He appears to have been completely rigid in his stand, with little time for anyone else's point of view, and although his parents supported him throughout his ordeal in the First World War they did not give him their support in the Second World War.

Other COs were, like Bert, prepared to undertake their share of firewatching as long as they were not compelled to do it. Howard Marten was in his late fifties but despite his age he was 'more or less conscripted for the City of London Fire Guard. I dodged it often and avoided fire drill as much as I possibly could. I hated the idea of that regimentation.' Nevertheless, at the end of the war he was invited by Unilever, the firm which he then worked for, to a formal dinner at the Connaught Rooms to honour the company's Fire Guard Organisation.

Among the Bloomsbury Group Duncan Grant accepted commissions from the War Artists' Advisory Committee as well as joining the Home Guard, happily wearing khaki and a tin helmet and brandishing a rifle – although he did not have the right ammunition to fire it. Bunny Garnett 'completely abandoned' his pacifist opinions, got a commission in the RAF Volunteer Reserve and joined Air Ministry Intelligence.

Fenner Brockway, leader of the fight against conscription in the First World War, had already been tested by the Spanish Civil War and, like many Socialists, found there were limits to his pacifism. Faced with fascism he wanted the Socialists to win and it followed that 'I couldn't want them to win without doing something to help them win.' Looking back years later he said: 'It changed me from being an absolute pacifist ... emotionally I'm still a pacifist but politically and realistically I can't entirely justify it.' In the Second World War he remained a campaigner for the rights of conscientious objectors although he 'had tremendous sympathy for the victims of Hitler. I compromised by becoming sector captain of a fire brigade.'

He certainly was not alone in his conversion. Yet in the 1920s and well into the 1930s it had seemed for a brief time as though the peace movement, backed by the enormous emotional support of those determined to learn the lesson of the First World War, might change the way the world thought. In 1920 the League of Nations held its first session. The hope was that somehow it could impose its will without the force of arms to back it up. In 1933 the Oxford Union passed its famous motion that 'this house will in no circumstances fight for King and Country'. In 1934 in a letter to *The Times* the Anglican clergyman Dick Sheppard, broadcaster and popular preacher, invited people to sign a simple pledge: 'I renounce war and I will never again support or sanction another one.' He was overwhelmed with replies, the Peace Pledge Union was born and it soon had more than 100,000 members and 800 branches. But there could be no tougher test of a pacifist's belief than Adolf Hitler.

For some the problem was not so much Hitler but the Treaty of Versailles, which had imposed such swingeing terms on Germany at the end of the First World War. But as the historian Peter Brock wrote, this meant the pacifist press 'only too often served up the German viewpoint and pleaded for its acceptance on grounds of moral principle'. However, faced with Hitler, many of the peace pledgers simply melted away, as one CO put it: 'like an early morning mist on a hot June day'. Even Bertrand Russell wrote, 'If I were young enough to fight myself I should do so.'

Albert Einstein was the best-known figure in the peace movement in the late 1920s to suggest that if no more than 2 per cent of the male population of the world refused to fight then wars would cease. But, after Hitler came to power, when Einstein was asked to speak on behalf of two COs awaiting trial in Belgium, he replied: 'Were I a Belgian, I should not, in the present circumstances, refuse military service; rather I should enter service cheerfully in the belief that I would hereby be helping to save European civilisation.'

The writer A.A. Milne was another whom pacifists felt betrayed by. In 1934 he wrote *Peace with Honour* 'as an ordinary man who hated war. My soul revolted against it; my heart revolted against it; but most of all my mind revolted against it.' Six years later he published *War with Honour* and said that anyone reading his earlier book 'must read it with that one word HITLER scrawled across every page'. Now he argued that 'Nazi rule is the foulest abomination with which mankind has ever been faced. I believe that if it is unresisted it will spread over and corrupt the whole world. I believe it is the duty of mankind to reject such a world. I see no way of doing this save by the use of force.'

Among the next generation, Howard Marten's son joined the air force. His father recalled: 'He had no pacifist inclinations at all. He joined not so much because he was patriotic, but because he saw no alternative.' Harry Stanton's son joined the Friends Ambulance Unit. However Norman Gaudie's son Martyn followed his father down the same conscientious objector route – although it did not end in a death sentence. Martyn Gaudie died in September 2007, but a couple of years earlier, when looking back on the stand he had taken, he felt slightly guilty about how easy the whole thing had been. The first thing his tribunal did was to put off his hearing from January 1943 until September so that he could finish his exams.

When it was eventually time for his hearing he came before a tribunal in Newcastle headed by a judge who, he later discovered, had two sons fighting in the war, one of whom had already been killed in action. Gaudie had the sense that the tribunal members 'wouldn't understand what we were doing at all'. Unlike his father, he was at least allowed some help from a 'supporter' who had been a CO in the previous war.

Gaudie told the tribunal that he was trying to follow the Christian principles that he had learned from childhood and the next question was 'Are you a Quaker?' 'When I answered yes immediately the whole thing changed. It felt as though they were thinking "if he's a Quaker we haven't a hope of persuading him to do anything." I felt quite upset about this because I was in the room when the next fellow came in and he was a young fellow, a good broad Geordie who hadn't had any education worth speaking of and they gave him a very rough time.' Gaudie was not sure what happened to the Geordie but he himself was given 'land work' and went straight back to the farm where he had been working over the summer.

Conscription had been brought back in 1939 – with minimal opposition – by Prime Minister Neville Chamberlain who had had the advantage of sitting on a tribunal in 1916 and had discovered what was possible and what was futile: one CO remembers Chamberlain treating him 'completely as a gentleman'. With this experience behind him Chamberlain told the House of Commons that the new law would recognise three categories of conscientious objector: those who were prepared to accept non-combatant work with the army; those who were prepared to undertake work of 'national importance' as long as it was not connected with the military; and the absolutists – those who would do nothing even to 'aid or comfort those who are engaged in military operations'. He went on: 'It often happens that those who hold the most extreme opinions hold them with the greatest tenacity. We learned something about this in the Great War and I think we found that it was both useless and an exasperating waste of time and effort to attempt to force such people to act in a manner which was contrary to their principles.' Bert Brocklesby and the other absolutists of the First World War had made absolute opposition to any kind of war effort an acceptable position by the time of the Second War – however unpopular that stand remained.

The statistics covering the Second World War period up to 1948 show there were just over 62,000 registered conscientious objectors, including about 1,000 women, and of these 2,868 men and 69 women were granted absolute exemption. This compares with 16,300 conscientious objectors in the First World War of whom 200 were given absolute exemption. In the Second World War COs still faced prison sentences and about 6,500 COs spent some time in prison, including 500 women, out of whom 1,000 were court-martialled and sentenced to military prison. However, for those who did go to prison in the Second World War the pattern was usually that (although there were exceptions) after a second sentence, the authorities became convinced that the CO was either genuine or too much trouble or both and released him or her.

In the first months of the Second World War, 2.2 per cent of those registering under the Military Training Act applied for conscientious objector status, although as the war went on this figure dropped steadily to under 0.5 per cent. The conscientious objector discovered that the process had become both easier and more acceptable. 'Many people still regarded COs as a bit queer but it was a queerness they could tolerate,' says Harold Bing who was imprisoned in 1916 and whose family had not been allowed to forget they had had a CO in their midst. 'They were not looked upon as traitors or skunks or cowards but as people who had a legitimate religious or moral or other acceptable objection.'

The tribunals, usually five-strong, had to be headed by a county court judge and one member had to be appointed in consultation with the trade unions. Sometimes there was a military man on the tribunal, although Lloyd George emphasised in the Commons that these people should not be 'pukka soldiers' and there was certainly no military representative trying to boss the tribunals about. Ronald Mallone, a twenty-three-year-old teacher who refused to collect a gas mask when war broke out – 'if I'm not going to be part of the war machine I'm not going to accept their protection either' – had his tribunal in Southampton. He reports that the trade union rep said nothing; an 'intellectual' – an authority on Shakespeare – was 'most unpleasant' while a military man 'was very fair'. Nevertheless 'the atmosphere was quite a frightening one. One of my friends was an open-air speaker and a Quaker and he went completely to pieces in front of that tribunal, he couldn't say a word for himself. If he hadn't been a Quaker I think he would have been put on the military register.'

Mallone's tribunal lasted for about twenty minutes and 'much to my astonishment I got what I wanted which was unconditional exemption'. He attended a number of tribunals after his own and he says they varied enormously. 'If there'd been a raid the night before, the judge was always in a very bad temper.' He remembers too a judge asking one Socialist: 'How can you go on living in England making money when soldiers are only getting a shilling a week?' The Socialist was bold enough to reply: 'How can you accept so many guineas a week for judging my conscience?' and he was immediately put on the military register ready to be called up by the army.

Jesse Hillman, who was working at Orpington in the underground control centre that kept the railways running during the German bombardments, found his tribunal even more threatening than Mallone's: 'it felt like being put in the dock with a bunch of old fogeys sitting high above me directing pretty antagonistic questions.' What made it worse for him as a committed trade unionist was that 'the trade union member was even more unfriendly than most of the others'. He was given non-combatant service but would not accept it and appealed.

The atmosphere on appeal was completely different and Hillman has only praise for this part of the legal process. 'It was conducted informally sitting around a table with the members of the tribunal. It was designed to set me at ease and a genuine attempt to explore what I believed in – a sensitive attempt to explore how far I could go along the line that the tribunal wanted me to go.' He was given exemption as long as he did hospital, land or civil defence work and he chose the Friends Ambulance Unit. When the war was over he was demobbed on exactly the same date as would have applied if he had been in the army and the railway had offered him his job back.

Even the Non Combatant Corps rose again from its first dismal beginnings and again, lessons were learned from the past. A minute by a Ministry of Labour official attending a meeting with the War Office in April 1940 noted: 'During the course of the discussion the chairman (Colonel J.V.R. Jackson) stressed the need for a broader and more humane treatment of conscientious objectors than obtained during the last war.' The work was not that much more imaginative than in the past but for the most part – although certainly not in every case – tribunals sent men to the NCC only if they were prepared to put on the uniform.

Ken Shaw, who registered as a CO 'much to my family's horror', agreed to join the NCC. He found himself being drilled on the promenade at Ilfracombe and living in one of the beach hotels that the army had commandeered. 'It felt like a junior Dad's Army . . . the outstanding feature of our training was a demonstration by a crusty old colonel who came to show us how to use a pickaxe.' From there they went to Bulford Barracks on Salisbury Plain where they were surrounded by crack fighting regiments and they faced a reception which at first was a mixture of 'hostility and indifference'. This eased once they had formed a football team and started beating some of the other units. Shaw got a drum kit, formed a jazz band and also played most nights of the week in an orchestra. 'In some respects it was a bit like an open prison,' he says, 'once a month we could have a weekend at home.'

Amidst all the books on peace in the Friends House library in London there sits a book of reminiscences by the commander of Number Three Non Combatant Unit which fairly bristles with pride at the spirit of the men he commanded. Major G.W. Clark MC had been a sapper in the First World War and his second-in-command, Captain

F.A. Peach, had lost his right arm at the battle of Loos in 1915. When Clark learned of his appointment it was greeted by his fellow officers in the mess as a 'cause for commiseration'. But both men obviously took considerable pleasure in the work done by the odd assortment of COs who made up their unit.

Major Clark's 'Golden Rule' for the NCC was: 'Get them behind the idea; get them to understand it; get them to agree with it.' It might be not be the traditional army but it turned his men into a 'a grand team of workers'. After the war there were annual reunions and when Captain Peach died in 1955 there was a wreath at his funeral inscribed 'With remembrance of a beloved skipper, from his troops No 3 NCC Association'. It was a far cry from the 'No Courage Corps' of the First World War.

Some members of the NCC actually became uneasy about the fact that their life was so comfortable. Some transferred to the Royal Engineers to work as bomb disposal experts, others to coal mining or to the smoke companies which produced smokescreens to help protect cities from air raids. Another 162 – sometimes called the 'right wing of the pacifist movement' – volunteered to become medical paratroopers, with D-Day being their frightening debut. Colonel Alistair Young, commander of 224 Parachute Field Ambulance, once asked one of his volunteers 'Don't you bloody conchies ever think of anything else but your bloody consciences?' Nevertheless he called them 'excellent in battle' and when one of them went missing – he was later found in a German prisoner of war camp – Colonel Young wrote to his parents: 'He was known by all ranks for his modesty and for the courage with which he bore his Christian convictions. Such men are rare.' Another received the Military Medal for rescuing wounded paratroopers from the drop zone during the 1945 advance over the Rhine after having been told by an NCO 'You'll never get there and back alive.'

It would be wrong to paint an entirely rosy picture of how COs were treated in the Second World War. Percy Wilding was working on land clearance in Epping. He was also taking a course in Esperanto, the universal language which in both wars seemed to attract many COs with its message of hope and togetherness. On one occasion a local farm worker came striding across the field and started addressing him and the other COs in language which was as far away from Esperanto as it was possible to imagine. 'I asked him to moderate his language whereupon he came up to me and punched me hard in the face.' Wilding proved his pacifist credentials by refusing to retaliate. This was rather different from a CO at the north-western tribunal in Manchester who, having heard the tribunal decide he would be sent to the army, attacked Judge Burgis so violently he put him in hospital and off work for several weeks.

John Radford wrote home from Dingle Vale near Liverpool where he and several others were badly mistreated. He told of being put in solitary confinement for refusing to work. In the middle of the night he was woken and told again he had to work. He refused. 'We were knocked about and dragged to the butcher's shop. Here we were bashed up a bit more – we stuck it out and were taken back after the hottest half hour I have ever known.' Night after night he was woken every two hours and marched around the yard and every time he fell the guard 'kicked me to my feet again'. Eventually, after a week of this, he gave in. 'I think it has nearly broken my heart. I never felt so unhappy in my life . . . people are trying to cheer me up. The padre says I can do more good spreading the gospel in the RAMC than dying on bread and water.'

Dennis Waters, a student at University College London, was sent to join the Non Combatant Corps at Ilfracombe – much against his will. He and three others refused to put on a uniform and one morning his sergeant, Maloney, an ex-wrestler, decided he had had enough. Waters says:

He went into the room next door and I heard him bawling and shouting and heard the sound of blows. He then appeared in my room and went through the same routine with me. I felt rage but I knew that if I lifted a finger against him I would be in deep trouble. Then he went off and did the same thing to the man in the next door room. By merciful providence very shortly afterwards we had a visit from the orderly officer of the day. A decent man. I let it all rip.

Sergeant Maloney was court-martialled, although eventually acquitted on all charges. Dennis Waters was court-martialled three times for disobeying orders and sentenced to twenty-eight days, fifty-six days and three months before eventually being released to work on the land.

In December 1941 Churchill introduced conscription for single women aged between twenty and thirty to do war work. For those who refused there was much less inclination to send them to prison. Kathleen Wigham, aged twenty-two, who came from a family in Blackburn so strongly pacifist that her brother was made to return a toy dagger he had swapped for his own Christmas toy, refused a direction to do hospital work. She was fined five pounds and summoned to court in Blackburn. The magistrate told her: 'We don't want to send people like you to prison, can you pay your fine?' She replied 'I can pay it but I'm not prepared to.'

'Well, would you pay it if we said five shillings a week?' When she refused – politely – she was given fourteen days in Strangeways prison. Her mother gave her a 'nice bag of cherries' and told her to 'keep her pecker up' and then she drove off to Strangeways with two policemen and one policewoman who were almost begging her to pay the fine rather than go into a prison they knew was not for nice girls like her. She learned how right they were when the wardress told her: 'Our men are out fighting for sluts like you . . . if I had my way you'd certainly be hanging from a rope.' But her two weeks there were made bearable by a doctor who was called to examine her and who told the wardress 'You can find her a bed in the hospital, she's barmy.' Whether or not he knew he was doing her a favour is unclear but life in the hospital ward was much less likely to drive her barmy than life in the cells of Strangeways.

Joan Williams lost her job in Shoreditch library in London when she refused the council's order to carry out firewatching duties. When she was brought before the magistrates for refusing to register for conscription she told the court: 'I recognise that the country has been very generous in its treatment of COs, but there is no conscience clause in the industrial conscription act. It is the principle of the act I object to . . . It is the organisation of the country for war purposes and I feel I cannot take part in it.' She spent six weeks in Holloway prison in addition to the two weeks she had already spent on remand; after her release she ignored three notices directing her to attend an interview and then heard nothing more – she and many others were not considered worth pursuing.

Looking back, Dennis Waters remembers how painful it was to be despised by one's contemporaries: 'If you haven't been through it yourself you cannot realise what a depressing thing this can be.' Yet when he applied for his first teaching post after the war his reception was much warmer than he might have expected. The headmaster who interviewed him had won the Military Cross in the First World War. 'It made not the slightest bit of difference as far as he was concerned. I didn't suffer any great disability from that point of view.' However, the majority of both county and city councils dismissed anyone who registered as a conscientious objector. The BBC banned the conductor of the Scottish Orpheus Orchestra from giving a radio concert because of his pacifist views and dismissed two CO technicians, one of whom had been granted total exemption by his tribunal on condition that he continued in his job. Their jobs were restored only after the intervention of Churchill, who told the House of Commons in March 1941 that 'anything in the nature of persecution, victimisation or manhunting is odious to the British people'. He also advised the technicians to be careful in their choice of music, suggesting that 'very spirited renderings of "Deutschland über Alles" would hardly be permissible'.

If there was one class of person who was undoubtedly discriminated against it was the Jehovah's Witnesses. They are not pacifists – they saw themselves then and still see themselves as neutrals in any wars of 'this world' as they wait for the coming of Christ at Armageddon. They suffered for their beliefs in 1914–18 and were to suffer again now. Their brand of proselytising Christianity seemed to particularly rile some of the judges who headed the tribunals. Judge Frankland in Leeds told one applicant: 'You have fallen for this very obvious money-making concern, Jehovah's Witnesses. You, a schoolmaster. I want you and your friend to leave the room. I don't want other people to be contaminated by your presence.' Judge Wethered in Bristol described them as a 'mischievous society, persuading people that they should refuse to take part in the defence of their country'.

The lawyer prosecuting Kathleen Fairweather in Ilfracombe for refusing to do the work in a hospital kitchen allocated to her went to what he thought was the heart of the matter: 'This woman and those who associate with her are willing to avail themselves of all the advantages of this free country without doing a single thing in the national effort.' Mrs Fairweather, who said her time was fully occupied 'preaching the Gospel of the Kingdom', was given the choice of £5 fine or a month in prison: she chose the latter.

While many Jehovah's Witnesses were happy to undertake alternative work in the hospitals or on the land, the problem came with the 1,500 'full-time servants' who had freed themselves from secular activities to devote their life to serving their God but were not recognised as 'regular ministers' by the government. By the end of the war some 1,249 male and 344 female Witnesses had been imprisoned.

Yet while Jehovah's Witnesses suffered for their 'neutrality' in Britain, in Germany they died for it. Unlike the Jews, they had a chance to recant and sign a declaration that they would go into the army – although it was not the most tempting of alternatives since the army posting was usually a front-line penal battalion. In any case very few signed. By September 1939 August Dickmann, aged twenty-nine, had already been held in Sachsenhausen concentration camp for two years. He had initially weakened and signed the declaration but changed his mind when he received his call-up papers. On 15 September the camp commandant lined up all the camp's prisoners, including the other Witnesses, and told them over the loudspeakers that Dickmann 'refuses military service, claiming he is a "citizen of God's kingdom" . . . He has placed himself outside of society and in accordance with instructions from SS leader Himmler he is to be executed.' Dickmann was shot by three SS officers with a fourth stepping up to his body and putting a bullet through his head. He was the first conscientious objector to be executed in Nazi Germany.

The cruellest touch was that, among those forced to watch his execution, was his brother Heinrich. Afterwards Heinrich was interviewed by two Gestapo officers:

'Did you see how your brother was shot?'
'I did.'
'What did you learn from this?'
'I am and I shall remain one of Jehovah's Witnesses.'
'Then you will be the next one to be shot.'

Although Heinrich and his wife survived the rest of the war in concentration camps, a further 271 German and Austrian Jehovah's Witnesses were sentenced by the courts and executed by the Nazis as conscientious objectors. Sometimes family members would be brought in to try to get a Witness to recant but they were seldom successful and Admiral Max Bastian, who presided over the State War Tribunal, recalled later that sometimes 'the relatives of the condemned man begged him to remain firm under all circumstances, not to give in but to suffer death rather than yield'.

In the Soviet Union the very liberal law on conscientious objection which Lenin introduced was slowly chipped away and in 1929 the last of the pacifist organisations – the Tolstoyan Vegetarian Society – was closed down. By 1939 no applications for conscientious objector status had been received for the previous two years – which was hardly surprising since the outlook for anyone who dared try was far from healthy. What remained of the law could now be removed from the statute book since there was no need for it – a very neat, Stalinist solution to the problem.

So while the stand taken by the COs in the First World War changed the way they were regarded and consequently the way they were treated in both Britain and indeed America in the Second World War, the effect certainly did not carry over to the Continent. Yet they had planted the seed and it continues to grow. Where conscription still exists today it rarely comes without a 'conscience clause', however weak that clause might be.

Of the four major European powers involved in the Second World War, Britain took the lead in ending conscription in 1960. This was the year after conscription was introduced again into Germany as part of the re-established army – albeit with extensive provision for conscientious objectors. In Germany today conscription and the alternative service that comes with it is as much a device for propping up the social services as it is for supplying men to the army. There is no need to argue your case before a tribunal since almost all applications for CO status are automatically granted. In 2005 it was estimated that 90,000 would be called up for nine months of alternative service while only 67,000 conscripts would go into the army. Those who refuse both forms of service are usually sentenced to between 62 and 84 days of arrest. There is an option which covers Jehovah's Witnesses, allowing those who object to being forced to do substitute service to be exempt if they promise to work in welfare institutions for a certain length of time.

In the France that emerged after the war, conscription was very much a part of life and pacifism was seen as a form of defeatism. It needed a man of Charles de Gaulle's war record to introduce reforms allowing conscientious objectors some rights. However, De Gaulle said 'I want a statute but no objectors', making quite sure that conscription continued and the reforms were limited. Recently France replaced conscription with a 'rendez-vous citoyen': a day when men and women aged sixteen to eighteen are asked to prepare for national defence. Since there are no uniforms, no arms and no military discipline, it is hard to object to.

In Russia where conscription still exists – although only between 10 and 30 per cent of conscripts get called up – a social services alternative for conscientious objectors was introduced in 2004, but those who are allowed to volunteer for it have to serve almost twice as long as a soldier.

In America the fight against the war in Vietnam and the conscription needed to fight it (the draft) has been well documented: the marches; the veterans who threw away their medals in disgust at American policy; the men called to fight who burned their draft cards; those like Presidents Bush and Clinton who in their younger days found a whole assortment of legal ways to avoid Vietnam; those like Muhammad Ali who went to jail for their beliefs; and those with neither the legal know-how nor the money who ended up fleeing to Canada instead. In all it is estimated that 170,000 received conscientious objector status during the Vietnam period and another 80,000 fled to Canada.

But what is much less well known is that a considerable number of soldiers who had joined the US army as volunteers, expecting a steady career and help with college fees, decided they wanted to leave the army as the war grew more intense. Between 1965 and 1973 about 17,000 serving American soldiers claimed conscientious objector status and applied for either total discharge from the army or non-combatant service. Although only 28 per cent of claims were approved in the early years, as the war went on so the army decided it did not want these doubting soldiers within its ranks. By the end of the war an extraordinary 80 per cent of claims were being approved.

The draft ended in 1973 and America's standing army has proved big enough to fight two wars in Iraq without the need to revive it. The reintroduction of the draft for Iraq would undoubtedly have triggered protests to make the anti-Vietnam war 'actions' look tame. However in both Gulf Wars the US army has still had to deal with a small but steady stream of soldiers applying for a discharge on the grounds of conscientious objection.

There were, for instance, 441 applications in 1991 and 110 in 2004. The picture is complicated by the fact that achieving a discharge on the grounds of conscience can take eighteen months and it is often much easier to obtain a quieter and faster discharge using other claims such as parenthood or health problems. But there are now enough of these soldiers with second thoughts for academics to be debating 'the new conscientious objection', which is defined by two conditions: the COs are already in the army and the 'old religious and communal grounds for objection' have been supplanted by a 'new secular and often privatised base'.

In Britain, too, the debate has moved on. Some 415 serving soldiers who became conscientious objectors in the Second World War went before an advisory panel and argued successfully for their release from the army. Serving soldiers today can apply for a discharge on the grounds of conscience, but it is by no means an easy or well-known route. Under new rules drawn up in 1970 a soldier has to go first to his commanding officer who, together with the chaplain, will examine the case and make a recommendation to the divisional officer. If the decision goes against him – or her – the soldier can appeal to an advisory committee appointed by the Lord Chancellor which will hold a public hearing. Since its inception the committee has heard thirty-seven cases with twelve cases being allowed and twenty-five being denied. Of the last four hearings three out of four have been successful. There was one in 1990 (which was successful), and two hearings in 1991 (one was successful, the other failed). The last hearing was in 1996 when a twenty-two-year-old marine told the committee he had spent two years thinking about his actions – having served part of the time in Northern Ireland – and he was now determined never to carry a weapon again. His application was successful.

But it is not exactly a well-publicised system. Thus when a Muslim reservist airman, Mohisin Khan, refused to take part in the Iraq War because of his religious beliefs, he did not apply for discharge as a conscientious objector but instead went absent without leave. He was fined nine days' pay and later discharged from the RAF. He took his case to the High Court in 2004, claiming a breach of his human rights. Although the judges agreed that he held a 'genuine and deep belief' that the war was wrong, they dismissed his claim, saying he should have applied for a discharge as a conscientious objector. They did add that the system for informing reservists of their rights 'could be improved'.

Back in 1916, those thirty-five men sitting in cells in Felixstowe, Harwich, Richmond, Seaford and Boulogne, wondering what their fate would be could hardly have imagined that ninety years on their rights would have become so established that yesterday's conchie would become today's 'new conscientious objector', and that even those who volunteer for the army now have a route – albeit limited – by which they can make their exit. It is a long way from Catherine Marshall and the NCF holding committee meetings and writing polite letters on behalf of COs back in 1916, to the Lord Chancellor's committee today holding a public hearing to decide whether a soldier is entitled to second thoughts. But without one there would surely never have been the other.

A Lonely Belief

Over the years Phil Brocklesby's doubts about the war, expressed so angrily in his letters home from the front, appear to have been forgotten completely. In his outward life at least there was never a hint of doubt. He was so active organising the Home Guard in the Second World War that he was awarded the MBE for his work. As guest of honour to celebrate the award, he told those assembled: 'I have so thoroughly enjoyed being in the Home Guard, that somehow to receive this honour for doing what I like seems not quite right.'

His interest in the Home Guard did not end when the war ended. In 1952 he called a public meeting to recruit more members in the very hall where he had signed his army entry forms in 1915. It was now not Germans that he was worried about but Russians, who, he warned, might be launching suicide paratrooper attacks. The Home Guard would have to be more mobile and he wrote to his local newspaper: 'Fifteen hours training in three months is not much to ask toward the safety of our Motherland.'

If anything his interest in remembering the First World War grew with age. 'If you gave him a chance he would talk for days about it,' says his partner in the chemist shop. Even in the 1950s Phil had a box of ammunition stored under a desk in the back room in the shop.

After his retirement he gave away much of his money and moved to a small bungalow in Lincolnshire where his existence became more and more frugal – he was determined as a point of honour to live on no more than the state pension. In his papers there is a detailed map he has drawn of the British trench system at Serre, with every trench named, showing very clearly how, in the minds of the military planners, the attack was going to work. But he was not satisfied with just a drawing and produced page after page of notes of what went wrong. In his bungalow he set up a table tennis table, covered it with sand and turned it into a permanent relief map of the battle. Immense amounts of his time and effort went into it; every trench was burrowed into the sand. The battle was fought and re-fought and, especially after his wife died, when friends or family went to see him, they knew exactly what he was going to talk about. 'He was replaying this over and over again,' says his nephew Malcolm. 'But it wasn't worrying him and he wasn't agonising over it.'

Phil took considerable comfort in theosophy but there was one question that always stayed with him: why was he saved when so many of his friends were killed? He had somehow been allowed to survive for some reason but he did not know why. He was in the Thirteenth Platoon of the Thirteenth Brigade and he always reckoned there were thirteen instances when out in France he had been saved by Divine Providence. Why? Twice he travelled back to France to what he called 'the land of my nightmare dreams', trips that were both a memorial to those friends who had been killed and part of his continuing search. He died in 1976 without ever quite finding the answer he was after.

While Phil ran his own chemist shop, which prospered when the National Health Service was introduced, Bert never reached anywhere near his potential. His daughter Mary, looking back now, says that her father's record as a conscientious objector was 'something that followed him all the way through his life. He never made any career in his teaching. At one point he talked about other people who were with him saying "Oh, you will become a headmaster." Well, he never achieved that.'

Being the kind of man he was, he was not prepared to help his cause too much either. As Mary says: 'He was always very positive; but he was never willing to fit in with what he might have had to do to make a career. No, he stuck to his convictions.' In the 1950s, for example, he played the piano at assembly at the school where he taught in Scunthorpe, but he would not play hymns that glorified war and sacrifice. Another teacher who remembers 'Brock' very fondly says: 'It was a prickly subject between Brock and Mr Ramsden [the head]. On one occasion Mr Ramsden chose a hymn at assembly "Oh Valiant Hearts" and Brock quietly and politely said he couldn't play it and would it be possible to choose another hymn. Mr Ramsden was furious and ordered him to play, but Brock just stood up and walked out with great dignity.'

From childhood, when Bert was around everyone knew it. He was the brother who would play tricks on his siblings, the one who would get people laughing, get people singing. His daughter says he would have loved sending the coded postcard from Boulogne: 'It's a good job they didn't send him to Vladivostock.'

Jovial yes, but stubborn too. The Bishop of Oxford, who supported the right of the conscientious objector, nonetheless called the absolutists 'an extraordinarily inflexible set of men' and he was right. Bert never gave up and he never tried to hide his views. He might have been just the sort of independent-spirited person the world needs to question everything from war to quinine but he was also the sort of person who could be very difficult to deal with. He had an absolute conviction that he was being guided by God and no one was going to change the way he thought. Even his daughter Mary says his stand at times 'seems a bit extreme to me . . . He says how he refused to peel potatoes or sew bags. I mean, some of these things I can't take as being part of the war effort.' However, a clue to Bert's philosophy lies in a letter to his brother Harold in the last years of his life, in which Bert asked 'For what do we have ideals but to make us uncomfortable and dissatisfied with the present state?'

As for Annie Wainwright, he never talked of her again. Yet his two daughters, Mary and Josie, both still hold on to her flame. 'We had always taken it that she would have been the person he would have married if there hadn't been the First World War,' says Mary. 'They never would have been faced with all this conflict.'

Annie's family continued to see the Brocklesby family over the years but they also continued to mourn her brother Gilbert – his having come so near to surviving the war almost made it worse. Annie's niece says, 'Behind the house where my grandparents lived there was a field and poppies used to grow in the cornfield. And I remember as a child picking poppies and taking them to my grandmother and she just wouldn't have them in the house. "We can't have poppies here" she'd say.'

Somewhere along the way the Annie that Bert knew became the slightly more mature Anne that her family and friends knew her as. She grew into quite a different woman – with a much more modern independent streak – than the woman that Bert knew. Walter Marsdin, the bank manager she married, was, like Bert, a lifelong Christian. But far from being a conscientious objector, he came back from the war as a second lieutenant – cited for conspicuous gallantry in the last days of the fighting.

Anne used to go off to Spain in the winter with a woman friend, driving her own Austin Seven – these were the days when women drivers were still something of a rarity. However the Austin Seven had to be abandoned in a hurry when she was evacuated from Barcelona during the Spanish Civil War. It was later replaced by a Rolls-Royce she used to drive for friends. They would sometimes turn up in it in Conisbrough and although the Rolls had seen better days (there was one part of the floor where you could see through to the road) her arrival still impressed her old neighbours. There is a picture of Anne standing glamorously on the seafront in the South of France among the palm trees and she looks a very different person to the one that Bert conjured up on the wall of his prison cell.

She continued to pursue her own way for the rest of her life, running a café in Devon before buying a hotel and turning it into flats. Her husband still preferred Yorkshire but he came down every summer bearing pies for all his friends, and when she eventually retired to Torquay he joined her there – and became a stalwart of the local Conservative Club.

But while pre-war Annie was a rather different person from the one who emerged after the war was over, Bert, on the other hand, remained as consistent as ever. In 1962, at the age of seventy-three, he was entertaining the Aldermaston 'Ban the Bomb' marchers with his accordion. In the same year there is a picture of him in front of Scunthorpe's War Memorial; he stood there for three hours holding up a placard upon which was written: 'Vigil for Peace Hiroshima August 6 1945'. He was there all alone and the local paper's report sounds slightly tongue in cheek: 'Mr Brocklesby has long been associated with any peace movements in North Lincolnshire (though they have been few and far between over the years).'

Bert told the local reporter: 'It is very good to remember the heroes on Remembrance Day but we ought also to remember the sufferers on Hiroshima Day . . . this is an individual activity but I think it is an idea that will grow.' He died four months later.

My research for this book involved not only a journey through England and Northern France, but also a journey through my own beliefs and feelings about these men and particularly about the thirty-five 'Frenchmen'. It was not a straightforward route: admiration for their steadfast determination was sometimes replaced by irritation at their overwhelming self-righteousness and in the background – always – was the sacrifice made by the men who did fight for their country. While I remained angry at how they had been treated, I still could not ignore the glimmer of enlightenment that Asquith and some of his fellow Liberals showed on occasions.

My travels started at Richmond Castle, where a tour of the cells provoked an uncomplicated outrage at the way they had been treated, and they ended at Richmond three years later. By then the sixteen topiary sculptures planted in memory of the COs held there had begun to take shape. But under a certain amount of local pressure they had become less a straightforward memorial to the sixteen and rather more a neutral 'acknowledgement of the struggle of the individual to express himself or herself'. So even as the garden starts to reveal itself and begins to soften the castle's stark outline, the argument over conchies lives on.

Richmond was my introduction to Bert Brocklesby's story. But before starting to write I visited Sheffield Cathedral, where in the chapel of his old regiment Phil Brocklesby had dedicated nine oak chairs to comrades who had fallen in the war that Bert had refused to fight.

Here was a chair for Captain John Normansell who had amazed Phil on the first day of the Somme by clambering out of his trench and sitting on the road, whistle at the ready, waiting to order the advance. He had survived that first day but he was killed by friendly fire – a Lewis gun 'nearly cut him in two' – eight months later. Here was a chair for Lieutenant Stephen Sharp from Conisbrough, the only man Phil knew when he joined the Thirteenth Battalion. They had a chance for one five-minute chat before the battle and the next thing Phil heard was that Sharp had been killed by a piece of shell setting off the Mills bombs he was carrying.

Here was a chair for Captain De Ville Smith who left his church to march off to the war and, the night before the battle, seemed to sense his death: 'before he died I had to step over Captain Smith's body to get to our correct position', wrote Phil. And here too was a chair for Colonel Addison who had given Phil a battle souvenir to deliver to his wife back in 1915. He had been killed on the first day of the Somme; his body was not found until September and the diary found with him showed he must have lived two or three days out in No Man's Land before his death. It was impossible not to be moved by the courage of these men whose memory Phil had brought back to life in this chapel.

But travelling to Northern France to see first where Bert had been imprisoned and then on to where Phil had fought and his comrades had died, I was surprised that amidst the understated beauty of the Commonwealth Cemeteries I found myself feeling more sympathy for conscientious objectors like Bert, not less. For this was a war waged as a war of attrition, which in the dictionary means 'a gradual wearing down of strength and morale by continuous harassment' but which translates on the ground to more and more cemeteries. In April 1916 Haig had discussed with the Chief of Imperial General Staff, Sir William Robertson, what sort of numbers he could expect from England in the summer months. Haig noted in his diary: 'I said that if I attacked say with 450,000 men the War Office should be prepared to provide 50 per cent wastage of that number in two months.' The Director of Recruiting complained that commanders in the field were beginning to see the men he sent to them as 'expendable stores' and there is the inescapable feeling of anger amidst these cemeteries that all this raw courage and sacrifice was so misused.

The pacifist would argue that if there had been enough Bert Brocklesbys there would have been no war. But the war was in progress well before conscription was introduced and was not going to be halted by conscientious objectors in Britain. It can be much more strongly argued that if there had been more Bert Brocklesbys refusing to fight, the army would have had to fight the war a different way. Men's lives could not have been offered up so easily and the wholesale slaughter at the Somme and a year later at Passchendaele might have been avoided.

It is easy to condemn a government that forced people to fight, but the Liberal government, however half-heartedly, did give rights to the conscientious objector and ensured that the thirty-five 'Frenchmen' survived. There was a very real chance that they might have been executed but in the end there were enough people who cared – from the Prime Minister downwards – to make sure this never happened.

And some of the COs realised that England was the exception to the Continental rule. Corder Catchpool in his penultimate court martial in October 1917 told the court: 'I believe that England will be honoured in history for having had the courage to introduce exemptions on conscientious grounds – had she not done so, some thousands of us would have been shot, a fate which overtook many under the less liberal regimes of Germany, Russia and Austria.' (Tactfully he omitted any mention of our closest ally, France.)

In the Second World War another conscientious objector, Ken Shaw, ended up giving lectures on the history of the Soviet Union to German prisoners-of-war. Whether they were interested in the Soviet Union he does not say but they were certainly interested in him: 'They couldn't understand what a conchie really was. They really didn't understand it. They thought the British were very peculiar actually to allow such things to happen because in Germany it wasn't allowed.'

Between Phil risking everything for his country and Bert being imprisoned and indeed blighted because he refused to fight, there is no squaring the circle. Phil was on the winning side; he was part of an army that ultimately achieved victory – albeit at a cost of 744,000 British dead. But what did Bert and his fellow 'Frenchmen' achieve? They clearly did not succeed in their ultimate aim of ending war. But never again would the conscientious objector be treated – at least in Britain – the way the thirty-five 'Frenchmen' were treated. They were accepted, however grudgingly, and those who followed were safe from the firing squad. They won the right not to fight, but lost the battle to stop wars. They failed to halt the First World War and failed to stop the Second World War and the wars that have followed.

But while the pacifists have got nowhere near the ultimate prize, the concept of the conscientious objector, such an alien thought ninety years ago, is now accepted almost universally. If Bert Brocklesby returned today he could speak his mind without having to endure the anger and the bitterness that he was put through in 1916. His case, based on religion, remains the easiest case to argue; however the idea of opposition to war based on a personal set of moral beliefs which are not religious has slowly become more accepted. The idea of being against one war but not against all wars remains the most difficult to present successfully, implying, as it does, that the citizen–soldier rather than the state can take his or her pick of wars.

Looking back, Phil Brocklesby admitted 'emotionally I agreed pretty much with Bert's attitude and during the war there were many occasions when I think I almost envied him being in prison. In other words he was a conscientious objector who stuck to his guns. I went in and I think I must have become eventually a problem officer to my commanding officer out in France.'

Bert, however, was not a man of many doubts and the only time he showed any sympathy for those who chose to fight came when the Methodist minister Mr Wardell who visited Maidstone prison told him he had lost a son in the war. Initially, he says, 'I am afraid I only felt his sorrow in a superficial way.' But years later Bert too looked back and decided: 'I minimised the great sense of duty (true or false) that drove these men along the hardest path of all, saying goodbye to all that makes life fair: home, kindred, sweethearts, careers and life itself. Poor bereaved Mr Wardell!'

Both brothers shared a determination under pressure. Though Phil could hardly be painted as likely VC material, nevertheless in one of his notebooks he tots up in his neat, organised way the many occasions when 'death could have claimed me but he stepped aside'. He was a safe pair of hands, endowed with both luck and canniness. He owed it to his men and to his own sense of self-worth to stick at it despite his growing despair and the knowledge that death was so close at hand. He brought them through and they respected him for it.

As for Bert, he needed enormous determination to stick it out when almost all around him were against him – his belief was a very lonely one. After the war was over Geoffrey Fisher, who eventually became Archbishop of Canterbury, told one CO who he had once taught: 'I think you were one of the loneliest people I have ever known.'

Before he died Fred Lloyd, one of the few veterans of the First World War who survived into the twenty-first century, spoke movingly to Sebastian Faulks, author of *Birdsong*, about what they had all been through: 'It was a terrible war. There was thousands of young boys killed for nothing. We lost forty-nine boys who went to school with me. There's no need for wars.' But he could say this with the advantage of hindsight. At the time it was a much, much more difficult thing to say, let alone to act upon.

Bertrand Russell, in a letter sent from prison where he spent five months in 1918, wrote: 'War develops in almost all a certain hysteria of destruction – self-destruction, among the more generous, but still destruction. We have to stand out against this hysteria, and realise, and make others realise, that Life, not Death (however heroic) is the source of all good.' But it was not an easy task Russell set himself and his fellow pacifists. In Bert's world there was no room for second thoughts. His argument was a simple one: 'Conscience is not the voice of God but it is the best that a man may know from his own experience, and woe betide him if he does not follow the best he knows.' He and his fellow absolutists followed where their experience led them; they made the case for Life. But just twenty-one years later Europe was at war again.

Yet what is most remarkable about the story of the two brothers, both as individuals and as symbols of opposing responses to war, is this: Phil chose to fight, Bert chose not to, but neither their family nor their country was torn apart by these profound differences over the value of life.

Bibliography

Adams, R.J.Q and Poirier, Philip P. *The Conscription Controversy in Great Britain 1900–18*, Macmillan, 1987.

Arthur, Max. *Forgotten Voices of the Great War*. In association with the Imperial War Museum, Ebury Press, 2002.

Atkin, Jonathan. *A War of Individuals: Bloomsbury Attitudes to the Great War*, Manchester University Press, 2002.

Baldwin, Hanson W. *World War I*, Grove Press Inc., 1962, Black Cat edition by arrangement with Harper and Row.

Barker, Rachel. *Conscience, Government and War, Conscientious Objection in Great Britain 1939–45*, Routledge and Kegan Paul Ltd, 1982.

Barry, Sebastian. *A Long Long Way*, Faber, 2005.

Boulton, David, *Objection Overruled*, Macgibbon and Kee, 1967.

Braunthal, Julian. 'War resistance in Austria and Germany' in Julian Bell (ed), *We Did Not Fight: 1914–1918 Experiences of War Resisters*, Cobden-Sanderson, 1935.

Brock, Michael and Eleanor (eds). *H.H. Asquith Letters to Venetia Stanley*, Oxford University Press, 1985.

Brock, Peter. *Against the Draft: Essays on Conscientious Objection from the Radical Reformation to the Second World War*, University of Toronto Press, 2006.

Brock, Peter. *Pacifism in Europe to 1914*, Princeton University Press, 1972.

Brock, Peter (ed). *Records of Conscience*, William Sessions, 1993.

Brock, Peter and Young, Nigel. *Pacifism in the Twentieth Century*, Syracuse University Press, 1999.

Catchpool, Corder. *On Two Fronts, Letters of a Conscientious Objector*, 3rd edn, George Allen and Unwin, 1940.

Chamberlain, W.J. *Fighting for Peace: The Story of the War Resistance*

Movement, No More War Movement, 1928.

Childs, Major-General Sir Wyndham. *Episodes and Reflections*, Cassell and Company, 1930.

Coombs, Rose E.B. *Before Endeavours Fade: A Guide to the Battlefields of the First World War*, After the Battle, 2006.

Cooksey, Jon. *Barnsley Pals: A History of Two Battalions Raised By Barnsley in World War One*, Pen and Sword, Barnsley, 1996.

Corns, Cathryn and Hughes-Wilson, John. *Blindfold and Alone: British Military Executions in the Great War*, Cassell, 2001.

Corrigan, Gordon. *Mud, Blood and Poppycock*, Cassell, 2003.

Crutwell, C.R.M.F. *A History of the Great War 1914–1918*, Paladin Books, 1986.

De Benedetti, Charles, with Chatfield, Charles, assisting author. *An American Ordeal: The Anti-War Movement of the Vietnam Era*, Syracuse University Press, 1990.

Egremont, Max. *Siegfried Sassoon: A biography*, Picador, 2005.

Evans, Cecil. *The Claims of Conscience*, Quaker Home Service, 1996.

Foley, Michael S. *Confronting the War Machine Draft: Resistance During the Vietnam War*, University of North Carolina Press, 2003.

Gardiner, Juliet. *Wartime Britain 1939–1945*, Headline, 2004.

Garnett, David. *The Flowers of the Forest*, Chatto and Windus, 1955.

Gaylin, Willard. *In the Service of their Country: War Resisters in Prison*, Viking Press, 1970.

Gilbert, Martin. *First World War*, HarperCollins, 1995.

Gioglio, Gerald R. *Days of Decision: An Oral History of Conscientious Objectors in the Military During the Vietnam War*, Broken Rifle Press, New Jersey, 1989.

Goodall, Felicity. *A Question of Conscience: Conscientious Objection in the Two World Wars*, Sutton Publishing, 1997.

Graham, John W. *Conscription and Conscience: A History 1916–1919*, George Allen and Unwin, 1922.

Hattersley, Roy. *The Edwardians*, Abacus, 2006.

Hayes, Denis. *Conscription Conflict: The Conflict of Ideas in the Struggle For and Against Military Conscription in Britain Between 1901 and 1939*, Sheppard Press, 1949.

Hirst, Margaret. *The Quakers in Peace and War*, Swarthmore Press, 1923.

Hobhouse, Mrs Henry. *I appeal unto Caesar*, George Allen and Unwin, 1917.

Holmes, Richard. *The Western Front*, BBC Worldwide Ltd, 1999.

Hughes, William R. *Indomitable Friend: Corder Catchpool 1883–1952*, George Allen and Unwin, 1956.

Jenkins, Roy. *Asquith*, Collins, 1964 (Revised 1978).

Johnson, Paul. *Ireland: Land of Troubles*, Eyre Methuen, 1980.

Jolliffe, John. *Raymond Asquith: Life and Letters*, Collins, 1980.

Lewis, Jon E. *True World War I Stories*, Robinson, 1999.

Keegan, John. *The First World War*, Pimlico, 1999.

Kennedy, Thomas C. *The Hound of Conscience: A History of the No Conscription Fellowship, 1914–1919*, University of Arkansas Press, Fayetteville, 1981.

Knightley, Phillip. *The First Casualty*, Andre Deutsch, 1975.

Marwick, Arthur. *Clifford Allen, The Open Conspirator*, Oliver and Boyd, 1964.

Mason, A.E.W. *The Four Feathers*, House of Stratus, 2003.

Moorehead, Caroline. *Troublesome People: Enemies of War 1916–1986*, Hamish Hamilton, 1987.

Moskos, Charles and Chambers, John Whiteclay. *The New Conscientious Objection: From Sacred to Secular Resistance*, Oxford University Press, 1993.

Moynihan, Michael. *People at War, 1914–1918*, David and Charles, 1973.

Oram, Gerald. *Death Sentences Passed by Military Courts of the British Army 1914–1924*. Francis Boutle, 1998.

Peace Pledge Union. *Refusing to Kill: Conscientious Objection and Human Rights in the First World War*, 2006.

Prasad, Devi and Smythe, Tony (eds).*Conscription: A World Survey*, War Resisters' International, 1968.

Rae, John. *Conscience and Politics: The British Government and the Conscientious Objector to Military Service 1916–1919*, Oxford University Press, 1970.

Remarque, Erich Maria. *All Quiet on the Western Front*, Vintage Classics, 1996.

Rosmer, Alfred. 'The fight against war in France during the war' in Julian Bell (ed), *We Did Not Fight: 1914–1918 Experiences of War Resisters*, Cobden-Sanderson, 1935.

Russell, Bertrand. *The Autobiography of Bertrand Russell*, 3 vols, George Allen and Unwin, 1967–1969.

Sassoon, Siegfried. *Memoirs of an Infantry Officer*, Faber, 1965.

Seymour, Miranda. *Ottoline Morrell: Life on the Grand Scale*, Sceptre, 1993.

Spalding, Frances. *Duncan Grant: A Biography*, Pimlico, 1998.

Stapledon, Olaf. 'Experiences in the Friends' Ambulance Unit' in Julian Bell (ed), *We Did Not Fight: 1914–1918 Experiences of War Resisters*, Cobden-Sanderson, 1935.

Stephen, Adrian. 'The Tribunal' in Julian Bell (ed), *We Did Not Fight: 1914–1918 Experiences of War Resisters*, Cobden-Sanderson, 1935.

Stevenson, David. *1914–1918: The History of the First World War*, Allen Lane, 2004.

Strachan, Hew. *The First World War: To Arms*, vol. 1, Oxford University Press, 2003.

Tatham, Meaburn and Miles, James E. *The Friends' Ambulance Unit 1914–1919: A Record*, Swarthmore Press Ltd, 1919.

Van Emden, Richard. *Boy Soldiers of the Great War*, Headline, 2005.

Van Emden, Richard and Humphries, Steve. *All Quiet on the Home Front: An Oral History of Life in Britain During the First World War*, Headline, 2003.

Vansittart, Peter. *Voices from the Great War*, Pimlico, 2003.

Vellacott, Jo. *Bertrand Russell and the Pacifists in the First World War*, Harvester Press Ltd, 1980.

Vellacott, Jo. *From Liberal to Labour with Women's Suffrage: The Story of Catherine Marshall*, McGill-Queen's University Press, 1993.

Waller, Ralph. *John Wesley – A Personal Portrait*, SPCK, 2003.

Wilkinson, Alan. *The Church of England and the First World War*, SCM Press Ltd, 1996.

Wilson, Jean Moorcroft. *Siegfried Sassoon: The Making of a War Poet. A Biography (1886–1918)*, Duckworth, 1998.

Woodward, David R. *The Military Correspondence of Field-Marshal Sir William Robertson, Chief of the Imperial General Staff December 1915–February 1918*, The Bodley Head for the Army Records Society, 1989.

Webb, Beatrice (ed Margaret Cole). *Beatrice Webb's Diaries, 1912–1924*, Longman, 1952.

Zweig, Stefan. *Beware of Pity*, Pushkin Press, 2003.

Manuscript sources

Bodleian Library, University of Oxford

The papers of Herbert Henry Asquith, 1st Earl of Oxford and Asquith, mainly 1892–1928.

The papers of Emma Alice Margaret (Margot) Asquith, Countess of Oxford and Asquith, 1862–1945.

Papers of Gilbert Murray.

The Liddell Hart Centre for Military Archives, King's College, London

The papers of Field Marshal Sir William Robertson.

The papers of Field Marshal Douglas Haig, 1st Earl Haig. (The papers are held at the National Library of Scotland in Edinburgh, but a microfilmed set is also held at the Liddell Hart Centre.)

The National Archives

The papers of Field Marshal Kitchener, 1st Earl Kitchener of Khartoum.

For the court martial of John Hasemore, see: PRO WO/71/465.

Other documents consulted include those in records class MH 47; WO 32; WO 71; WO 154; WO 158; WO 209; WO 213; WO 293; HO 45; Lab 6.

The Cumbria Record Office, Carlisle

The papers of Catherine Marshall.

The Imperial War Museum

A large number of interviews with conscientious objectors in both World Wars have been conducted by the Museum's Sound Archives, where they are to be found. In addition there are diaries, letters and other papers concerning conscientious objectors held by the Department of Documents, which have also been very helpful.

University of Leeds, Liddle Collection

The Collection's founder interviewed a number of First World War conscientious objectors and these interviews, together with diaries, letters and other documents from those interviewed and other COs are held here. Among the privately published manuscripts held here (see below) are those of John H. (Bert) Brocklesby, Norman Gaudie, Howard Marten, Fred Murfin, Frank Shackleton and Harold Stanton. Copies of Philip Brocklesby's letters are also in this collection.

Friends House Library

Among the many manuscripts, books and published sources on the subject of conscientious objection held at the headquarters of the Religious Society of Friends, there are manuscripts from Cornelius Barritt, John H. (Bert) Brocklesby and Fred Murfin.

Other papers consulted here include:

Duplicated papers of the No Conscription Fellowship.

Correspondence of Harvey T. Edmund with First World War conscientious objectors

The papers of Arnold Rowntree.

The Friend.

The Tribunal.

Winchester Whisperer, Clandestine Prison Magazine.

Further reading

The Absolutists' Objection to Conscription: A Statement and an Appeal to the Conscience of the Nation, Issued by direction of The Friends Service Committee, London, 1917.

Advisory Committee on Conscientious Objectors. Information updated by *Peace Matters*, Autumn 1996, and by the Ministry of Defence, December 2006, under the Freedom of Information Act.

Babbington, Caroline, Manning, Tracy and Stewart, Sophie. *Our Painted Past: Wall Paintings of English Heritage*, English Heritage, 1999.

Brown, Michael Barratt. *The Evolution of the Friends' Ambulance Unit (1914 and 1939),* reproduced from *Friends Quarterly Examiner,* vol. 77, 306–7, Friends Ambulance Unit, London, 1943.

Cemeteries and Memorials in Belgium and Northern France, Commonwealth War Graves Commission.

Goodall, John. *Richmond Castle, Easby Abbey,* English Heritage, 2001.

Greathead, June and Tony (ed Peter Tuffrey). *Photographs of Old Conisbrough,* Doncaster, 1990.

Gullace, Nicolette F. 'White feathers and wounded men: female patriotism and the memory of the Great War', *Journal of British Studies,* vol. 36, No. 2.

The Harwich Redoubt, The Harwich Society, 2005.

It's Different Now, essays by A.A. Milne, Dr Maude Royden, Bertrand Russell, Professor C.E.M. Joad, pamphlet, 1940.

Jehovah's Witnesses: Their Position. Issued by the International Bible Students' Association, London, 1942.

Manual of Military Law. War Office, HMSO, 1914.

Milne, A.A. *War with Honour,* Macmillan War Pamphlet No. 2, 1940.

Conscientious Objection to Military Service in Europe. Report submitted to the Council of Europe Legal Affairs Committee, Quaker Council for European Affairs, 1984.

The No Conscription Fellowship: A Souvenir of Its Work During the Years 1914–1919, No Conscription Fellowship, London, 1919.

The Right to Conscientious Objection in Europe, Quaker Council for European Affairs, 2005.

The Report of the Royal Commission on Militia and Volunteers, HMSO, 1904.

Snowden, Philip. *British Prussianism: the Scandal of the Tribunals. Full report of two speeches delivered in the House of Commons by Philip Snowden MP on March 22 and April 6 1916,* The National Labour Press Ltd., Manchester and London.

For the report of Bert Brocklesby's tribunal hearing: *Doncaster Gazette,* 3 March 1916.

For the obituary of Revd Robert Wardell: Minutes of the Wesleyan Methodist Conference, 1924.

For the report of the death of Revd George De Ville Smith: *Worsbro' Dale Parish Magazine,* August 1916 and *Barnsley Chronicle,* 15 July 1916.

www.ppu.org.uk: Website of the Peace Pledge Union, containing 'Learn Peace' resources.

Privately printed publications

Baker, George. *The Soul of a Skunk: The Autobiography of a Conscientious Objector*, Eric Partridge, 1930.

Brocklesby, John H. *Escape from Paganism.*

Clark, Major G.W. *3NCC: Being the Story of a Non Combatant Company in War Time told by Major G.W. Clark, MC.*

Marten, Howard. *White Feather: The Experiences of a Pacifist in France and Elsewhere 1916–1918.*

Murfin, Fred. *Prisoners for Peace: An Account by Fred J. Murfin of His Experiences as a Conscientious Objector During the 1914–18 War.*

Shackleton, Frank (under the pen name Christopher Hurst). *All My Tomorrows.*

Stanton, Harold. *Will You March Too?*

Every effort has been made to trace copyright holders and the author and libraries holding documents would be grateful for any information which might help to trace those whose identities or addresses are not currently known.

Acknowledgements

This book would not have been possible without the help of Malcolm Brocklesby, Bert and Phil Brocklesby's nephew, and Mary Brocklesby, Bert's daughter. I would like to thank them both for their insight, their incredible support and their patience with my attempts to dig out an answer to every query however small. I would also like to thank other members of the Brocklesby family, in particular Malcolm's wife, Molly, and also Harold's son, Ian, and Bert's second daughter, Josie.

The resources of Britain's libraries are the other essential in this book. In particular the University of Leeds, Special Collections, where, through the foresight of Dr Peter Liddle, an extraordinary number of first-hand individual experiences of the First World War have been gathered together, including interviews with key conscientious objectors, and where Richard Davies and his staff make finding this material a pleasure. The same is equally true of the Imperial War Museum. The Sound Archive, headed by its Keeper Margaret Brooks, has a wide collection of interviews with conscientious objectors, including some whom she interviewed herself. The Department of Documents, under its Keeper, Roderick Suddaby, provides a good source of contemporary material and diaries of COs. The third key library is the Society of Friends Library where, again, Heather Rowlands and her staff are equally helpful in providing material to both Quaker and non-Quaker alike. Other libraries which have been extremely useful include the Cumbria Records Office in Carlisle; the Bodleian Library, University of Oxford; the Liddell Hart Centre for Military

Archives; the British Newspaper Library; and the National Army Museum.

My thanks too to the Trustees of the Liddell Hart Centre for Military Archives for permission to quote from Sir William Robertson papers; the Bonham Carter Family Trustees for permission to quote from H. H. Asquith's unpublished papers; Mr Christopher Osborn for permission to quote from Margot Asquith's papers; and to individual copyright-holders of papers held by libraries who have always been very willing to give copyright approval.

There are many, many people who helped with this book and in naming some of them I can only apologise to those who I fear I may have inadvertently left out. Mick Brown at *The Telegraph Magazine* gave me great encouragement from the start and never flagged either in his enthusiasm for the project or his helpful advice. Don Berry, who Sir Max Hastings rightly calls 'a man of profound and unobtrusive integrity', gave me his usual key advice at decisive moments as well as reading and making the first edit of the manuscript. Other journalists who helped with encouragement or advice or both include my former colleagues on *The Telegraph Magazine*; Emma Soames, now editor of *Saga Magazine*; and Jon Connell, founder of *The Week*.

Outside journalism I would like to thank Lorraine Cooper at Richmond Castle for her help when I first started out on this book, and David and Margaret Gray, Quakers living in Richmond who were among the first to raise the issue of the COs imprisoned at the castle. Martyn Gaudie and his wife entertained me splendidly on their farm while he recounted the history of his father and himself. Tony Greathead, a local historian, was so helpful on the history of Conisbrough – facts he did not know he would hunt down. He also introduced me to several others in the area, including Gerald Wright, Phil Brocklesby's partner in the chemist shop, who helped on Phil's life following the war. My thanks too to Shirley Bracewell, both niece and god-daughter of Anne Wainwright, and her cousin Bob Wainwright for their considerable help on filling in Anne Wainwright's life after the war ended.

Bill Hetherington, Honorary Librarian with the Peace Pledge Union, has an immense knowledge of the whole subject and his help was considerable. Peter Forsaith, co-ordinator at the Methodist Studies Unit, Oxford Brookes University, dragged both information and pictures out of the files showing just what a star Bert was on his way to becoming before the war arrived. Gary Perkins was kind enough to share his detailed knowledge of the Jehovah's Witnesses. At the splendid Harwich Redoubt, which – amazingly – is run by a group of volunteers, Andy Rutter, the secretary of the Harwich Society, was very helpful. The Rev. Geoff Holmes, the former vicar of St Thomas's Worsbrough Dale, kindly dug out obituaries of the Rev. George de Ville Smith. Peter Francis, at the Commonwealth War Graves Commission, helped with the cemeteries that I needed to visit. Mariella and Richard Ardron, teachers who have often taken their charges on visits to the trenches, were two others who encouraged me to tell this story, Mariella being particularly insistent on the subject of the white feather.

I would like to thank my agent Kate Jones at ICM for her confidence in me and her determination to get this book published, and all at Aurum Press – in particular, Natasha Martin, whose perceptive editing has made such a difference.

Finally, I want to thank my wife Barbara and children Lara and Daniel, who have had to grow used to a book which sometimes must have seemed like an obsession. They have put up with countless recitations of facts and discoveries which must, at times, have seemed boring to them but seemed all-important to me; they too have given strong advice and encouragement whenever it has been needed.

The mistakes are mine alone.

Index